A Brief History
of Afghanistan

A Brief History of Afghanistan

Shaista Wahab

University of Nebraska at Omaha,
Arthur Paul Afghanistan Collection

and Barry Youngerman

Facts On File
An imprint of Infobase Publishing

A Brief History of Afghanistan

Facts On File, Inc.
An imprint of Infobase Publishing
132 West 31st Street
New York NY 10001

ISBN-10: 0-8160-5761-3
ISBN-13: 978-0-8160-5761-0

Library of Congress Cataloging-in-Publication Data

Wahab, Shaista.
    A brief history of Afghanistan / Shaista Wahab and Barry Youngerman.
        p. cm.
    Includes bibliographical references and index.
    ISBN: 0-8160-5761-3 (alk. paper)
  1. Afghanistan—History. I. Youngerman, Barry. II. Title.
    DS356.W34 2006
    958.1—dc22   2006043979

Facts On File books are available at special discounts when purchased in bulk quantities for businesses, associations, institutions, or sales promotions. Please call our Special Sales Department in New York at (212) 967-8800 or (800) 322-8755.

You can find Facts On File on the World Wide Web at http://www.factsonfile.com

Text design by Joan M. McEvoy
Cover design by Semadar Megged/Anastasia Plé
Illustrations by Sholto Ainslie

Printed in the United States of America

MP Hermitage 10 9 8 7 6 5 4 3 2 1

This book is printed on acid-free paper.

CONTENTS

LIST OF ILLUSTRATIONS

LIST OF MAPS

LIST OF CHARTS

INTRODUCTION: THE CHALLENGE OF AFGHANISTAN

By the late 20th century, the world agreed on a simple standard to judge whether a territorial unit was a country: full membership in the United Nations. Afghanistan easily passes that bar; it is almost a charter member, having joined in 1946, a scant year after the world body was formed. By that standard, it has remained independent ever since, despite periods of foreign control.

A more difficult question is whether the lands enclosed by Afghanistan's borders now constitute, or can soon develop into, a viable, unified state. In some ways, the country just does not make sense.

Afghanistan is not unified in any ethnic or linguistic sense, like Italy or Japan is. Many of its dozens of ethnic groups have long histories of conflict and enmity with one another. Many, in fact, had more in common up to the recent past with their fellow ethnics across international borders than with their fellow Afghans across the country—or across the street in the major cities.

Nor does Afghanistan have natural geographical borders, like Australia or Greece does, nor any obvious unifying feature like Egypt's Nile. Relatively brief stretches of border are defined by rivers—the Amu Darya (Oxus) in the north, the Hari Rud in the northwest, and the highly variable Helmand in the southwest—but no seas or mountain ranges create natural frontiers. In fact, the towering Hindu Kush mountains, an extension of the Himalayas, which provide natural northern borders for Pakistan and India, split Afghanistan in two; the lowlands on either side are contiguous to similar topographic zones across the northern, western, and southern borders and have from time immemorial welcomed invasion and migration in either direction.

Perhaps what most unites the Afghans are the things they are not.

Although most of the people speak languages that are related to Farsi, the official language of their western neighbor Iran, they differ from most Iranians in their continued adherence (apart from the Hazara minority) to the Sunni stream of Islam, which Iran abandoned in the 16th century in favor of the Shia sect or tendency.

While northern Afghanistan shows linguistic, cultural, and geographic continuity with the Central Asian republics across the Amu Darya, its people were spared the destructive if transformative experience of two generations of czarist Christian suzerainty followed by 75 years of Soviet communism. In fact, many Uzbeks and Turkmen first arrived in Afghanistan as refugees from the Russian or Soviet empires. Once in the country, they have shared the Afghan experience of a more organic, gradual transition from premodern ways, where traditions and institutions may evolve but without the shock or humiliation of heathen rule.

The eastern border with Pakistan may be the least natural in that it bisects the huge Pashtun ethnic group, which maintains the same way of life on either side to the present day. The line simply reflects the limits of British imperial power in the 19th century. But just beyond the Pashtun zone lies the Indus Valley, whose ancient cultural, economic, and linguistic heritage never spread very far or deeply into the Afghan world; besides, Pakistan underwent its own transformation as part of the British Empire, which the fierce Afghans kept at bay for more than a century.

Until 1747, when Ahmad Shah founded the Durrani Empire, Afghanistan had never been ruled as one country, except as part of larger foreign empires. In fact, it had been exposed to thousands of years of invasion and migration from every direction. But ever since that historic date, the peoples of present-day Afghanistan have lived under unified native rule, albeit with a large degree of local autonomy. For more than 250 years, their rulers managed to stave off Persian, Russian, and British control, often at great cost. This defiant isolation may itself have provided the foundation for a distinct Afghan national identity that could transcend ethnic or tribal loyalty.

If Afghanistan were located in a peaceful region, surrounded by stable countries, the question of national unity and identity might not loom so large. But three decades of war, revolution, terrorism, and foreign intervention by Russia, Pakistan, the Arab world, and the United States have made that question vitally important, both within and outside the country's borders. History can help elucidate the problem; it can also contribute to a positive answer, by reinforcing a sense of the antiquity and special nature of Afghanistan.

***

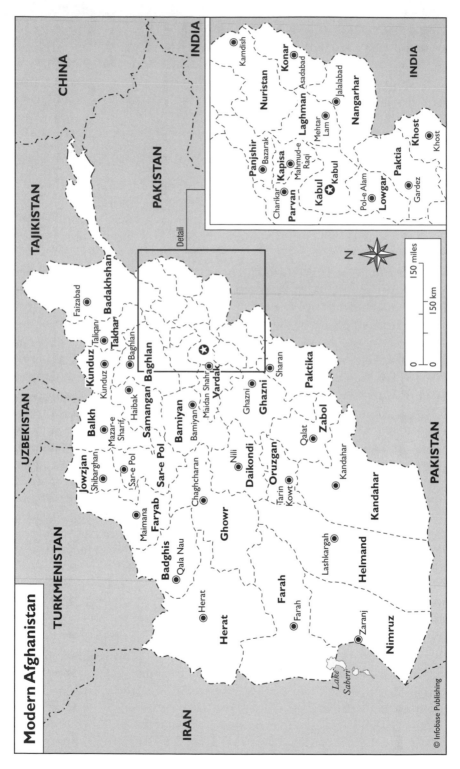

Modern Afghanistan

CHINA

INDIA

TAJIKISTAN

PAKISTAN

Detail

UZBEKISTAN

Faizabad ◉

Badakhshan

Taliqan ◉

Takhar

Kunduz ◉ **Kunduz**
◉ Baghlan

Samangan **Baghlan**

◉ Haibak

Mazar-e ◉ Sharif

Balkh

Maidan Shahr ◉ **Wardak**

★

Ghazni ◉ **Ghazni**

Sharan ◉

Paktika

Bamiyan
Bamiyan ◉

TURKMENISTAN

Shibarghan ◉ **Jowzjan**

◉ Sar-e Pol **Sar-e Pol**

Chaghcharan ◉

Nili ◉ **Daikondi**

Oruzgan

Tarin ◉ Kowt

Qalat ◉ **Zabol**

Kandahar ◉

Faryab

Maimana ◉

Badghis

◉ Qala Nau

Ghowr

Lashkargah ◉

Helmand

Kandahar

◉ Herat

Herat

Farah

Farah ◉

Zaranj ◉ **Nimruz**

Lake Saberi

IRAN

PAKISTAN

© Infobase Publishing

N

150 miles
150 km

0
0

Detail map (inset):

INDIA

Kamdish ◉

Nuristan

Konar ◉
Asadabad

Konar

Laghman
Mehtar Lam ◉

Jalalabad ◉

Nangarhar

INDIA

Panjshir
Bazarak ◉

Charikar ◉ **Kapisa**
Parvan Mahmud-e Raqi ◉

Kabul ◉ **Kabul**
★ Kabul

Pol-e Alam ◉ **Lowgar**

Khost
Khost ◉

Paktia
Gardez ◉

x

Historians could make a case to begin the story of Afghanistan in 1747, when the country was united under Ahmad Shah. The borders later changed, but at least some state institutions have functioned continuously since that time, usually from the capital of Kabul; the city has long had the most diverse population in the country, situated as it is near the border between Pashtun, Tajik, and Hazara ethnic zones. Of course, earlier Muslim Afghans had ruled large empires for short periods, such as the shahs of the Ghurid dynasty (1148–1206) and the Suri dynasty (1540–55), but their legacies did not outlast their rule.

Others might suggest starting the epic a thousand years before Ahmad Shah, in the eighth century C.E., when Islam first established itself in much of the country, profoundly changing its cultural, social, and political life. After all, the common religious faith is perhaps the strongest element of the Afghan national identity; old legends even trace the Pashtuns back to ancestors from among Muhammad's companions, or to the 10 lost tribes of ancient Israel.

But even to begin the story with the first Arab incursion deep into the country in 699 C.E. would still be ignoring the first two millennia of civilization in the country, the era when the majority of its peoples probably settled within its current boundaries. The pre-Islamic polities that Afghans sometimes point to as forerunners of their nation include the Buddhist Kushan Empire (c. 50 B.C.E.–250 C.E.); the Bactrian or Indo-Greek kingdoms that arose in the centuries after Alexander's conquest (330–326 B.C.E.); the Persian Empire of the Achaemenids (c. 550–331 B.C.E.), whose Zoroastrian religion may have arisen in Afghanistan; and even a putative Aryan entity near Balkh, "the mother of cities," in the second millennium B.C.E.

Of course, detailed accounts of the Persian Empire, for example, or of the reigns of Ashoka (third century B.C.E.), Genghis Khan (13th century), or Babur (16th century), whatever their powerful impact on Afghanistan, belong more in histories of Iran, Central Asia, and India. This book takes a middle path.

After a preliminary survey of the country's natural and human resources, from its famously harsh topography to its rich ethnic diversity and culture, the historical narrative begins with a brief account of the prehistoric period, as illuminated by archaeological remains and ancient literary allusions. As the book moves across the centuries, the pace slows down to accommodate the available information (including cultural and economic) and its relevance to modern Afghanistan. In-depth discussion starts with the Durrani Empire and continues with the dynasty of Dost Muhammad, the Anglo-Afghan Wars of "the Great

Game," and the turbulent events of the 20th century. Inevitably, the largest part of the work treats the violent era from the overthrow of the monarchy in 1973 to the fall of the Taliban almost 30 years later. The experience of mass destruction, death, exile, and tyranny touched every Afghan. Whether the legacy of civic strife can be overcome by the shared experience of suffering is the challenge Afghanistan faces today.

The book concludes with a discussion of two topics of special interest—popular culture and the role of women—and a survey of basic facts on the country.

1

LAND AND PEOPLE

Natural Setting

Afghanistan's geography helps explain its troubled modern history. A landlocked Central Asian country of modest size, it rests mostly on bare mountain ranges and high rocky plains far from the dynamic centers of modern civilization.

Its position astride the ancient trade and invasion routes between East Asia, South Asia, and the Middle East once made Afghanistan a crossroads of cultures. In the modern era, however, it served as the end point of two expanding empires—Britain and Russia. Both powers were eventually content to allow the country, with its forbidding topography and sparse resources, to remain as a buffer state outside their formal control and beyond the networks of railways, telegraphs, and cultural infrastructure that were then stretching across the rest of Eurasia.

For 150 years, therefore, the world stopped at Afghanistan. The country's traditional culture, economy, and political life did not experience the challenge of modern ways. A people tough and resourceful enough to scratch a living from an unpromising land, the descendants of conquerors and founders of great cities, the Afghans endured a very low literacy rate and a shockingly short life expectancy right into the 21st century. With few paved roads to connect the hundreds of steep valleys and widely spaced lowland towns, the country remained almost ungovernable from its capital in Kabul.

Ultimately, of course, isolation was not sustainable. The cold war brought decades of violent destruction, followed by years of civil war and imported religious fanaticism. Hopefully, the latest incursion, in the form of U.S. and NATO (North Atlantic Treaty Organization) peacekeeping troops and major international aid programs, will be more constructive and will finally allow the Afghan people to apply their talents to repairing and developing their starkly beautiful land to its full potential.

Topography

Rugged mountains cover about half of the country's 250,000 square miles (647,500 km²), giving it an average elevation of 6,500 feet (1,980 m) above sea level. Most of these mountains are part of the Hindu Kush range, which spreads over the center of the country in a generally northeast to southwest direction, separating the Central Asian plains from the Indian subcontinent. The average mountain elevation is 9,000 feet (2,740 m). This snow-covered range is the source of nearly all of Afghanistan's rivers.

The range begins in the Pamir Knot in the country's northeastern spur, where it abuts the northwest extension of the Himalayas. It then rises as it moves west toward Nurestan and Badakhshan, reaching 24,557 feet (7,485 m) above sea level at Nowshak Peak near the northern end of the Pakistan border and 25,400 feet (7,742 m) at Tir Ajmir Peak, a short distance away across the border. The range then gradually declines before petering out as it reaches Iran. Several passes cut through the Hindu Kush. The most important, the Salang Pass, leads from the Surkhab River valley in the north to empty into the Kabul Valley; it is the only pass open during the winter snows, thanks to the Salang Tunnel, built in 1964.

Other ranges branch off from the Hindu Kush: the Badakhshan in the northeast, the Paropamisus in the northwest, and the Safed Koh (or Sulaiman Range) in the south, which extends across the eastern Pakistan border through Pashtun tribal territory, defeating all attempts at border security. The Safed Koh rises to 15,620 feet (4,761 m) at Mt. Sikaram and is breached by the celebrated Khyber Pass connecting Kabul to Peshawar in Pakistan.

A multitude of valleys crisscross the Hindu Kush at every angle; they are often suitable for agriculture, which is supported by elaborate irrigation channels and tunnels. Many of the mountain slopes and high plateaus are covered with scrub and short grasses in the warm months, inviting nomads to pasture their flocks.

The mountains of the center are surrounded on three sides by lowland areas: the Turkestan Plains in the north, the Herat-Farah lowlands in the northwest, the Sistan Basin and Helmand River valley in the southwest, the Registan Desert in the south, and the Ghazni-Kandahar Plateau in the southeast. The wide semicircle formed by these areas

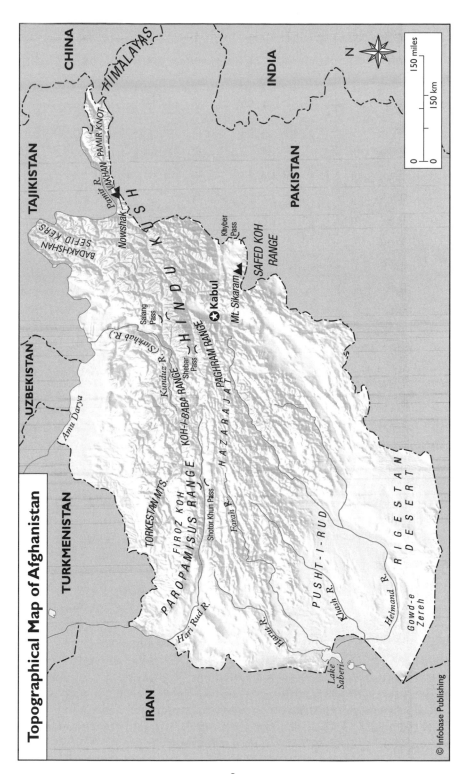

Topographical Map of Afghanistan

CHINA

HIMALAYAS

TAJIKISTAN

PAMIR KNOT

Pamir R.

WAKHAN

BADAKHSHAN

SEFID KERS

H I N D U   K U S H

Nowshak

Salang
Pass

Surkhab R.

Kunduz R.

Shebar
Pass

KOH-I-BABA RANGE

PAGHRAM RANGE

Kabul

Mt. Sikaram

SAFED KOH
RANGE

Khyber
Pass

INDIA

PAKISTAN

H A Z A R A J A T

UZBEKISTAN

Amu Darya

TORKESTAN MTS.

FIROZ KOH

PAROPAMISUS RANGE

Shotor Khun Pass

Farah R.

TURKMENISTAN

Hari Rud R.

Harut R.

Khash R.

P U S H T - I - R U D

Helmand R.

R I G E S T A N
D E S E R T

Gowd-e
Zereh

IRAN

Lake
Saberi

150 miles

150 km

0

0

N

The Hindu Kush mountains, as seen from the Khyber Pass, which connects Kabul and Jalalabad (Photo by Bruce Richardson)

served as an invasion route by mounted hordes from Central Asia for thousands of years, who thus avoided the impassable Himalayas to the east and the high Caucasus-Elburz system to the west.

Of the many rivers that rise in the Hindu Kush, only the Kabul system has an eventual outlet in the sea. The Kabul River rises in the Paghram Mountains to the west of the capital, flows through the fertile plains around Jalalabad, picks up tributaries from the high eastern summits along the way, cuts a pass through the Safed Koh into Pakistan, and joins the Indus River 100 miles to the east.

The Helmand River begins just one ridge away from the source of the Kabul, but it flows to the southwest, providing life-giving irrigation along its 800-mile path. It empties into the Sistan marshes along the Iranian border, which are also fed by a series of seasonal rivers rising in the western Hindu Kush, such as the Farah Rud.

The Hari Rud arises in the Koh-i-Baba Range of central Afghanistan and flows west and northwest. It passes through the fertile plains south of Herat and serves as the northern border with Iran. It eventually disappears into the (Caspian) Kara Kum desert of Turkmenistan.

EARTHQUAKE

Afghanistan is located on the trans-Asiatic seismic zone, or Alpine Belt, that runs from the Azores in the Atlantic through the northern Mediterranean to Iran, the Hindu Kush, the Himalayas, Burma, and Indonesia. In Afghanistan, the earthquake zone is at a depth of many miles.

The country experiences an average of 5,000 earthquakes a year, 500 of them significant, concentrated mostly in the northeast. One ninth-century earthquake destroyed a quarter of the town of Balkh; another in 1832 caused major mudslides and killed a great part of the population of Badakhshan, according to contemporary reports. The most powerful documented episode occurred in 1921 in Badakhshan Province, with a Richter magnitude of 8.1. Two much less powerful, but more devastating quakes hit Takhar Province in winter 1998, together killing some 8,000 people. Most recently, in March 2002, a series of powerful earthquakes occurred in the northeast, the strongest measuring 6.0 on the Richter scale, killing several hundred people and leaving thousands homeless. The Kashmir earthquake of October 8, 2005, that killed tens of thousands of people, primarily in the Pakistan-administered region of Kashmir, and left more than 3 million people without a home, had only a minimal effect on Afghanistan.

The rivers that flow north from the central mountains to water the terraced loess plains of the north either disappear into the semiarid ground (in the west) or join the Amu Darya, which forms the border with Tajikistan and Uzbekistan. The Amu Darya's source is in the Pamir; it accepts a multitude of tributaries before turning north to reach the Aral Sea, now fast disappearing as a result of generations of abuse under the Soviet regime.

Afghanistan enjoys a generally temperate climate. Winter brings fierce weather systems from the north, dropping deep deposits of snow, particularly in the eastern mountains. Strong winds prevail in the mountains even in the warmer months. December is the coldest month, but even then, temperature readings rarely fall much below freezing in the heavily populated valleys and plains. Summers are fairly moderate in Kabul and the center, but the lowlands can be quite hot, and temperatures can reach as high as 120 degrees Fahrenheit (49 degrees Celsius) in the southwest desert zone.

Rugged roads, such as the Shibar Pass shown here, make traveling difficult in winter. (Photo by Shaista Wahab)

Average rainfall is less than 10 inches a year. Only a few areas jutting into Pakistan in the east benefit from the annual monsoon of the subcontinent.

The country has more than 3,317 miles (5,529 km) of borders with neighboring countries. It shares borders to the north with Tajikistan (749 miles; 1,206 km), Uzbekistan (85 miles; 137 km), and Turkmenistan (462 miles; 744 km); to the northeast with China (47 miles; 76 km); to the east with Pakistan (1,509 miles; 2,430 km); and to the west with Iran (581 miles; 936 km). Rivers separate the country from Tajikistan and Uzbekistan; the borders with China and Pakistan mostly bisect mountain ranges; and the borders with Turkmenistan, Iran, and western Pakistan lie across lowlands and desert.

Mineral Resources

Afghanistan has extensive mineral resources that have barely been tapped, apart from natural gas in the north central region, which also has modest untapped oil reserves. Potential commercial deposits have been found of chrome, beryllium, copper, lead, zinc, uranium, manganese, asbestos, gold, silver, iron, sulfur, mica, nickel, slate, and salt.

The precious stones and gems of Afghanistan, on the other hand, have been exploited for thousands of years and continue to provide export income. They include lapis lazuli, amethyst, beryl, emerald, sapphire, ruby, alabaster, tourmaline, jade, and quartz. U.S. geologist Chamberlin Bonita has identified 91 different minerals, metals, and gems that have been produced at 1,407 mining sites in the country.

Agriculture and Plant Life

Afghanistan has an agriculture-based economy, although only 12 percent of the land is suitable for crops; more than 40 percent can be used as pasture. The country's main crops traditionally included wheat, rice, barley, fruits, cotton, poppy, and a large variety of vegetables. The country produces a rich variety of high-quality fruits and nuts, including grapes, apples, apricots, cherries, peaches, quinces, pears, plums, pomegranates, melons, walnuts, almonds, and pistachios. Many of these products were first developed in Afghanistan from wild varieties.

Much of Afghanistan's fresh and dried fruits has typically been exported to European and Asian countries. Sugar beets used to supply a small sugar industry in the north; a refurbished sugar factory was opened in Mazar-e Sharif in 2005. With the exception of drought years, the country was nearly self-sufficient in food before 1978.

Most farmland, such as this in Bamiyan Province, is situated in valleys. (Photo by Shaista Wahab)

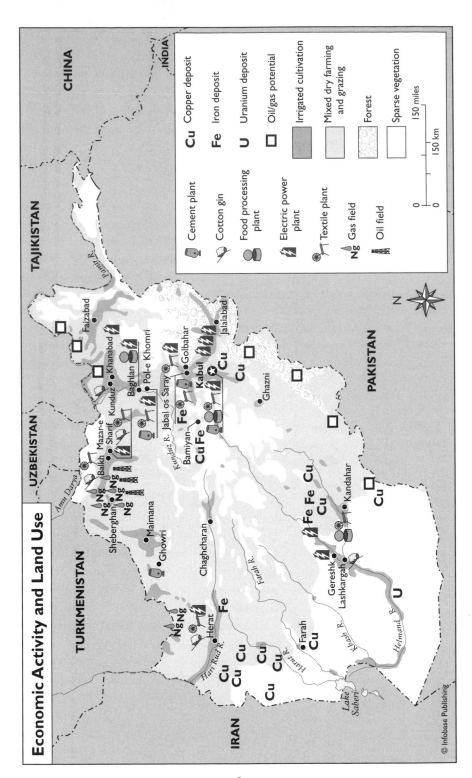

Economic Activity and Land Use

CHINA

INDIA

TAJIKISTAN

UZBEKISTAN

TURKMENISTAN

IRAN

PAKISTAN

Cu Copper deposit

Fe Iron deposit

U Uranium deposit

Oil/gas potential

Irrigated cultivation

Mixed dry farming and grazing

Forest

Sparse vegetation

Cement plant

Cotton gin

Food processing plant

Electric power plant

Textile plant

Ng Gas field

Oil field

150 miles

150 km

N

Faizabad

Khanabad

Kunduz

Baghlan

Pol-e Khomri

Golbahar

Jalalabad

Kabul

Cu

Cu

Ghazni

Mazar-e Sharif

Balkh

Fe

Jabal os Saray

Kunduz R.

Bamiyan

Cu Fe

Fe

Amu Darya

Ng

Ng

Ng

Ng

Sheberghan

Maimana

Ghowri

Chaghcharan

Fe Fe Cu

Fe Cu

Kandahar

Cu

Farah R.

Ng Ng

Herat

Fe

Hari Rud R.

Cu Cu

Cu

Cu

Cu

Harut R.

Farah

Cu

Khash R.

Gereshk

Lashkargah

U

Helmand R.

Lake Saberi

Pamir R.

© Infobase Publishing

Grain production fell steadily from the record prewar figure of 4.5 million tons in 1976, until returning refugees and massive assistance from nongovernmental organizations (NGOs) pushed the 2003 crop to a new record of around 5 million tons, despite dry conditions. Yields have always varied dramatically depending on winter precipitation and will probably remain so barring major infrastructure development.

In the 1980s, opium poppies became the country's most valuable crop; in fact, opium refinement became the country's major industry, and opium, its only lucrative export. Production reached 4,200 tons in 2004, enough to meet 87 percent of global demand. As profits feed crime and terrorism, the government, the United Nations, and the U.S. military launched a major campaign in 2005 to try to suppress the industry.

Because annual rainfall is low, most farmlands are located near streams and rivers for easy access to irrigation water. Traditionally, most farmers also depended on deep wells, canals, and intricate hillside *kariez,* or underground water channels, built up over the centuries, but they unfortunately were heavily damaged during the years of war. About 85 percent of crops were traditionally irrigated, with the rest depending directly on rain.

Forests covered about 3 percent of the land before 1978, mostly in Nurestan and the east along the Pakistan border. Warfare and unrestricted illegal logging has cut back tree cover by two-thirds. Native species include pine, spruce, fir, hemlock, larch, cypress, juniper, alder, birch, willow, oak, poplar, ash, rhododendron, wild hazelnut, almond, and pistachio.

Traditional Afghan doctors or healers use a variety of domestic plants and herbs to treat different illnesses. Healers are called *hakim* (wise men), and their medicines are called *dawa-i-yunani* (Greek medicine). Medicinal plants found in Afghanistan include anise seed, asafetida, caraway, coriander, cumin, garlic, licorice root, saffron, and sage.

Livestock and Wild Animals

The country supports large herds of sheep and goats. They are pastured by nomads in the warm months in the watered highlands. Sedentary farmers keep cattle, including buffaloes, and poultry. Cattle are used for plowing and other labor as well as being a source of food.

In December 2003, the UN Food and Agriculture Organization published the results of the first livestock census ever conducted in Afghanistan, covering about 3 million families. Some 3.7 million cattle were counted, along with 8.8 million sheep, 7.3 million goats, 1.6 million

9

A donkey is used for transportation in Bamiyan Province. (Photo by Shaista Wahab)

donkeys, 180,000 camels, 140,000 horses, and 12.2 million poultry; the figures were believed to have been somewhat lower than the previous year due to drought. Livestock yields commercially important quantities of wool; animal hides, especially from *qaraqul* (Karakul, or astrakhan sheep); meat; and dairy products.

Donkeys, mules, and horses are widely used to carry merchandise and as the most common form of transport in rural areas. During the war years (1978–2001), these three species played a noble role in transporting supplies and weapons and wounded fighters. Camels are used primarily by *kuchis,* or nomads, for transportation and as a source of meat and dairy products.

Afghanistan also boasts a variety of wild animals. Some of them traditionally were important as sources of fur, in sports hunting, and as pets. Several species of wild goats live in the mountains, including markhor and ibex. The rare Afghan wild sheep known as Marco Polo live primarily in the Pamir region; they were brought to Europe by their namesake, the famous Italian merchant-traveler, who visited the area in the 13th century. Their curved horns grow a remarkable 60 inches (152 centimeters) long. Another rare species native to the country is the Bactrian wapiti deer; several of them now live in the San Diego Zoo.

The San Diego Zoo now houses several Bactrian wapiti deer. (Photo by Shaista Wahab)

Animals traditionally hunted for fur and trophies included red foxes, jungle cats, jackals, stone martens, wolves, wild sheep, goats, and snow leopards. Hunters and trappers typically sold furs and skins in regional centers such as Mazar-e Sharif, Maimana, Kunduz, Andkhui, Khanabad, Ghazni, and Herat, from which merchants would bring them to the large fur market in Kabul. From Kabul, they were exported to international markets.

In the 1960s, in response to increased demand from Europe and the United States, numbers in the wild were drastically depleted. In 1973, the government banned the sale of fur products for three years, to give the species a chance to recover.

The Afghan hound (*tazi*) is famous around the world for its speed: It can sprint at 50 miles per hour. Its speed and superior eyesight make it an excellent hunter of deer and rabbit. Many other species of domesticated and wild dogs live in Afghanistan, some of which are trained as sheep dogs.

Unfortunately, years of war, deforestation, and drought have decimated many wild natural habitats in Afghanistan, with results that have yet to be adequately researched; some of the endangered species may have disappeared entirely. Other species that used to be found in the

HUNTING

In response to drops in species' numbers, since the 1970s the Afghan government has regulated hunting seasons and required permits to hunt the following animals:

Animal	Area	Season
Marco Polo (Ovis ammon poli)	Pamir	July–October
Urial (Ovis orientalis)	Lataband	January–March
Ibex (Capra ibex)	Pamir	July–September
	Ajar	December–March
Markhor (Capra falconeri)	Nuristan	December–March

Source: Afghanistan Tourist Information

country include the argali, badger, brown bear, *qaraqul,* ferret, gazelle, gerbil, gopher, groundhog, hamster, hare, hedgehog, hyena, jerboa, leopard, lynx, mole, mongoose, monkey, mouse, otter, porcupine, polecat, rat, shrew, squirrel, tiger, weasel, and wild pig.

The Afghan hound (tazi) is a fast-running dog often used in hunting. (Photo by Shaista Wahab)

For a largely arid country, Afghanistan boasts a large population of wild birds, with an estimated 460 species, of which 235 breed in the country. The country straddles the Indian and Central Asian habitat zones, which accounts for much of the diversity. However, several years of drought dried up the Sistan wetlands in the southwest, which usually serve as breeding grounds for thousands of migratory waterfowl.

The most common birds in Afghanistan are partridges, pheasants, storks, cranes, starlings, ducks, geese, orioles, paradise flycatchers, kingfishers, finches, sparrows, eagles, falcons, quails, owls, nightingales, and swallows. Afghanistan does not restrict bird hunting, which is common throughout the country, as Afghans are fond of keeping birds as pets, with canaries being the most popular species. The Taliban prohibited keeping birds in cages, but the practice resumed after the regime's demise. Some birds are trained for game shooting, including partridges, cocks, falcons, and pigeons.

The People

Ethnic Groups

Afghanistan lacks an accurate recent census of its population, due to the wars and internal and external migrations that prevailed for 25 years. In July 2004, the Central Intelligence Agency (CIA) estimated the population to be 28,513,677, as compared with the last official census in 1979, which registered a population of 15,551,358.

Citizens of Afghanistan are called Afghans, a term that originally referred to Pashtuns alone. Today's Afghans are ethnically and linguistically diverse. Their varied physical appearance, with Mediterranean, East Asian, and South Asian types, shows the imprint of the many conquering nations that passed through or settled.

Despite the multiplicity of ethnic groups, tribes, languages, and dialects, certain qualities bind Afghans together. Religion is the strongest unifying factor, but many other social customs and traditions are shared among the varying groups, as are many economic technologies and patterns. Furthermore, during wars and foreign invasions, Afghans have always put their differences aside and united against the common enemy, as they did against the British several times in the 19th and early 20th centuries and against the Soviet Union in the 1980s.

Population statistics for the major ethnic groups are highly controversial in the absence of an accurate official census. Many people, especially in the cities, are of mixed cultural heritage; even villages and communities of mixed ethnicity can be found. Furthermore, nomads and local tribes are

A Pashtun man, wearing a traditional turban, in Matun (Photo by Bruce Richardson)

often assigned to different ethnic groups based on different criteria. Nevertheless, the CIA made the following estimates in 2004: Pashtun, 42 percent; Tajik, 27 percent; Hazara, 9 percent; Uzbek, 9 percent; Aimak, 4 percent; Turkmen, 3 percent; Baluchi, 2 percent; and "other," 4 percent.

The Pashtun have been the politically dominant group since the mid-18th century. Most of them live south of the Hindu Kush, though sizable concentrations are also scattered across the north. The Uzbek and Turkmen are both concentrated in the north-central border regions, while the Tajik and other Dari speakers occupy a broad swath of the country from east to west, north of the Hindu Kush. The Hazara dominate the mountainous center of the country, with the Aimak situated to their west. Kabul is situated at the juncture of Pashtun, Tajik, and Hazara regions and close to the Pashai-Nuristani homeland.

The origins of the various ethnic groups are the subject of much speculation and legend. The Pashtun at one time commonly considered themselves to be the descendants of the 10 lost tribes of ancient Israel, who were exiled from the Holy Land by the Assyrians in the eighth century B.C.E., according to the Bible; others claim that Afghana, a grandson of King Saul, was the progenitor of the race. Since the establishment of the State of Israel and the spread of anti-Israel sentiment in the Muslim world, another legend has taken precedence, asserting that the Pashtun are descended from Qais, one of the companions of the prophet Muhammad. The Durrani tribe claims descent through Qais's eldest son; the Ghilzai, through his second son. Historians speculate that various ancient invaders gave rise to the Pashtun; the Scythians, who are known to have settled where most Pashtun live today, are a prime candidate.

Pashtun tribes (and clans) traditionally enjoyed a great deal of autonomy. The major tribes are the Durrani, Ghilzai, Momand, Afridi, and Yusufzai. All of them follow a strict code of honor called Pashtunwali, whose main principles are hospitality and asylum to all guests seeking help, justice and revenge for misdeeds or insults, fierce defense of "Zan, Zar and Zameen" (women/family, treasure, and property); defense of the homeland; and personal independence. Local government is regulated by village or tribal elders, who hold *jirgas* (councils) to discuss tribal affairs and resolve problems. Feuds between tribes are often carried on from generation to generation. The majority of Pashto speakers are sedentary farmers, though a large minority lives as nomadic herders.

The Pashtun are notorious for their strict gender role division, and women are often kept isolated in their home compounds. However, families are reported to be matriarchal; it is often mothers, sisters, and wives who encourage their men to be courageous in defense of the family's interests and honor.

The Tajik, Uzbek, and Turkmen each share a language, culture, and history with millions of compatriots in the Central Asian republics of Tajikistan, Uzbekistan, and Turkmenistan. Their numbers in Afghanistan were increased by refugees fleeing first the advance of the Christian czarist forces in the 19th century and then the triumph of Soviet atheism

A Tajik boy carries a large sack. Children in Afghanistan work hard from an early age. (Photo by Shaista Wahab)

in the 20th. All three groups traditionally followed a less tribal political organization than the Pashtun and instead usually accepted the rule of various regional khans.

Of the country's major ethnic groups, the Tajik are the most urbanized, better educated, and more likely to run businesses or hold government jobs. The Turkmen are famous for raising *qaraqul* and for their beautiful wool carpets and rugs.

The Hazara, many of whom have East Asian features, may well be descendants of the Mongol invaders of the 13th and 14th centuries, yet they all speak a dialect of Dari. A small ethnic group called Mogholis, who live in pockets among the Aimak and elsewhere, spoke Mongolian until recently. Nearly all Hazara are Shiite Muslims, possibly dating from the time that the Mongols first converted to Islam, or else from the time of the Safavid dynasty, which militantly imposed Shiism in Iran and tried to do the same in its Afghan realms.

The Hazara were often oppressed on religious or racial grounds. Traditionally, most of them were semisedentary, moving seasonally from lowland farms to high pasture lands. In the 20th century many moved to urban areas where they worked as physical laborers or domestics. They formed the backbone of the country's small labor union movement. A Hazara cultural movement flourished in Quetta in Pakistan, where many Hazara fled in the late 19th century; it helped form the basis for a political and cultural revival in recent years within Afghanistan as well.

A Hazara boy in Bamiyan (Photo by Shaista Wahab)

Many legends exist about the origins of the Nuristani, all of which try to account for the rather high local incidence of blond or red hair and light-colored eyes, especially in the more remote valleys of Nurestan, which is located in the high eastern Hindu Kush. In their tribal lore, many Nuristani claim descent from the soldiers of Alexander the Great. Some observers, pointing to their apparently archaic language, speculate that the Nuristani may be remnants of a putative "original Indo-European tribe."

Nuristan (land of light) was called Kafiristan (land of infidels) until the late 19th century, when the Kafir exchanged their polytheistic faith for Islam, at the demand of the emir Abdur Rahman Khan. Several thousand Kafir living across the border in Pakistan still practice their ancient faith. Nuristan is one of the few well-wooded areas in the country, and the local people build wooden houses perched on the steep slopes of the valleys they farm.

Many Brahui appear physically related to South Indians. They may be either a remnant of the presumed original founders of the Indus Valley civilization, or they may have migrated to the area from a homeland in southern India. They generally occupy a lower social status in relation to their neighbors, the Baluchi. The Baluchi include many fishermen, a rare trade in Afghanistan. They fish the marshes and seasonal lakes of the Sistan; others farm the fertile banks of the Helmand River.

KUCHIS

From time immemorial, there has been a large population of seasonal nomads in Afghanistan known as *kuchis*. Ethnically, most of them are Pashtun (or Baluchi), but they do not fit neatly into the Pashtun tribal structure.

In the cold months, *kuchis* pitched their black tents in lowland camps in various parts of the country or in Pakistan; they often farmed their own land. In the warmer months, they generally pastured their flocks in the central highlands, taking all their possessions with them. Blessed with an entrepreneurial culture, they sold animal products in the villages they passed through and provided cash credit to farmers.

The ethnic tensions stoked by years of war have alienated *kuchis* from many of their Uzbek, Turkmen, Tajik, and Hazara neighbors, who have taken their farmlands or blocked their migration routes, despite attempts by the present government under Hamid Karzai to preserve their rights. The constant dangers of war and the millions of mines drove many *kuchis* to refugee camps near Herat or Kandahar, or out of the country to Pakistan. Severe drought in the early years of the 21st century drastically reduced their herds.

Their exact numbers are unknown and controversial, as they are usually added into the Pashtun total. A recent study by the UN World Food Program estimated that the number of *kuchis* declined from 2–2.5 million in the early 1980s to 1.3–1.5 million in 2004.

Language and Religion

Like ethnic population figures, the number of speakers of each of the languages of Afghanistan is often disputed—one person's "language" is another's "dialect." Using CIA figures again, the 2004 linguistic breakdown was Afghan Persian (Dari), 50 percent; Pashto, 35 percent; Turkic languages (primarily Uzbek and Turkmen), 11 percent; 30 minor languages (primarily Baluchi, Brahui, Pashai, and Nuristani), 4 percent; and "much bilingualism."

Dari has traditionally been the language of literature and government, a remnant of the centuries of Persian rule; all Tajiks speak Dari. Pashto is Afghanistan's other official language. Millions of Afghans, whatever their ethnicity, can speak both languages.

With the exception of the Turkic languages and Brahui (a Dravidian language spoken by scattered groups in the southwest totaling perhaps 200,000 people), nearly all languages and dialects in Afghanistan belong to the Iranian branch of the Indo-European language family. Persian and Pashto are major components of Iranian; Baluchi is closely related to Pashto. Pashai and Nuristani are often considered to constitute another language family on a genetic par with Iranian.

Ninety-nine percent of Afghans are Muslims. About 80 percent belong to the Sunni sect of Islam, and 19 percent are Shiites, with perhaps 1 percent Ismailis. Hindus, Sikhs, and Jews together make up less than 1 percent of the population.

During the 1980s, approximately 50,000 Hindus and Sikhs lived in urban areas. They were mainly traders, merchants, and moneylenders. Afghan Hindus and Sikhs speak Hindi or Punjabi in addition to Dari and Pashto. Several thousand Jews used to live in Kabul, Herat, and Kandahar. They were free to practice their religious ceremonies and attend synagogues; they spoke Dari or Pashto, and some could also read and write Hebrew.

The Soviet invasion of Afghanistan, the civil war, and Taliban rule forced most Jews to leave the country. In 2002, of the entire Afghan-Jewish population, only two individuals remained, both living in Kabul. During the years of war, many Hindus and Sikhs left as well, but some returned following the fall of the Taliban in November 2001.

The constitution of 2004 grants freedom of religion to all citizens. All religious groups, including Christians, are free to practice their faith.

Music and Dance

Music, singing, and dance play essential roles in Afghan family gatherings, parties, weddings, holidays, and special occasions. The various

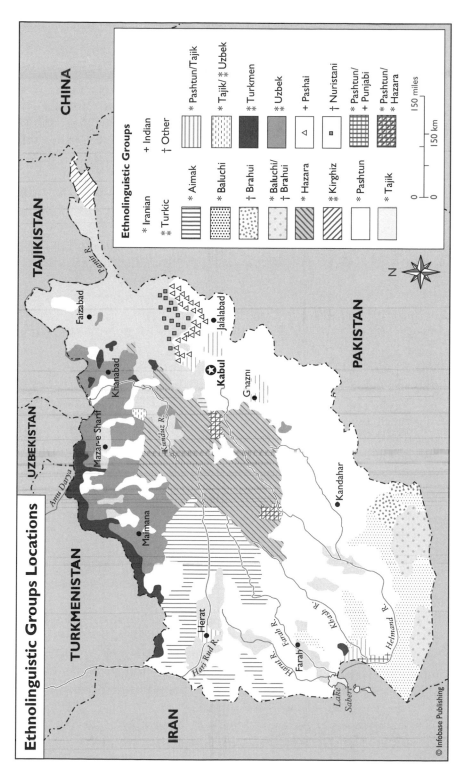

Ethnolinguistic Groups Locations

Ethnolinguistic Groups

* Iranian	+ Indian	* Pashtun/Tajik	
** Turkic	† Other	* Tajik/** Uzbek	
* Aimak		Turkmen	
** Baluchi		** Uzbek	
† Brahui		+ Pashai	
* Baluchi/† Brahui		† Nuristani	
* Hazara		* Pashtun/+ Punjabi	
** Kirghiz		* Pashtun/Hazara	
* Pashtun			
* Tajik			

CHINA

TAJIKISTAN

Faizabad

Khanabad

Mazar-e Sharif

Jalalabad

Kabul

Ghazni

UZBEKISTAN

Amu Darya

Kunduz R.

Maimana

Kandahar

TURKMENISTAN

Herat

Hari Rud R.

Farah R.

Hamu R.

Farah

Khash R.

Helmand R.

Lake Saberi

PAKISTAN

N

0   150 miles
0   150 km

© Infobase Publishing

19

ethnic groups in Afghanistan have their own styles of folk music, but certain common elements are shared by all.

Traditional Afghan music has different scales, intervals, and rhythms than Western music, although it generally sounds less "foreign" to Westerners than Indian music might, for example. Afghan classical and folk music has undergone a revival in recent decades, even as modern Western and Indian music has penetrated the country and been imitated locally.

At most celebrations, men and women stay in separate rooms and dance in separate groups. The *attan-i-milli,* which originated as an open-air Pashtun victory dance, has been adopted as the national dance of Afghanistan, often performed at the end of a celebration. It is a circle dance performed to the accompaniment of *dhol* (drum) and *surnai* (reed pipe) in the unique "mogholi" rhythm. During the dance, the pace gradually picks up, ending with wild exuberance among those remaining on their feet.

Under the Taliban, it was illegal to play musical instruments, listen to music, or dance; the law was strictly enforced by the religious police (Rasanayagam 2003, 198). Taliban authorities destroyed thousands of audio and video music tapes, often in large bonfires. Following the fall of the Taliban, people returned to their traditional musical tastes; peddlers began offering CDs on the streets of Kabul the very day the Taliban withdrew in November 2001.

Afghan musical instruments resemble those used in Central Asia, Iran, and India. The most commonly used are the following:

The *dhol* is a type of barrel-shaped drum made from wood and stretched goatskin. Cords passed through brass loops are used to tighten the goatskin.

The *zerbaghali* is a large vase-shaped drum with a narrow neck and wide head. The body is made of baked clay and is often decorated with drawings and designs. The head is covered with stretched goatskin. It is also played in Iran and Turkey.

The *daira* is a kind of tambourine made from a wooden ring approximately $10^1/_4$ inches (26 cm) in diameter and $2^1/_3$ inches (6 cm) in depth. One side is covered with stretched goatskin. Brass rings or bells are often attached to the inner side of the wooden rim for additional sound effects. The *daira* is played primarily by women, who strike the skin with their hands.

The *rebab* is an ancient short-necked lute with 18 gut and metal strings. The face is covered with stretched goatskin.

The *tambur* is a stringed instrument made of hollowed wood with metal strings; it is played with a metal pick on the index finger. The number of strings can vary, but the most common type of *tambur* has 18 strings.

Other stringed instruments are the *shashtar, richak, waj,* and *sarani.*

Handicrafts

Important handicrafts in Afghanistan include woodworking, leather crafting, basket weaving, and carpet weaving. The fine quality carpets made in Afghanistan are known internationally.

Most carpets are designed and produced by women. Girls begin making carpets at an early age and tend to continue throughout their lives. During the Soviet occupation, many Afghan women continued to make carpets in the refugee camps in Pakistan and Iran.

Sports and Games

Buzkashi (goat grabbing) is the national sport that helped give Afghanistan its fierce reputation among 19th-century Europeans. It

Buzkashi *(goat grabbing) is a national sport in Afghanistan that dates back to Genghis Khan.* (Photo by Shaista Wahab)

21

remains very popular, especially during Independence Day and New Year's Day festivities and other important events.

The sport probably arrived with Mongol or Turkic invaders and is particularly popular among the Tajik, Uzbek, and Turkmen of northern Afghanistan. It is a dangerous game with no explicit rules (until recently), played by expert, powerful horsemen. Players compete to grab and carry the headless carcass of a goat from a starting point to a designated finishing point. It can be played by individuals or by two opposing teams.

Buzkashi demands extraordinary communication between horse and rider and between players on a team. The size of the field varies and can be as large as several miles across; in the autumn, plowed fields are turned up and fertilized by the action of the horses. The horses are trained for at least five years before they can participate. Today's polo was developed by British colonial soldiers in imitation of Afghan *buzkashi*. *Buzkashi* was outlawed by the Taliban, but a large public match was arranged in Kabul as early as December 2001.

Most poor Afghan children are required by their families to work from a very young age to help supplement family income. Children may work on farms with their parents or in shops, factories, offices, or wealthy households as domestics. Consequently, they have little time to play, and the games they do participate in are usually simple and inexpensive. Some are played only by boys, and others, only by girls.

The most common games are the following:

Gudiparan bazi (kite fighting) is normally played by boys, although many adults participate as well. Once the kites are aloft, each player (or team of two players) guides his kite so that its string crosses the string of another player. The players (usually numbering around 25) continue to cross their strings, which are coated with ground glass, until one of them breaks. Onlooking children then try to capture the defeated kites.

Kites are made from bamboo and tissue paper and are typically around $3^{1}/_{2}$ feet (1 m) long, although they can often be as tall as an adult. The sport was banned by the Taliban.

In *juz bazi* (hopscotch), girls draw a rectangular shape on the ground, around 6 feet (1.8 m) long and 3 feet (almost 1 m) wide, and divide it into eight boxes. It is played one person at a time. The player throws a small flat pebble into the first box and tries to kick it out by hopping on one foot. If she succeeds without stepping on any line, she proceeds to the next box. Her turn contin-

Tukhum jangi *(egg fighting) is played by Afghans on special occasions, such as Nawruz or the Eid festivals.* (Photo by Shaista Wahab)

ues until she completes all boxes; if she fails, the next player begins her turn.

Cheshem putakan (hide-and-seek) is played by both boys and girls; they can even play together. One person is blindfolded and counts to 10 while all the other players hide; the game proceeds exactly as it does in the West.

Tukhum jangi (egg fighting), as the name implies, uses an egg as a weapon—but it is hardboiled. It is usually played during Nawruz or either of the Eid festivals (see below). One player holds a hard-boiled egg end up; the other player taps the egg until one of the shells cracks. The player with the cracked shell loses the game. The game is played by children and adults, usually outdoors.

Religious and National Holidays

In the 20th century, Afghanistan began celebrating secular national holidays, but the Muslim religious holidays still evoke the most intense celebrations. Most Afghans try to buy new clothing for Eid al-Fitr, Eid al-Adha, and Nawruz. They mark the holidays with visits to relatives

23

and friends, communal meals, and traditional games. Locally made Ferris wheels, swings, and other entertainments are erected to mark these special occasions.

Nawruz (New Year) is celebrated on the first day of spring, which is considered the first day of the Afghan solar calendar. The holiday dates back to the Zoroastrian period and is celebrated in Iran as well. Afghans celebrate Nawruz by planting new trees throughout the country in *melah-i-nihalshani* (tree planting celebrations).

Special food is prepared for Nawruz. Women spend all night cooking, singing, dancing, and playing the *daira*. They bake colorful cookies called *kulcha-i-Nawruzi* and prepare special dishes like *samanak,* a pudding made from wheat sprouts and whole walnuts cooked together for several hours, and a preparation of white rice and spinach. Afghans also prepare a fruit drink called *mewa-i-Nawruzi* using nuts and dried fruit, including walnuts, almonds, apricots, raisins, pistachios, and *senjet* (lotus fruit).

Ramadan, the ninth month of the Muslim lunar year, is devoted to daylight fasting and evening celebrations. The first day of the month and the first day of the following month (Shawwal) are holidays. During Ramadan, Muslims refrain from eating, drinking, taking medi-

Many Afghans celebrate Nawruz at the site of the holy shrine of Sakhi in Kabul. (Photo by Shaista Wahab)

This Hazara family is on its way to visit relatives in Kabul during Eid celebrations in 2003.
(Photo by Shaista Wahab)

cine, or smoking from sunrise to sunset. Children, the sick, and travelers are exempt. Since the lunar calendar is not connected to the solar year, Ramadan can occur at any season. People may prepare food before sunset to break the fast. Most Muslims break their fast by eating dates, praying, and then eating dinner.

Eid al-Fitr (festival of ending the fast) begins on the first day of the month of Shawwal, which follows Ramadan. It is a three-day holiday in Afghanistan. Tea, cookies, and candies, especially sugar-coated almonds called *nugul,* are served to guests. Younger family members receive gifts of money, called *eidi,* from their relatives.

Eid al-Adha (festival of the sacrifice) is marked on the 10th day of the last month of the lunar calendar. Those who have the means sacrifice lambs or cows to mark the sacrifice of Ishmael, as told in the Qur'an (Koran). The sacrificial meat is shared with family, friends, and poor people. Those with the time or money go on hajj (pilgrimage) to the city of Mecca during Eid al-Adha. The hajj is the fifth and last pillar of Islam, all of which must be undertaken at least once during a Muslim's lifetime, if at all possible.

Maulud-Sharif marks the birth of the prophet Muhammad and falls on the 12th day of the month of Rabi al-Awal. Muslims around the world celebrate this day and offer prayers. Afghans make *halva*, a sweetened sesame paste, and share it with family and friends.

Ashura is a Shiite festival that commemorates the martyrdom of Muhammad's grandson Husayn, who was murdered at Karbala, in Iraq, on the 10th day of the month of Muharram in 680 C.E. Shiites visit *takiyakhanahs,* special halls where they publicly mourn. As a further sign of mourning, devotees stage marches through the streets while beating themselves with whips, chains, and sharp objects, typically drawing blood.

Jeshen (Independence, or Liberation, Day) takes place on August 18; it starts a three-day official holiday and a full week of festivities, including military parades, fireworks, music, and concerts. Jeshen marks the day in 1919 when Afghanistan won full independence from Great Britain by signing the Treaty of Rawalpindi. For the previous 40 years, the British had official control of all Afghan foreign affairs.

Labor Day is celebrated on May 1 to honor the country's working people. May 4 is officially Remembrance Day for Martyrs and the Disabled.

Major Cities
Kabul
Kabul became the capital of modern Afghanistan in 1775 when Timur Shah, the son of Ahmad Shah Durrani, moved his court there from Kandahar. It is strategically located in east-central Afghanistan between the Asmai and Sher Darwaza mountains, on a plateau about 6,000 feet (1,830 m) above sea level. The Kabul River runs through the city on its way to Pakistan and the Indus River.

Historically Kabul was an important town on the ancient trade routes between India and Central Asia. It also played a significant role in social and cultural exchange between various peoples and civilizations. The remains of the old city wall, built by the Hephthalite Huns in the fifth century C.E., are still visible at the BALA HISSAR (citadel). The wall was 23 feet (7 m) high and 9 feet (3 m) thick. In the 16th century, Babur, founder of the Mughal dynasty, made Kabul one of his capitals. Babur died in Agra, India, in 1530, but his body was buried in Kabul on a hillside in his famous Bagh-i-Babur mausoleum, in accordance with his wish. The gardens he laid out still remain as a public park.

Kabul was just a small village when the Durranis arrived. It grew to a town of 10,000 by the end of the 18th century and to the country's largest city over the following hundred years. Today, it is a growing metropolitan city that serves as the social, economic, political, and cultural center of Afghanistan. It is connected via major highways (currently

Downtown Kabul, crowded with pedestrians and cars (Photo by Shaista Wahab)

being rebuilt) to all other parts of the country: The Salang Pass leads to the northern regions and Central Asia, the eastern areas are connected through the Mahipar and Tangi Gharu Gorges, and the south and west are reached via the Kabul-Kandahar-Herat highway. The city's roads and streets were mostly destroyed during the war years.

The population has increased from 600,000 in 1978 to more than 3 million people in 2005. A large number of refugees from Pakistan and Iran, and a smaller number from the United States and other parts of world, settled in Kabul upon their return to Afghanistan after the fall of the Taliban in 2001. The city, lying at the intersection of the main Pashtun, Tajik, and Hazara zones of the country, has long been the country's melting pot.

Owing to the large number of international aid workers and diplomats in Kabul, many business owners and shopkeepers speak some English. The U.S. dollar is the second most popular currency, after the Afghani, used in retail transactions.

Kandahar

Kandahar (Qandahar) became the first capital of modern Afghanistan when Ahmad Shah Durrani set up his court there in 1747. It is located in the south-central region, not far from the Pakistan border.

KABUL MUSEUM

The Kabul Museum reopened to the public on February 4, 2005, with an exhibit of 17 carved wooden effigies from Nuristan. The objects, including life-sized equestrian sculptures, had been cut up by the Taliban but carefully restored since 2001.

The museum, founded in 1931, was once world famous for its rich collections of treasures from many of the cultures that influenced Afghanistan, dating from the prehistoric era to the Greek, Kushan, Buddhist, and other periods. Enriched by finds unearthed by archaeologists around Afghanistan, the museum was testimony to the country's role as a crossroads of civilization.

In 1993, during the brutal mujahideen factional fighting, the Kabul Museum was bombed, and some of its artifacts were looted. The chief curator and his staff transferred as much as could be salvaged to the building's basement. However, looting continued, and despite a 1994 United Nations attempt to seal the building, many artifacts were removed and sold in Pakistan, and from there to unscrupulous dealers and collectors around the world. In 2001, the Taliban destroyed some 3,000 pre-Islamic artifacts, which the regime considered an offense to the Muslim prohibition of images.

Reconstruction began in 2002, along with a concerted effort to locate and repatriate the stolen treasures. Fortunately, some 22,000 gold Bactrian objects believed to be lost were recovered after the fall of the Taliban from a vault beneath the old Presidential Palace.

Artifacts from the Kabul Museum were stolen and destroyed after 1992. Many treasures have recently been recovered. (Photo by Shaista Wahab)

In 329 B.C.E., Alexander the Great entered Kandahar, where he founded the Greek city Alexandria of Arachosia. In the 16th and 17th centuries, the Safavids of Iran and the Mughals of India contended for control of the city, which dominated the main land route between those two empires. In the 18th century, Afghans under Mir Wais Khan fought against the Persians to win independence for the city, and it was in the Kandahar region that Durrani Pashtuns united to choose Ahmad Shah as the first ruler of what became the independent state of Afghanistan. For five years, beginning in 1996, Kandahar was the spiritual capital of Afghanistan under the Taliban regime; Mullah Mohammed Omar had claimed the authority of the Prophet there by publicly wearing the Cloak of Muhammad, the most sacred relic in Afghanistan, brought to the city by Ahmad Shah.

Kandahar is the second largest city in Afghanistan, with an estimated population of several hundred thousand, most of them Durrani Pashtuns. The city is famous for its pomegranates and grapes.

Herat

Herat is located in northwestern Afghanistan, in a region historically known as Khorasan that spanned northeastern Iran and southern Turkmenistan. A cultural and economic center for at least 2,000 years, Herat played an important role in Persian cultural history.

Alexander the Great entered Herat and founded the Greek city Alexandria Arion there. Arab armies passed through in 650 C.E. in pursuit of the last Sassanian emperor and conquered the city around the year 700. By the 11th century, Herat was a famous gathering place for Muslim scholars. It was destroyed in 1220 by Genghis Khan, who slaughtered most of its residents, and again in the 14th century by Timur (Tamerlane). After Shah Rukh Mirza rebuilt the city, it became a famous cultural center where art and literature flourished. The Timurids raised magnificent buildings there. Some of them are still standing, though much was destroyed in 1885 when British officers dynamited the famous Musalla Complex to create a clear field of fire to defend against a feared Russian attack.

Herat is Afghanistan's third largest city. Its economy depends on the region's rich farms, which grow cotton, rice, wheat, and pistachios.

Mazar-e Sharif

Mazar-e Sharif, "the Tomb of the Saint," capital of Balkh Province and the largest city in the north, is named for Ali, son-in-law of Muhammad.

It was founded in the 12th century after a local mullah dreamed that Ali (known as Hazrat Ali in Afghanistan) was buried there. Thousands of Afghans visit every year to pray at his shrine. Sultan Ali Mirza built the beautiful Blue Mosque over the shrine in 1420.

The majority of the city's inhabitants are Uzbek, although many Hazara, Turkmen, and other Afghans live there as well. The region has an agricultural-based economy. It is famous for its watermelon, cotton, and silk products and is also known for rugs, the *qaraqul* industry, and horses.

Ghazni

Ghazni, known as Ghazna in ancient times, is located on a high plateau more than 7,000 feet (2,134 m) above sea level on the main trade route between Kabul and Kandahar. The city reached its zenith as the capital of the Ghaznavid empire (994–1160). Sultan Mahmud, Muslim conqueror of India, built a magnificent mosque there. Most of the city's historic monuments have been destroyed by foreign invaders, including Genghis Khan in 1221.

Ghazni is famous for embroidered sheepskin (*posteen*) coats and vests. It is also a market for sheep, wool, corn, and skin.

2

EARLY HISTORY
(PREHISTORY–651)

Remote and uninviting as Afghanistan may sometimes seem to outsiders, the land has hosted human populations since earliest times. The people who first hunted the plains and foothills and those who first broke the soil and herded animals set the patterns that have continued to recent times. Even then, Afghanistan's geography made it a crossroads for peoples and ideas; never truly isolated, its inhabitants benefited from contact and cultural continuity with their fellows in neighboring lands.

The First Human Inhabitants

Most prehistoric digs in Afghanistan took place between the 1950s and 1970s; foreign scholars led the way, later joined by a growing body of trained Afghan academics and archaeologists. During these three decades of exploration, a few dozen important sites were discovered and studied, revealing tantalizing clues that demanded further and more extensive study. Unfortunately, most work stopped following the Communist coup of 1978 and the Soviet invasion of 1979, and almost nothing was accomplished in the succeeding decades of war, privation, isolation, and ideological hostility to pre-Muslim exploration. In fact, most sites remained exposed to the elements, vandalism, and systematic looting. Archaeologists believe that the existing sites still hold many undiscovered secrets; furthermore, hundreds of other promising sites (caves and rock shelters, suggestive mounds) were identified in the past that can be studied once security is restored and research funds become available.

The limited amount of digging that has been done so far has uncovered rich remains of early human habitation, by *Homo sapiens sapiens*

Archaeological Sites in Afghanistan

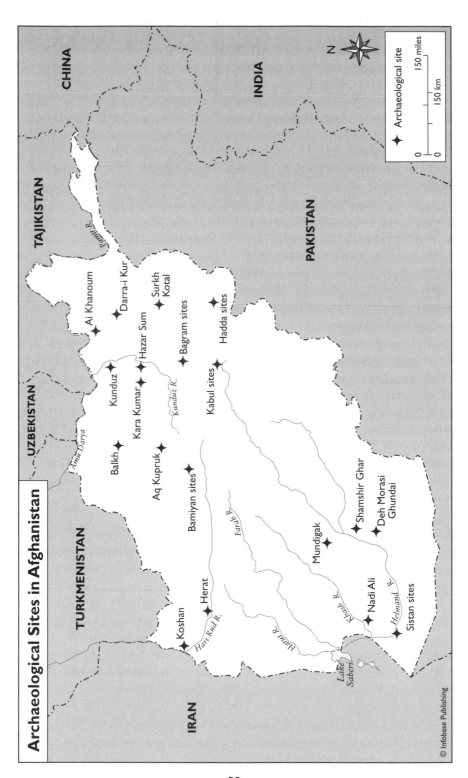

N

Archaeological site

150 miles

150 km

CHINA

INDIA

PAKISTAN

TAJIKISTAN

UZBEKISTAN

TURKMENISTAN

IRAN

Ai Khanoum

Darra-i Kur

Surkh Kotal

Hazar Sum

Bagram sites

Hadda sites

Kunduz

Kara Kumar

Kabul sites

Kunduz R.

Balkh

Aq Kupruk

Bamiyan sites

Amu Darya

Panj R.

Shamshir Ghar

Deh Morasi Ghundai

Mundigak

Farah R.

Koshan

Herat

Nadi Ali

Sistan sites

Hari Rud R.

Harut R.

Khash R.

Helmand R.

Lake Saberi

© Infobase Publishing

32

ASSAULT AGAINST THE LEGACY OF THE PAST

Abdul Wasey Feroozi, director general of the National Institute of Archaeology reflected on the disastrous effects of war on Afghanistan's artifacts and legacy for the Archaeological Institute of America.

> *Afghanistan, which stands at a crossroad of the ancient civilizations in the East and West, has kept a great unique treasure in different parts of its land, and due to that reason some scholars and researchers of different countries decided to start their archaeological activities in this area...*
>
> *The catastrophe of war annihilated seventy years of our hard work and accomplishments.... Over 70% of the Kabul National Museum [collection was] stolen and looted.... Illegal excavations and extensive clandestine digging started at most historical sites and thousands of valuable objects were transported to other countries...*
>
> *The priceless treasures of Mir Zaka in the Paktia Province were illegally excavated from 1993 [to] 1995 by the local people and commanders with the encouragement of Pakistanis and Afghan dealers. The finds, consisting of ornaments, coins, vessels, stamp seals, and animal figurines made of gold, silver, copper, and bronze metals weighing tons, were stolen and smuggled to Pakistan and according to a French publication, from there to Japan, London, Switzerland, Italy and the United States, among other countries. Also Aï Khanum [Ai-Khanoum], which is a Greco-Bactrian city, was badly damaged by looters using bulldozers during illegal excavations.... During the oppressive Taliban regime cultural activities were severely restricted and diminished.... Bamiyan's two colossal statues, along with others in the Foladi valley and Kakrak, were dynamited and hundreds of statues in the collection of the Kabul Museums were destroyed in 2001.... Tepe Shutur-e-Hadda, the great Buddhist Temple, which was an immovable museum and a masterpiece of Gandahara art was demolished and all its unique moldings were plundered. The [Buddhist] Minaret of Chakari, one of the most important monuments of the first century A.D., was also blown up.*

Abdul Wasey Feroozi. "The Impact of War upon Afghanistan's Cultural Heritage." Archaeological Institute of America. Available online. URL: http://www. archaeological.org/pdfs/papers/AIA_Afghanistan_address_lowres.pdf. Posted January 3, 2004.

and possibly by Neanderthals as well. The earliest finds, dated to the Lower Paleolithic of 100,000 years ago, were made in the 1970s at a site 150 miles southwest of Kabul on terraces above Lake Dasht-e Nawur. No clearly Neanderthaloid bones have been found in the country; however, plentiful stone tool sets dating from c. 50,000 years ago were found at the Darra-i-Kur site in northeast Afghanistan. These finds resemble tools associated with *Homo sapiens neanderthalensis* remains in Uzbekistan, not far to the north.

More impressive cultural remains, left by modern humans, have been found at a variety of Middle and Upper Paleolithic sites (35,000–15,000 years ago) in the northern foothills of the Hindu Kush. Tens of thousands of stone tools have been collected, including cores, flakes, handaxes, scrapers, blades, awls, and spear points, made of flint or limestone. A variety of bone implements have been uncovered as well. Judging from animal bones, these hunters had a diet of wild sheep, goats, horses, deer, cattle, and sometimes jackal, fox, tortoises, and even voles.

The fine craftsmanship of the tools dug up at the Aq Kupruk hill site 75 miles south of Balkh, in northern Afghanistan, represents a local tradition that persisted for some 5,000 years (20,000–15,000 years ago). The inhabitants put their craftsmanship to nonutilitarian use as well, judging from a remarkable find in a hearth at the site in the 1960s: a carefully carved $2^1/_2$-inch (6-cm) limestone pebble, some 17,000 years old, whose rounded oblong shape was incised with human features. This is the oldest piece of sculpture unearthed in Asia, though older examples have been found in Europe and, possibly, in Africa. Other possible evidence of early symbolic thinking in the country are geometric markings on microliths that were found in sand dunes near the Oxus River (Amu Darya) 100 miles farther north and dated some 10,000 years ago; such a date makes these artifacts only a bit younger than the earliest geometric finds in Europe, where archaeologists have had much more time to rummage around.

Neolithic Era

Primitive agriculturalists tilled the soil of Afghanistan quite early in the Neolithic era, perhaps 9,000 years ago in the north of the country (Aq Kupruk site), while herders of domesticated sheep and goats were beginning to develop the tradition of seminomadic pastoralism that continues to the present. The elevated foothill terrain that yielded the earliest Afghan Neolithic remains constitutes the eastern end of a climatic and topographic zone that stretches west through northern Iran to modern Turkey. This zone, still home to wild wheat, rye, and other grains, may well have been the original home of the wheat-barley-sheep-goat economy of the Middle East, which underlay the development of the first great ancient civilizations.

At least until the recent past, the isolated mountain valleys and hills of Afghanistan were also home to a great variety of wild fruits, including grapes, cherries, apples, pears, peaches, apricots, pomegranates, almonds, walnuts, and pistachios, some of which are ancestors to current domesticated varieties grown around the world. The massively destructive ordinance of modern warfare removed much of this legacy, and part of the rest was chopped down for firewood by a population reduced to penury.

While some Afghan Neolithic sites show Middle Eastern affinities, a later site at Darra-i-Kur in the northeast (dated 4,000 years ago) bears more resemblance to sites occupied by ancient nomadic or semi-nomadic shepherds in southern Siberia and Kashmir. Darra-i-Kur included jewelry, geometric-decorated pottery, and ritual human burials containing goat heads and horns. Goat horns can still be found associated with graves and shrines in Afghanistan.

Archaeologists have uncovered sedentary Neolithic farming villages at several sites in the country, generally in the low-lying river valleys, more amenable than the hill country to large-scale agriculture. The site at Deh Morasi Ghundai near Kandahar dates as far back as 5000 B.C.E. Morasi, together with neighboring Said Qala and a larger site at Mundigak 40 miles to the north, show a near-continuous record of settlement, allowing scholars to trace the development of agricultural and then urban technologies right down to the mid-first millennium B.C.E.

Early levels at these southern Afghan sites already show pottery, clay human and animal figurines, sundried brick, and small copper implements. Pottery drains and copper tubing followed not long after. Cultural remains show some similarities with Iran and Central Asia.

Early Civilization

By the Bronze Age strata (c. 2000 B.C.E.), these settlements show an obvious relationship with the Indus Valley civilization. They may well have been part of the trading and agricultural network that supported the great urban centers of Mohenjo-daro and Harrapa in present-day Pakistan. At Morasi, a large brick shrine complex shows evidences of a Mother Goddess fertility cult. The Mundigak site became a significant town, with a large monumental complex that may have witnessed human sacrifice, according to some archaeologists. Other Indus Valley cultural artifacts have been found in Sistan in the southwest and Turkestan in the north.

A more culturally eclectic site dated c. 2300 B.C.E. was discovered at Khosh Tapa near the Khawak Pass 150 miles northeast of Kabul, an ancient crossroads between the Middle East, India, and Central Asia. The site yielded gold and silver objects showing animal motifs from all those regions. Nearby deposits of lapis lazuli helped tie the region to Mesopotamia, where Afghan lapis appears in objects from the third millennium B.C.E., and to the Aegean, where it has been found in second millennium B.C.E. strata at Mycenae. The same region may also have been a source of tin for the Middle East.

Another impressive Bronze Age urban site is Dashli in the central northern plains near Mazar-e Sharif, dated at c. 1500 B.C.E. It contained fine local and imported Iranian pottery, bronze and copper weapons, and the remains of a monumental palace.

In the absence of any written remains, scholars cannot make any confident assertions about the language or ethnicity of the early urban residents. Perhaps they were related to the peoples living in the advanced civilizations of that era—in the Indus Valley to the east or Mesopotamia to the west. But in the first half of the second millennium B.C.E., the linguistic picture, at least, becomes a bit clearer.

Earlier, the ancient town located at Mundigak had survived two short-lived episodes of destruction, apparently caused by marauders from the Iranian plateau to the West and Ferghana in Central Asia. But the town was unable to survive new attacks in the mid-second millennium, when a series of more lasting invasions began. For the next two millennia, the region's history would be refashioned by repeated invasions of nomadic groups speaking Indo-Iranian languages.

The Aryans and Their Faiths: Brahminism and Zoroastrianism

The Indo-Iranian, or Aryan, tribes probably entered the country in force c. 2000–1500 B.C.E., as part of a mass migration that brought their language and much of their culture to present-day Iran and India. A few historians speculate that some were present even earlier. In either case, it remains unclear how these people were related to the ancient European peoples who spoke other tongues within the wider Indo-European language group.

Most Afghans today (apart from members of the Uzbek and Turkmen ethnic groups) speak languages descending more or less directly from the Aryan invaders. Many Afghans may themselves be descendants of these migrating tribesmen and -women. The pre-Aryan populations of Afghanistan were never as numerous as those in the Indus Valley and may have been driven out or replaced by the Aryans in certain areas.

The Vedas (c. 1500–900 B.C.E.), the most ancient scriptures of the Hindu religion of India (written in Sanskrit, the ancestor of Hindi and other Indian languages), describe the Aryans as a pastoral people, led by warriors with iron weapons driving horse-drawn chariots. Historians long believed the Aryans came from the Central Asian steppes, but other theories place their origin in the Middle East. Their appearance in South Asian history about the time of the abrupt end of the Indus Valley civilization led earlier historians to postulate a rapid, destructive invasion of India by Aryans passing through Afghanistan; these historians identified place-names in the Vedas with Afghan sites, marking the country's first appearance in recorded history. More recent historians consider it just as likely that the Aryans migrated more gradually; some even believe the language family was present in India long before the time of the Vedas.

The Vedas and other semilegendary material paint an idyllic picture of the Aryans; they were organized into tribes (each with its own dialect), clans, and families, ruled by leaders chosen by councils of all adult males. Women moved about freely and sometimes participated in battle. Primarily a pastoral people, the Aryans also settled the city of Balkh (Bactria) in north-central Afghanistan, calling it "the mother of cities." From Balkh, limited trade was conducted via Samarkand with China, via the Kabul Valley to India, and via Herat to Persia. By the first millennium B.C.E., Vedic religion (later called Brahminism, or Hinduism) was probably honored by most people in northern India and by many in adjacent areas of Afghanistan.

The modern Afghan languages are more closely related to the languages of Iran than to those of India; the Iranian branch of the Aryan peoples may have come in a second migration that passed through northern Afghanistan into Iran and eventually spread to the south of the country as well. The Avesta, the ancient scriptures of Zoroastrianism (the religion of ancient Iran) clearly refers to place-names in Afghanistan, such as the city of Balkh. Zoroaster himself (Zarathustra in Iranian) may have been born in the country and probably died there as well. He is said to have encouraged the local Aryan tribes to adopt agriculture and to have preached unity in the service of the supreme god Ahuramazda, the spirit of good, represented by a ritual flame.

Northern Afghanistan can thus be seen as the original heartland of the Zoroastrian religion. The Avestas report punishing raids from the north, in one of which Zoroaster himself was apparently killed, at Balkh, some time between 900 and the late sixth century B.C.E.

If the latter date is accurate, the prophet was extremely successful in his own day, as the Avesta was put to writing during the reign of the Persian emperor Cyrus the Great (559–530 B.C.E.), who spread the religion throughout the vast Achaemenid Empire (so named for the rulers' semilegendary ancestor Achaemenus). Zoroastrianism became institutionalized as the official religion of the Persian Empire at least by the time of Darius I (522–486 B.C.E.). It remained the national faith throughout the Achaemenid, Parthian, and Sassanid dynasties, and declined only after the Muslim conquest of the seventh and eighth centuries C.E. The Zoroastrian faith, which still survives in small communities in India and Iran (but no longer Afghanistan), may represent a transition between earlier polytheistic religions and the ethical monotheistic religions and universalist philosophies that dominate the world today. Its adherents (and some scholars) claim that Zoroastrian ideas influenced classic Greek philosophy as well as early Judaism, Christianity, Islam, and Buddhism.

Assyrians, Medes, and Persians

According to the Roman historian Arrian, the first Middle Easterners to conquer Afghan territory were the Assyrians (eighth century B.C.E.). They ruled much of Iran, and they may have reached as far as Kandahar in southern Afghanistan; if so, they left no lasting impression on the country.

The Medes, a group of tribes in northern Iran related to the Persians, followed the Assyrians. Sometime before 600 B.C.E., their cavalry helped carve an empire that reached from Anatolia and the Caucasus to Central Asia; it is reasonable to assume, with Arrian, that they ruled northern and western Afghanistan as well. They were soon eclipsed by the Persians, who conquered them around 550 B.C.E. and proceeded to carve out the largest political entity yet known.

History as taught in the Western tradition starts with the ancient Fertile Crescent and then moves on to Greece; it looks at the Persian Empire from the standpoint of a Westerner looking east. We learn that Cyrus the Great, who founded the empire on the Iranian plateau, conquered Babylon to the west and allowed the Old Testament Jewish exiles to return to Jerusalem; Darius I conquered Thrace and invaded

Greece; and Alexander of Macedon brought his armies from Europe to subdue the vast Achaemenid realms. But half of the empire Alexander conquered lay to the east of the royal capital of Susa (Iran). The satrapies of Bactria in northern Afghanistan, Ariana in the west of the country, Arachosia in the south, and Ghandara in the east were named on the famous inscription carved by Darius at Behistun (Iran) listing his inherited lands. Together with Drogiana in the southwest and Sogdiana in Central Asia, these eastern territories (including all of modern-day Afghanistan) were integral parts of Persia and figured in its history and literature in all subsequent eras.

Thus, wherever the Iranians originated, by historic times their political, religious, and cultural patrimony covered much of Afghanistan. To this day, Dari, a form of Persian that is closer to the classic tongue than the dialects spoken in Iran, is one of the official languages of Afghanistan and is spoken in one dialect or another by 50 percent of the population; it was the court language even under the Pashtun-speaking emirs and kings of modern times.

Cyrus devoted at least two campaigns to securing his Afghan lands. One campaign took him through the southwestern desert (where his army might have succumbed without the help of the local Ariaspians), across southern Afghanistan, and up to Bagram (near present-day Kabul), where he built a garrison town called Kapisa. He also battled Scythian tribes north of the Oxus River (Amu Darya) and established several cities there; his final, fatal battle was near the Jaxartes River (Syr Darya).

Cyrus was the founder of Persian power; Darius I was its consolidator. Satrap of Parthia (which stretches across both sides of the current Iran-Afghanistan border), Darius seized the imperial throne in a bloody coup and added territories to the state. His greatest legacy, though, was bureaucratic. He reorganized his realms into 20 provinces, governed by Persian satraps watched over by military governors and royal inspectors. The armies were reorganized on rational principles. Communication lines were secured to enable the steady collection of taxes levied at every locality. The Persian language was put to writing for the first time (in a cuneiform syllabic and later alphabetic script), but Aramaic, already the lingua franca of the Middle East, became the official government language. Afghanistan thus became tightly integrated into the wider civilized world.

Much of ancient Persian history is known only thanks to Greek (and Greek-based Roman) historians, who relied on firsthand accounts. The Achaemenid emperors employed many Greeks for their military and other skills, and Greek colonists were planted in the far-flung border regions to help maintain control. The first Greek settlers in Afghanistan thus preceded Alexander the Great by one or two centuries; whatever their military skills, however, they were unable to keep the satrapies to the south and east of the Hindu Kush within the empire for long stretches of time.

Herodotus, a fifth century B.C.E. Greek historian, was the first to record any nonlegendary details about Afghanistan. He wrote about the warlike Paktuyke tribe in the east of the country, whom some identify with today's Pashtuns, the largest Afghan ethnic group. Their clothing and arms, he wrote, resembled those of the Bactrians to the north; they were subdued by Darius in his Indian campaign and forced to pay annual tribute of 170 gold talents.

Alexander of Macedon

Afghanistan's role as a cultural middleman or transit point, already played during the Neolithic era and the Aryan migrations, emerged even more strongly as a result of the career of Alexander of Macedon, called Alexander the Great. The warrior-king or later apologists speaking in his name, justified his bloody career as a campaign to spread Greek values, and/or to join the best of East and West in a unified civilization. Whatever his intentions, he did in fact leave a lasting legacy in the East, though transmuted in ways he could not have foreseen.

The later Achaemenid emperors no longer reliably controlled the Afghan satrapies; nevertheless, warriors from Bactria (northern Afghanistan) joined the mobilization to help Darius III (c. 380–330 B.C.E.) face the Macedonian threat. In 331, B.C.E. their cavalry under the satrap Bessus fought valiantly (according to Greek sources) at the crucial battle of Gaugamela in northern Iraq, but they were unable to prevent the rout that doomed the empire. Alexander soon added fabled Babylon to his dominions, burned the sacred capital city Persepolis, and pursued Darius toward the Caspian Sea, where the latter was murdered by Bessus and two other treacherous satraps.

The peoples of Afghanistan were to get better acquainted with Alexander than any of his other subjects, as he spent four of his remaining seven years living and fighting in their neighborhood, founding several cities there, and marrying the Bactrian princess Roxana. He left a strong impression, judging from the many folktales still told about Alexander throughout the country; so did Roxana, whose name has remained popular with Afghan parents (although she and her son did not long survive her husband's premature death).

Alexander entered the country in 330 B.C.E., in order to round out his conquest of the entire Persian world and to avenge Darius's murder, but the local tribes and satraps proved more slippery and rebellious than those in the west. Founding Alexandria Arion near present-day Herat, the conqueror followed the time-honored invasion route south to the Sistan; east to the region of Kandahar, where he built Alexandria Arachosia; and north to the Kabul Valley, where he founded Alexandria ad Caucasum. After two years crisscrossing Central Asia, he returned over the Oxus, rebuilt Balkh as another Greek Alexandria, trekked back across the Hindu Kush, and left his footprints in the Indus Valley. At the Beas River, his victorious but exhausted troops finally forced him to turn back.

Greco-Bactrians

Though all his eastern conquests eventually fell away, Alexander's civilian and military garrisons lingered—13,000 troops in Bactria alone. After his death, they were reinforced by thousands of colonists lured from mainland Greece by Alexander's successor in the East, Seleucus I Nicator (c. 358–281 B.C.E.); it was one of the greatest peaceful migrations in ancient history.

The new colonists reinforced Alexander's cities and created new ones, spearheading Hellenistic culture as far as India and Central Asia. Seleucus was forced to cede most of the land south of the Hindu Kush after a crushing defeat in 303 B.C.E. by Chandragupta Maurya (r. c. 321–297 B.C.E.), founder of the Mauryan Empire in India, but he retained the Bactrian lands. An era of peaceful relations, diplomacy, trade, and cultural exchange ensued between the two powers, which allowed the new urban civilization in the north to thrive.

The Greek colonists left behind in Bactria were soon freed of their Seleucid overlords when nomadic Parthians from the north reestablished an independent Persian state, interposing a formidable barrier between Afghanistan and the Greek-speaking West. The "Greco-Bactrians" eventually achieved full independence after 250 B.C.E. under Diodorus II. Within two generations their descendants ruled all of Afghanistan north of the Hindu Kush plus a vast swath of Central Asia. Their empire, or at least their raids, extended to the borders of Han China, or so the Greek historian Strabo claimed; Greek soldiers are occasionally represented in local frontier Chinese art of the period.

41

These contacts were duly noted by the Chinese court. The emperors were impressed by tales of settled cities with civilized ways and a taste for Chinese luxuries, located in a land beyond the barbarian zone; thus was the first regular contact made between China and the rest of the civilized world. Perhaps the first technological innovation to make the westward journey was a practical copper-nickel alloy, used in China for armor and in Bactria for its famous coins. More lastingly, the Silk Road began to be blazed sometime in the second century B.C.E., providing a source of commercial profit to Afghan intermediaries that continued (with ups and downs and some major interruptions) for 1,700 years. From its early days, the Silk Road became a cultural channel as well, as Indian religious ideas, modified by Hellenistic intermediaries, began to trickle into China and, eventually, the rest of East Asia.

Excavations between 1964 and 1978 by French scientists at the northern Afghan site of Ai-Khanoum on the Amu Darya revealed an impressive Hellenistic city, with a theater, gymnasium, a temple to Zeus, Greek-style homes with Corinthian columns and marble statues,

This "Vase of Pharos," showing the lighthouse of Alexandria, was found at Begram near Kabul in 1937. It dates to the first century C.E.
(Afghanistan: Ancient Land with Modern Ways, Ministry of Planning of the Royal Government of Afghanistan, 1961)

and numerous Greek inscriptions. Persian artistic motifs also abound in the city, which may have been one of Alexander's own foundations. Unfortunately, after the dig was suspended, the city's treasures were looted freely for 20 years. The entire site was bulldozed by the Taliban in 2000, but enough probably remains for many fruitful seasons of archaeological work.

Greco-Bactrian rule, whether by one state or a series of local dynasties, eventually stretched down to the Indian Ocean, where local and Silk Road trade was continued with Hellenistic Egypt. In 180 B.C.E., the Greco-Bactrian king Demetrius I pushed south over the mountains and invaded India. For the next two centuries, most of northern India was ruled by

Indo-Greek kings, many of whom, like the revered Menander, became Buddhists. In fact, Buddhism came to play an important role in the civilization of the eastern Greeks, who at their peak (around 150 B.C.E.) held sway from the Ganges to the Aral Sea. The northern Greco-Bactrian kingdoms disappeared in the face of fresh invasions from the north around 125 B.C.E. by Scythians and the Indo-Iranian Kushans, while the southern rulers succumbed to the same invaders after another century or so.

The Greek language eventually disappeared from Afghanistan, where it probably had never been adopted by the rural subjects of the Greek cities; the colonists appear to have blended in with the local population or disappeared. In the isolated valleys of Nuristan northeast of Kabul, however, the local population includes many people with blond or red hair and blue or intermediate color eyes. Europeans who first encountered the Kafirs (from the Arabic for "infidel"), as the local people were called before their forcible conversion to Islam in 1895, theorized that they were the remnant of Alexander's legions. Indigenous legends, as well as perceived similarities with ancient Greek mythology, music, and sports, supported this theory. However, the local languages constitute an archaic branch of the Indo-Iranian family; perhaps the Kafirs in their isolation preserved prehistoric Indo-European traits coincidentally shared with the Indo-European Greeks. Later ethnic and religious incursions would have removed those traits from the rest of Afghanistan; indeed, similar incursions later modified Greece as well, where no one any longer worships Zeus, and most people are not blond (if indeed they were in classic times).

Mauryan Empire

Before the Greek kings pushed south of the Hindu Kush, southern Afghanistan was ruled for 150 years as an integral part of the great Mauryan empire. The Mauryan dynasty presided over one of the glorious eras of ancient Indian history.

The state was founded by Chandragupta Maurya, a militant Hindu who, with the help of Macedonian troops, established a kingdom on the Ganges. He returned to the Indus Valley to overthrow Alexander's Greek colonies there around 320 B.C.E. and went on to defeat Seleucus I Nicator (the victorious) at a great battle in southern Afghanistan in 303. Seleucus ceded all his lands below the Hindu Kush, and the two monarchs set up friendly diplomatic and trade relations. The 500 elephants Chandragupta gave to seal the pact played a major role in Seleucus's later victories in the Middle East. By thus repelling

Alexander's successor from the region, the Mauryans allowed their Greco-Bactrian neighbors to the north to flourish and eventually win their own independence.

The founder's celebrated grandson Ashoka (r. 273–232 B.C.E.) completed the conquest of nearly all of India (though he never breached the Hindu Kush line in the north). Seized by remorse after slaughtering 100,000 people in his final campaign (as he explained in extant writings), he converted to a pacifistic Buddhism and devoted the rest of his reign to building a centralized structure for the empire governed by principles of right behavior and laying the precedent for the idea of India as a single unified country. In his missionary zeal, he built thousands of Buddhist stupas or monuments all over his domains and sent emissaries to spread the faith to Burma, Sri Lanka (where it still thrives), and Greek cities throughout the eastern Hellenistic world, including the contemporaneous Greco-Bactrian kingdom. A Buddhist community probably took root in Egyptian Alexandria at this time. The Greek historian Megasthenes resided at Ashoka's court and wrote the first detailed work describing the land and peoples of the subcontinent.

The king erected pillars with Buddhist inscriptions throughout his empire, usually written in the local languages; these are collectively known as the Edicts of Ashoka. One such pillar was uncovered near Kandahar in 1958, inscribed in Greek (apparently still a major local language) and Aramaic (the official language of the Persian Empire and widely used in diplomacy and government throughout western Asia until Roman days). Other similar Ashokan inscriptions were later unearthed near Jalalabad. Like the other inscriptions, the Kandahar texts extol dharma, or "righteousness," and reveal a pious humanitarianism. They decry cruelty against people or animals and call for moderation in behavior.

The empire declined after Ashoka. The last king in the line was assassinated in 185 B.C.E. by a Brahmin commander, who launched a persecution of Buddhists. This attack against a pro-Greek monarch may have triggered the Greco-Bactrian invasion by Demetrius I (described above), which resulted in the liberation of the Buddhists of northern India and Afghanistan and allowed the continued fusion of Hellenistic and Indian art and philosophy, whose greatest fruits were yet to come.

Kushan Empire

The interaction of Indian and Hellenistic art and philosophy, begun under Greco-Bactrian and Mauryan patronage, reached its creative peak

EDICTS OF ASHOKA— KANDAHAR PILLAR INSCRIPTION

Ten years being completed king Piyadassi [beloved of the Gods] showed piety [dharma] to men. And from that time [onward] he made men more pious. And all things prosper throughout the whole world. And the king refrains from [eating] living beings, and indeed other men and whosoever [were] the king's huntsmen and fishermen have ceased from hunting, and those who were without control [over themselves] have ceased as far as possible from their lack of [self-] control, and [have become] obedient to father and mother and to elders, such as was not the case before. And in future, doing all these things, they will live more agreeably and better than before.

"Kandahar Bilingual Rock Inscription." In Translation of the Edits of Asoka. Available online. URL: http://www.tphta.ws/TPH_ASK1.HTM. Accessed December 1, 2005.

under the rule of the Kushan empire, which encompassed all of Afghanistan as well as large parts of Central Asia and northwest India and which survived in some form for nearly 500 years. Its two most influential legacies were Indo-Hellenistic, or Gandharan, art and Mahayana Buddhism.

Sometime in the third century B.C.E., there began a period of more than usual turmoil and conflict among the nomadic peoples of Mongolia, Sinkiang (Xinjiang), and Central Asia. Many theories have been proposed to explain this phenomenon, which drove waves of Parthians, Scythians (Sakas), and Huns to overrun the civilized zones of South and West Asia and, later on, of Europe, with often cataclysmic results. Some say the new Great Wall of China changed migration patterns; others speculate that bad climate deprived the nomads of food, or, conversely, that good climate encouraged a population explosion requiring new geographic outlets.

In any case, the first to break through in Afghanistan were the Scythians, who were apparently content to live off the land without imposing any formal rule. Large numbers of them are reported at this time in what is now referred to as Pashtunistan. Perhaps the Pashtuns are their descendants, at least in part.

The Scythians were soon followed by the Kushan tribe, which spoke an archaic Indo-European tongue belonging to the obscure Tocharian branch. They were part of a larger confederation known by their Chinese name Yuezhi (Yüeh-chih), who had previously lived in Sinkiang. The Yuezhi began infiltrating Afghanistan in the second century B.C.E., displacing the Greco-Bactrian rulers in the north around the year 135. Some 60 years later, Kujula Kadphises, leader of the Kushan tribe, forged a tight alliance between several tribes, consolidated his rule in the north, and moved through the passes toward the south. For governmental purposes, the Kushans adopted the Greek alphabet and Greek-style coinage, but they apparently retained their native Indo-Iranian faith, a version of Zoroastrianism; a fire-ritual Kushan temple has been discovered from this era.

By around 100 C.E., after withstanding a serious military challenge from the Parthian empire of Persia and its Scythian allies, the Kushans reached their apogee when they crowned their third emperor, Kanishka I (c. 100–150 C.E.). This king is remembered as a glorious monarch who pushed the borders to their greatest extent and ruled from three capitals, including Bagram (Kapisa), north of present-day Kabul.

All the trade routes, by land and sea, between the three major centers of Old World civilization now passed through one rather well-governed and tolerant realm; the land routes all converged in Afghanistan. Under Kanishka's rule, the Silk Road flourished, bringing Chinese and Indian wares to Rome and Western goods to China, and stimulating the growth of literate urban centers in previously marginal zones. Exports from the Roman Empire (including Syria and Egypt) included precious metals, wool and linen cloth, topaz, coral, Baltic amber, frankincense, glass products, and wine. India contributed cotton to the trade mix, as well as indigo, spices, pearls, ivory, semiprecious stones, Kashmir wool, steel swords, and fur. From China came raw and embroidered silks, Siberian and Manchurian fur, jade, and eastern spices. All regions exported their own characteristic fine pottery and crafts, appreciated by connoisseurs throughout the civilized world. From this period on, rare foreign objects turn up at random in ruins in northern Europe and provincial China, mute testimony to the vibrancy of the ancient Silk Road.

Bagram, Kanishka's summer capital, sat astride the Indian branch of the road. Excavations in the 1930s and 1940s of two rooms of the second-century royal palace revealed a remarkable international collection of some 2,000 objects of art. The treasure included elaborately carved ivory panels from India, Han dynasty lacquered boxes, Greco-

Bamiyan, at an altitude of about 8,200 feet (2,500 m), is located 145 miles (223.3 km) northwest of Kabul. Set along the famous Silk Road that linked China with Europe, Bamiyan was a major Buddhist center prior to the spread of Islam during the ninth century. In March 2001, the Taliban destroyed the monumental statues of Buddha (120 and 175 feet [36 and 53 m] high) that were carved into the rock face. (Afghanistan: Ancient Land with Modern Ways, Ministry of Planning of the Royal Government of Afghanistan, 1961)

Roman bas-relief sculpture and plaster-cast medallions, Pompeian-style bronze statues, Egyptian silverware, Phoenician glass vessels, and more.

More impressive still are the treasures of Indo-Greek art known as the Gandharan style, after the Gandhara region of northeast Afghanistan that straddles the Pakistan border. Thousands of sculptures, reliefs, and architectural elements have been unearthed in the region dating from the late first to the mid-sixth centuries C.E. Many of them depict the Buddha, previously portrayed only symbolically as a footprint, lotus, wheel, or swastika. The Gandharan Buddha typically appears as a serene Apollo-like deity. The hair, clothing, and sometimes posture is rendered with Hellenistic realism; the face, however, is usually given a stylized cast, and the setting and accoutrements are Indian. Various Greek gods, such as Heracles and Atlas, were borrowed to embody Buddhist concepts, including the Boddhisatvas; their attributes, even hairstyles, were ritually copied for centuries. Gandharan Buddhas set the pattern for all subsequent Buddhist art throughout East Asia. The most dramatic specimens were the monumental Buddhas, 120 and 175 feet (36 and 53 m) high, carved into the rock face at Bamiyan in north-central Afghanistan on the trade route to Balkh. The statues were surrounded by numerous monastic caves; thousands of monks were reported to live in Bamiyan as late as the seventh century, just before the Muslim conquest.

The self-proclaimed Persian prophet Mani (c. 217–275 C.E.), who founded the ancient Manichaean religion, is said to have been active in Bamiyan. His religion, which won many powerful adherents all over the ancient world from Rome to China, was a deliberate fusion of such earlier religions as Christianity, Judaism, Buddhism, and Zoroastrianism. It may in turn have influenced later Christianity as well as Buddhism, but in Afghanistan, it probably did not long survive the arrival of Islam.

Kanishka has been revered as the patron of Buddhist Indian philosophy and literature, although he apparently supported Hindu and Zoroastrian institutions as well as the newer Persian cult of Mithra. Many contemporary Hindu temples and other remains have been found in eastern Afghanistan. The Mahayana (northern school) Buddhism that evolved in cosmopolitan Gandhara soon spread via the Silk Road to China, Mongolia, and Korea, and from there, later on, to Japan. The new view of the Buddha as a man-god may have been influenced by Greek models (for example, Alexander himself), and Stoic notions of duty, virtue, and equality may have contributed to the belief that each individual has a Buddha nature. On such a speculative level, we can surmise that Buddhist notions of respect for the weak and pardon for sinners, attested by the earlier Ashokan edicts, may have traveled through Greek intermediaries and influenced early Christianity. The pattern of the Buddha's life and the willingness of Boddhisatvas to endure the pains of reincarnation to help others achieve enlightenment may similarly have influenced the story of Jesus.

Sassanians and White Huns

The Kushans were weakened and much of their territory taken away by the new Sassanian dynasty of Persia. The dynasty's founder, Ardashir I (r. 224–c. 241 C.E.), overthrew the Parthians in 224. He was supported by nativist tribes from southern Persia determined to reject the Parthian intruders and restore the glories of the old Achaemenid regime. He succeeded in bringing western and southern Afghanistan back to the Persian fold, not for the last time in history.

The Kushans held on in northern India, though they lost ground there, too, this time to the Hindu nativist Gupta rulers. Petty Kushan states continued in parts of Afghanistan as well, sometimes as satrapies under the Sassanians. Buddhism continued to be practiced and

Kabul Bala Hissar (Kabul high walls) was built by the White Huns in the fifth century. During the 19th century, it was used as a residence by the British. (Photo by Shaista Wahab)

enriched in the diminished Kushan realms in northwest India and northern Afghanistan, but its glory days were numbered. Battered by the old Indo-Iranian religions (Zoroastrianism and Hinduism) and later by the destructive Hun invasions, Buddhism barely survived until the Muslim conquest, after which it ceased to exist as an important force in Afghanistan.

Successive invasions of nomadic tribes into the settled areas of the Near East were a familiar phenomenon by this time. The new peoples were usually accommodated and eventually integrated into the mix of cultures. But Afghanistan and north India were now faced with a more serious barbarian challenge.

The Ephthalites, or White Huns, may have originated in Mongolia and may have been ethnically related to the Huns and Avars who later terrorized Europe and the Middle East. When they crossed the Oxus in the mid-fifth century, they impressed the settled population both by their fierce, brutally efficient fighting methods and by their horrid appearance; they are said to have bound their children's heads to distort their skulls and to have slashed the cheeks of young boys to create unnatural looking beards. Such visages had never been seen; in the West, the unbeatable Huns were at first perceived as nonhumans.

It did not take the White Huns long to subdue Afghanistan and northern India, razing cities, slaughtering populations, and suppressing religious institutions in their path. They wisely ceased their depravations after their rule was secure, but they never entered the cities to establish successor empires as their predecessors had done. After a century of rule with little to show for it, the Huns were defeated around 565 in a joint attack by a Sassanian army led by Khosrau I (r. 531–579) and his Turkish allies, who took over all the lands north of the Oxus.

From then until the Muslim invasions more than a century later, Afghanistan was ruled as a stable part of the restored Sassanian Persian Empire, with Hun satraps in the north and Kushans in the south. To the east, the Hindu Guptas ruled India. After a millennium of foreign invasions and cultural change, the region was once more under unchallenged control of Indo-Iranian ruling elites—Persian Zoroastrians in the west and Indian Hindus in the east—along a border usually defined by the western rim of the Indus Valley.

3

FROM THE RISE OF ISLAM TO THE AFGHAN STATE (651–1747)

Historians of Europe traditionally used the sack of Rome by the Vandals in 472 as a convenient marker for the end of the ancient world and the start of the Middle Ages. For the lands to the south and east, all the way to Central and South Asia, a more appropriate year might be 632, when Muhammad died and his followers began their first raids out of the Arabian Peninsula toward the ancient settled lands of the Fertile Crescent. Within 20 years of that date, Arab armies were roaming the borderlands of Afghanistan 1,500 miles away; by the early 700s they ruled an empire from Spain to Central Asia—though it took them at least another 150 years to subdue the tough tribesmen of Afghanistan.

Islam

In some ways, the Arabs who so quickly conquered a huge chunk of the civilized world resembled many other nomadic invaders before them, from the Aryans of the distant past to the Goths and Huns of the previous few centuries. In each case, the conquering armies were composed of tough nomadic or seminomadic tribesmen with a proud fighting culture. Skilled at rapid mobile warfare, they were all able to exploit momentary weaknesses among their more civilized enemies.

The Arabs were helped by the exhaustion of the Byzantine and Sassanian treasuries and armies as a result of decades of brutal war between the two powers. In addition, the Sassanian Persian state had experienced political and social decline, and many of its subject peoples had little reason to fight for their rulers. Many Christians under Sassanian rule (like many Jews and Copts under Byzantine rule) may even have welcomed the Arabs as liberators from religious persecution.

But this invasion was different. The usual motives of power, material gain, and tribal or ethnic glory were accompanied by a remarkable religious zeal. The fractious tribes of central and western Arabia had only recently been united under the charismatic political, social, and religious leadership of Muhammad, the founder and prophet of Islam. With each of their astonishing early victories, the Arab armies gained more confidence in their mission to spread the truth revealed by Muhammad in the Qur'an (the record of his prophesies and other utterances) throughout the known world.

Muhammad considered the Qur'an to be the revelation of Allah (God) to the Arabs, parallel to the earlier revelations to the Jews and Christians (the Old and New Testaments). At first, many of the conquerors proudly asserted their Arab origins, even preserving their original tribal and clan affiliations. But the universalistic tendencies of the faith prevailed before long.

In the end, the Arabs' message proved far more lasting than their armies. Arab military supremacy lasted only 200 to 300 years, and the Arabic language itself only spread a couple of hundred miles in Asia, from the western bank of the Euphrates to the eastern bank of the Tigris, and from the Syrian Desert to the Mediterranean coast. But Islam, the legacy of Muhammad and those who developed its traditions, rather quickly prevailed over a vast area, becoming the majority religion in the most ancient centers of civilization—Egypt, the Fertile Crescent, and the Indus Valley. Subsequent nomadic conquerors, most notably the Turks and Mongols in Asia and the Berbers in Africa, were soon converted and, in turn, became agents in the further spread of the faith.

In Afghanistan, Islam eventually crowded out all previous religious traditions, and Islamic law and custom took root all over the country. Arabic became the language of religion (Muslims around the world still read the Qur'an in Arabic), and to a degree of law and culture. All of the older writing systems in Afghanistan were replaced by the Arabic alphabet, and many Arab words entered the local languages. Islam has proven to be the strongest, and at times the only, unifying factor for Afghanistan's varied ethnic groups.

The Early Conquests

After wresting Syria from the Byzantines in 635, the Arab armies turned to Mesopotamia. At the historic battle of Qadisiya two years later, they routed a vast Sassanian army and seized the Persian capital, Ctesiphon (near present-day Baghdad). The remaining Sassanian forces were anni-

FIVE PRINCIPLES OF ISLAM

There are many different traditions within Islam, some of them with contrasting beliefs and customs. But the more than 1 billion Muslims throughout the world all accept the Arabic Qur'an as their holy book, and all accept the five basic principles, or "pillars," of Islam.

1. The creed, or *kalima-e shahadat:* Muslims must proclaim that there is no God but Allah, and Muhammad is the messenger (*la illaha illa allah, Muhammadan rasul Allah*).
2. Prayer, or *namaz:* Muslims are required to pray five times a day—in the morning before sunrise, at noon, in the afternoon, at evening, and at night before retiring. If for any reason a Muslim is not able to pray at the appointed times, he or she is required to append the missed prayer(s) to the evening prayer.
3. Charity, or *zakat:* Muslims with the means are required to give charity. The rate is determined by the individual's income and type of property. *Zakat* is given to Muslims who are less fortunate.
4. Fasting, or *roza:* Muslims fast between sunrise and sunset every day during Ramadan, the ninth month of the year; no food, drink, smoking, or sexual relations are allowed. Since the Muslim calendar is strictly lunar, it lags several days behind the solar year, and Ramadan eventually falls in every season, including the long days of summer. Children, the ill, and travelers are not required to fast.
5. Pilgrimage to Mecca, or hajj: Muslims who are financially capable must make a pilgrimage to Mecca, in Saudi Arabia, at least once in their life, to visit and pray at the Kaaba, the sacred black stone monument. Thereafter, he or she is called *hajji.* Muhammad declared that Muslims who perform the *hajj* ceremony properly become free of all sins. In recent years, some 2 million Muslims from all over the world have gone on pilgrimage each year.

hilated at Nihawand in northwest Iran in 642, and over the next several years, the Arabs gradually asserted their authority in most of the vast empire.

In their long pursuit after the last Sassanian emperor, Yazdegerd III (r. c. 632–651), Arab forces passed through Herat and Balkh in northern Afghanistan around 650 and annexed the Seistan region in the southwest soon after. Yazdegerd was murdered shortly thereafter, either in Balkh or in Merv (modern Turkmenistan). The Arabs, preoccupied with digesting their vast conquests (in Africa as well as Asia) did not at first try to subdue the remaining Sassanid provinces in the east, which included most of Afghanistan. They contented themselves with occasional raids for booty; various towns or mountain valleys would submit, and even convert, only to revert once the raiding parties departed.

Even the population in the fully conquered provinces of Iran and Iraq did not all convert to Islam in the seventh or even eighth century. The urban population, more exposed to Arab rulers and soldiers and tempted by the economic and career advantages of conversion, rapidly accepted Allah; many Jews and Monophysite Christians similarly may have found it easy to accept the Muslim affirmation of faith that "There is no God but Allah." But most Persian landowners and peasants held fast to their ancient traditions until the ninth century. Afghan tribesmen, whether Zoroastrian, Buddhist, Hindu, or shamanist, apparently resisted more strongly; they exacted a continual small toll of casualties on the invaders.

Muhammad had accepted Jews and Christians (who were widely dispersed throughout the Sassanian Empire) as "People of the Book," to be tolerated on payment of special taxes. Omar (d. 644), the second caliph, or successor to Muhammad, extended that recognition to Zoroastrians, but subsequent Muslim rulers (Arab and Persian) worked to suppress the religion. Many Zoroastrians fled to India in the eighth century; those left behind eventually dwindled to tiny communities in Iran proper and disappeared entirely in Afghanistan, the probable original home of Zoroaster.

Around the year 700, an Arab army marching from Seistan annexed Herat and Balkh (which at the time boasted 100 Buddhist monasteries), while another took Kandahar and finally Kabul, then ruled by the Hindushahi dynasty. The local rulers were left in place on payment of tribute but "protected" by Arab military governors; the Arabs continued on to conquer Sind (southern Pakistan).

The Hindushahis (of Kushite, Hun, or Turkic origin) may have presided over a Hindu revival, before and after the appearance of Islam. The idea of the elephant god Ganesh may have originated or spread in Afghanistan in this era. The dynasty ruled Kabul until 870 and continued to rule Gandhara in eastern Afghanistan and parts of Pakistan for another hundred years.

Islam probably took on a more welcome face in the Afghan region under the early Abbasid caliphs, who reigned in Baghdad starting around 750. The dynasty, while of Arab descent, had been installed by a Persian general leading a Muslim army from Khorasan (eastern Iran, northwest Afghanistan, and the lands to the north). Ethnic Persian officials (and some Afghans) became prominent in the political and cultural life of the Abbasid Caliphate. From that point on, Islam ceased to be an exclusively Arab project, and Persian cultural elements and traditions had their impact on subsequent religious, artistic, and literary trends; many of the Arabic-language writers and scholars of that golden age were of Persian or Afghan background.

In this peaceful era, trade flourished, and a great Persian cultural revival began under Muslim auspices; the eastern cities took a major part in this trend, including Herat, Balkh, and especially Bokhara and Samarkand to the north. Once again, as in Greco-Bactrian and Kushite days, the Afghan region proved hospitable to a blending of diverse cultures.

Early Muslim Dynasties: Saffarids, Samanids, and Ghaznavids

Abbasid rule began to crumble after the death of the fabled Harun al-Rashid in 806 (though his successors kept formal power for another 450 years). By the mid-ninth century, many semi-independent principalities had emerged, especially in the eastern provinces. Tahir Foshanj of Herat and his descendants, the Tahirids, ruled Khorasan from 821 to 873. They lost Herat in 867 to Yaqub bin Layth Saffari, a fanatical Muslim coppersmith's apprentice from Zaranj in Seistan. Saffari united all of present Afghanistan (plus parts of Iran and the Indus Valley) under his somewhat erratic control. He conquered Kabul for Islam around 870 and effectively broke the back of Hindu and Buddhist rule everywhere in the country; a brief Hindushahi revival in the next century failed to last. Saffari's descendants ruled Seistan as vassals of other empires and dynasties for another 600 years.

At about the same time, the Samanids, a Muslim Persian dynasty founded by Saman Khuda (r. 819–864) was establishing itself at the capital of Bokhara and at Samarkand; their patronage made those cities, and later Balkh in Afghanistan, centers of learning, poetry, architecture, and art, as celebrated in their day as Baghdad. Among the famous poets of this period from the Balkh region were Abu Abdullah Jaffar, known as Rodaki, Shaku Balkhi, Shahid Balkhi, and the tragic poetess Rabia Balkhi, whose tomb was discovered in 1964. The Samanid writers laid the groundwork for most of subsequent Persian-language literature.

In 900, the Samanids won dominion over all the Saffarid lands, thereby uniting Afghanistan (together with Khorasan and Transoxiana, the lands north of the Oxus River) under a stable, tolerant Muslim regime that lasted 100 years. By around 960, however, they were feeling pressure from nomads to their north, the vanguards of a new wave of Central Asian conquerors—Turks and Mongols—whose descendants would play a central role in Muslim history up until the dawn of modern times. In 990 the Ilak Khan Turks captured Bokhara; nine years later, they finished off the Samanids for good.

The Samanids had been known for orthodox Muslim piety and patronage of Persian culture and for their rather lax rule. The next prominent Muslim dynasty in Afghanistan, the Ghaznavids, were known for military prowess and fierce promotion of Islam.

The peculiar circumstances surrounding the birth of the Ghaznavid dynasty set a pattern that became quite common in the Muslim world. Muslim armies began to be staffed, and soon led, by slaves captured in raids beyond the Dar al-Islam, the region controlled by Muslim rulers. Such slave commanders often assumed effective power in provincial areas, and even in the capitals, and eventually rose to power in their own rights.

One such slave general was a Turk named Alptigin who headed the Samanid garrison in Khorasan. He staged an unsuccessful coup and then fled with his Turk supporters to the small fortress of Ghazna, northeast of Kandahar, which he then ruled on behalf of the Samanids from 961. His own slave (and son-in-law) Subuktigin later extended Ghaznavid control to all of Khorasan south of the Oxus River by 994, taking advantage of the fall of the Samanids at the hands of the Ilak Khan Turks.

Subuktigin's son Mahmud of Ghazni (r. 988–1030) was the founder of the Ghaznavid empire per se, the first large Muslim state to be ruled from within Afghanistan. He personally led 17 campaigns into India, adding Baluchistan, Punjab, Kashmir, and the upper Ganges region to his rule; sacking cities; and using the vast treasuries of Hindu temples to finance his rule (and their slaves to do his labor).

Not content to be a mere overlord, he and his mullahs waged determined campaigns of mass conversion in both India and Afghanistan. Hinduism was effectively extirpated from the latter for the first time. Afghanistan eventually became one of the most purely Muslim countries in the world, lacking even a significant Christian minority. In Ghazni itself, archaeologists have dug up the worn-out remains of many Hindu statues on the approach to the ruined mosque in Ghazni, where they were apparently used as stepping stones. In Indian history, Mahmud is known as the "idol breaker" by Muslims or the "scourge of India" by Hindus. His destruction of the great temple at Somnath and his alleged slaughter of tens of thousands of Hindus became rallying symbols for 20th-century Hindu nationalists.

Mahmud also expanded the borders to the west, seizing much of Iran from another Turkish dynasty there, the Shiite Buwahids. The caliph in Baghdad, who was a Sunni like Mahmud, supported this campaign.

Once firmly established on his throne, Mahmud used the spoils of war to rebuild Ghazna into a large, splendid city. Remains of some of his mosques and palaces still stand at various sites in Afghanistan, especially in Bost in the southwest (but not much remains in Ghazni,

SUNNIS AND SHIITES

The two major religious communities among Muslims are the Sunni and the Shia, also known as Shiites. Today, the Shiites are concentrated in Iran, southern Iraq, and the Persian Gulf coast, with substantial minorities in Pakistan, India, Afghanistan, and a few other countries. This geographic distribution is partly the result of happenstance, as one ruler or another was won over to the Shiite camp; for example, Iran became predominantly Shiite only under the 16th-century Safavid rulers.

The division arose in the very beginning of Muslim history, in a dispute over the rightful succession to Muhammad, who did not have a son. The Shiites supported the claim of Muhammad's son-in-law Ali ibn Abi Talib, husband of his daughter Fatima. The disputes led to the assassination of Ali in 661 and of his son Husayn in 680. The two have been honored as martyrs by Shiites ever since. The Shiites believe that the leadership of Muslims rightfully belongs to the descendants of Muhammad; various factions within the movement disagree on the precise line of succession in the early centuries, but they all reject the early caliphs as illegitimate.

Shiites gained some strength under the Abbasid caliphs, who were Sunni Arabs themselves but found allies and supporters among the Shiite factions. Over the years, some more substantive differences emerged between the Sunnis and the Shiites, especially concerning which of the hadiths (the early traditions about Muhammad and his companions) are valid. Some Shiite factions seemed more open to mystical theories and practices; the Druze and Bahai movements, for example, began within Shiite communities.

which was repeatedly destroyed in later years). The sultan built universities that taught mathematics, religion, medicine, and the humanities. Though the Ghaznavids were Turks, Persian became the language of the court and empire, in imitation of the Samanids. Mahmud is said to have brought 900 scholars, poets, and Muslim philosophers to the city; he appointed as court astrologer the scientist and historian Al-Biruni (973–1048), who wrote in Arabic; Al-Biruni's book *India* is an important historical source. Mahmud also supported the historians Al-Utbi and Baihaqi, the philosopher Farabi, and a group of major Persian poets including the great Ferdowsi. These writers helped spread the

FERDOWSI

The following is excerpted from a biography of Ferdowsi provided by the Iran Chamber Society.

> Ferdowsi is considered as the greatest Persian poet, author of the Shahnameh ("The Epic of Kings"), the Persian national epic, to which he gave its final and enduring form, although he based his poem mainly on an earlier prose version. For nearly a thousand years the Persians have continued to read and to listen to recitations from his masterwork...
>
> The Shahnameh, finally completed in 1010 CE, was presented to the celebrated sultan Mahmoud of Ghaznavid, who by that time had made himself master of Ferdowsi's homeland, Khurasan.... Ferdowsi came to Ghazna in person and through the good offices of the minister Ahmad-ebn-Hasan Meymandi was able to secure the Sultan's acceptance of the poem. Unfortunately, Mahmoud then consulted certain enemies of the minister as to the poet's reward. They suggested that Ferdowsi should be given [only] 50,000 dirhams, and even this, they said, was too much, in view of his heretical Shi'ite tenets.... In the end Ferdowsi received only 20,000 dirhams. Bitterly disappointed, he went to the bath and, on coming out, bought a draft of foqa' (a kind of beer) and divided the whole of the money between the bath attendant and the seller of foqa'.
>
> Ferdowsi died inopportunely just as Sultan Mahmoud had determined to make amends for his shabby treatment of the poet by sending him 60,000 dinars' worth of indigo.

"Hakim Abol Qasem Ferdowsi Tousi." Iran Chamber Society. Available online. URL: http://www.iranchamber.com/literature/ferdowsi/ferdowsi.php. Accessed December 2, 2005.

dynasty's glory and preserved a record of beautiful buildings, gardens, and a life graced with fine objects of art and splendid ceremonies. The ruler is said to have kept 2,500 elephants in his stables, and thousands of slave soldiers in the barracks.

The Ghaznavid Empire did not remain intact after Mahmud's death in 1030. Turkish peoples from the steppes, including the Seljuks (who conquered Iraq and Iran around this time), encroached from the north and west, pushing Mahmud's successors to concentrate instead on securing India, where small independent states had sprung up. Mahmud's son Masud I set the example; A kind but incompetent ruler, Masud fled Ghazna after his defeat at Taloqan in 1040, taking his father's treasures with him to Marikala in India. His army followed, seized the treasures, and killed the sultan.

Ghurids and Khorasanians

The dynasty held on to Ghazna itself until the middle of the next century, but in 1151 the city was sacked, its people massacred, and its famous buildings and libraries burned by Allaudin, head of the Ghurids, another Afghan Turkish dynasty. Allaudin thus earned the title *jahansuz* (world burner); the remaining population did, however, rebuild the city. Ghaznavid rulers held on in India until 1186, when the last king was killed at Lahore by Ghurid forces.

Ghor was an old kingdom in the mountains of north-central Afghanistan, possibly founded by Kushans or Huns; the region was subdued and converted to Islam by the Ghaznavids. Under Turkish Muslim chieftains, the people emerged from the mountains early in the 12th century to make their first capital at Herat. One campaign at a time they gradually supplanted the Ghaznavids in all their Afghan and Indian domains.

The new dynasty did not leave as glorious an imprint on history and literature as its predecessor, but it did leave some monumental physical remains, including the foundations of the Friday Mosque (Masjid Jami) in Herat (begun by Sultan Ghiyasuddin in 1201 and later extensively remodeled) and two great victory towers, probably based on earlier Ghaznavid models. One is the famous sandstone Qutb Minar near Delhi, at 238 feet (72.5 m) the tallest minaret in the world. The other, only 20 feet (6 m) shorter, stands in the otherwise desolate Jam Valley in the Hindu Kush.

Beautifully decorated with blue-tile kufic inscriptions and lacey geometric and floral motifs in brick and stucco, the tower at Jam (built by

The Friday Mosque, or Masjid Jami, in Herat, begun by Ghaznavid sultan Ghiyasuddin in 1201 and later extensively remodeled (Photo by Shaista Wahab)

Ghiyasuddin in 1194) has puzzled archaeologists since its rediscovery in 1943, due to its remote location in the central mountains. Remains of a palace, fortress, bazaar, and a possible Jewish cemetery have since been uncovered, suggesting that the site may be the lost Ghurid summer capital of Firozkoh, reportedly destroyed by the Mongols in the 13th century (as was the other Ghurid capital at Bamiyan).

The Ghurids were defeated by the Khorasanian Shah Turks, who poured into Afghanistan and Iran from their capital at Samarkand around 1200. The Khorasanians defeated the Ghurids in 1215, overthrew the Seljuks to the west, and briefly established their suzerainty from Turkey to India. Financed by Silk Road profits, they might have developed from rough conquerors to civilized rulers, as had the earlier Turkish dynasties, but their reign was cut short by the Mongol invasions, which changed the course of history in so many ways.

The Khorasanians were weakened by resistance from their Persian subjects and from the Baghdad caliph, who still retained some moral authority in the Muslim world. But no power would have been able to resist the Mongol cavalry under Genghis Khan. The vast size of his armies (perhaps 2 million strong) and their speed, maneuverability, and discipline made all resistance futile.

The Mongols

The widespread, ruthless, and systematic destruction carried out by the Mongols in Afghanistan may have permanently changed the character of the country. Historic cities and large settled regions with towns, villages, and farms in the northern, southern, and southwestern regions were wiped out, some never to recover. Irrigation systems built up over the centuries were carefully demolished by the conquerors, and the people who knew how to rebuild them were killed. Cities such as Balkh and Ghazni lost their status as creative centers of Islamic culture. The fall of the larger trade cities and oases farther north, once rivals to Baghdad, and the murder of their educated elites pushed Afghanistan further from the centers of world civilization.

The more nomadic tribes of the country, on the other hand, may have found it easier to evade the conquerors by retreating to the mountains, where the Mongol advantage in horsemanship and tight organization was less effective and where tribesmen could hide in caves and irrigation tunnels, according to contemporary accounts. Afghanistan's reputation for decentralized tribal or clan rule and its martial, almost feudal code of values, little tempered by cosmopolitan sophistication, owes a great deal to the Mongol invasions. The gradual progress of urban civilization was set back hundreds of years.

Genghis Khan, or "ultimate leader," had begun his life as a lowly orphan and spent his early career in endless fighting that brought all the Mongol and Turkic nomads in the region north of China into one unified force. Chosen leader of this huge confederation in 1206 (at the age of 51), he imposed a unified legal and religious system on the tribes, adopted an alphabet for the Mongol language (the Mongols had been among the least civilized of the northern peoples), reorganized the army under brutal discipline that long outlasted his own death, and brought great generals up from the ranks to assist him and his sons.

After subduing China and carrying back enormous treasures and armies of slaves, Genghis turned his attentions to the west. According to medieval historians, the fighting started when the powerful Khorasanian shah rashly rebuffed Genghis's offer of alliance, killing his gift-laden envoys instead. This untimely gesture gave Genghis whatever pretext he needed. The shah had just dispatched an army to subdue Baghdad, when as many as 200,000 heavily armed Mongol horsemen swarmed through the Khorasanian heartland in 1219, accompanied by Chinese siege engineers; they reduced Bokhara to flames, culled the population for useful craftsmen and slaves, put Samarkand to the torch, and then turned south to sweep up their defeated enemy's subject peoples.

As so often in the past, Afghanistan was the first stop on the campaign; it was subdued in 1221. The contemporary Persian historian Juvaini wrote: "a world which billowed with fertility was laid desolate, and the regions thereof became a desert, and the greater part of the living dead, and their skin and bones crumbling dust" (Afghanan Dot Net 2005).

While other Mongol columns swept undefeated across northern Iran and through the Caucasus to the Ukrainian steppes, Genghis's generals suffered their first defeat of the campaign in Afghanistan, north of Kabul, at the hands of a mixed Khorasanian-Afghan tribal army. In revenge, Genghis annihilated the entire human and animal population of Bamiyan Valley (vowing to destroy every plant as well) and ordered it forever desolate. Ghazna, hardly recovered from the Ghurid destruction of 70 years before, was razed to the ground once more.

Despite these clear lessons, when Genghis moved on to India, the Afghan cities rebelled. Genghis turned back from the hot Indus Valley, which he deemed unsuitable for his horses, and promptly annihilated the citizens of Herat and Balkh. It took seven days to complete the slaughter at Herat; 2,000 citizens who managed to hide were later murdered by a Mongol force returning for that purpose. However, the rebellions, and the constant bandit attacks against supply stores, may have served a purpose. Uninterested in India, the Mongols may have concluded that Afghanistan was not worth the trouble of a sustained campaign.

After Genghis's death in 1227, the empire was divided into four realms; the border between two of them bisected Afghanistan. What was left of Balkh, Kabul, and Ghazna was allotted to the Jagatai Khanate of Central Asia. Mongol garrison troops stationed in the mountains may have been the ancestors of today's Hazara ethnic group, most of whom appear to be of East Asian origin.

Herat and the west of Afghanistan went to the Il-Khanate of Iran and Iraq, which in 1245 assigned the territory to the capable Kart dynasty of Tajiks as governors. The Karts revived the city and gradually occupied all of Khorasan as well as Kandahar to the south, declaring their independence of the khans in 1232. To this day, a significant minority of Afghanistan's Tajik ethnic group live in Herat and its region and other pockets in the west. The Karts held on for 50 years, until they were overcome by the next wave of Mongol conquest under Tamerlane.

Genghis's troops were not Muslims, although there were already many Muslims in his base areas. In 1258, the Mongol khan Hulagu (1217–65) killed the last Abbasid caliph in Baghdad for refusing to submit, putting an end to a 500-year dynasty. Hulagu's Christian wife and sisters persuaded him into an alliance with Christian crusader kings, and together they captured Syria. But by the end of the century, Islam reasserted itself. The Mamluk slave dynasty of Egypt, devout Muslims, defeated a Mongol army in Syria in 1260. Gradually, the new invaders succumbed to the same fate as other barbarian conquerors—cultural submission to the civilizations they had conquered. In China, they became Buddhist; in the west, they adopted Islam.

In 1295, the new il-khan, Mahmud Ghazan (1271–1304), declared himself a Muslim and forced his court to convert as well; he became a great patron of Muslim learning and arts, which subsequently showed a strong East Asian influence. By the next century, the Mongols had become defenders of Islam, helping its spread in border regions. As the century progressed, however, the various khans lost much of their barbarian vigor, and the political scene in the eastern Muslim world was ready for a new player.

Timur and the Timurids

Claiming to be a descendant of Genghis Khan, Timur (known as Tamerlane in the West) was actually born to a petty chieftain of Turkish-Mongol origin in an agricultural region south of Samarkand, in c. 1336; even at his most powerful, he was known as "the great emir" rather than by the more kingly title of *khan*. Many of the loyal soldiers who helped him carve out the last steppe empire in South and West Asia were Uzbek Turks, who comprised the core of his infantry; Uzbeks are the third largest ethnic group in Afghanistan today. Timur is considered the Uzbek national hero.

Timur established himself as master of Transoxiana through years of clever politics and tough fighting—an arrow wound during his early years as a bandit in Afghanistan gave him his name Timur-i Lang, which means Timur the Lame. In 1370, he marched out of his native Transoxiana determined to revive Genghis's empire; he proved at least as brutal and vindictive as his claimed forebear, judging by the number of cities he destroyed and the high pyramids of severed heads he built. His armies went even farther than Genghis's, at one time or another reaching Delhi in the east, Ankara and Damascus in the west, and Moscow in the north.

Timur's record in Afghanistan was mixed. On the one hand, he took ruthless revenge in Seistan in the southwest when his horse was shot out from under him; he systematically destroyed the Helmand irrigation systems and consequently is traditionally blamed for the region's desolate condition ever since. In fact, the unpredictable moving sand dunes of the region are also partly to blame for converting what had been known as "the granary of the East" into a desert. Timur tried, without much success, to subdue the mountain tribes, on his way to and from Delhi, where he massacred Hindus and impiously plundered the Muslim sultan's property. In the north, he destroyed but then rebuilt Balkh and Herat.

Most of Timur's conquests proved ephemeral, but his successors, the Timurids, remained in power in Central Asia and Afghanistan until the early 16th century. The spoils and captive artisans brought back by Timur to Samarkand jump-started the last major cultural and artistic flourishing in Central Asia. Commerce on the Silk Road reached its peak.

Samarkand and Herat benefited from the destruction of the cities of Iran during the two Mongol invasions. Timur's youngest son, Shah Rukh (r. 1405–47), a patron of the arts, established his capital at Herat. His celebrated wife, Gawhar Shad, who helped him emerge victorious in the succession struggles, supervised massive construction projects in that city using the finest imported architects. Much of the work is still standing, including parts of the Musallah, a combination house of worship, school, and mausoleum, world renowned for its delicate beauty, and the reconstructed Friday Mosque.

Minarets of Herat built in the 15th century by the Timurids (Photo by Shaista Wahab)

The Musallah, a mausoleum built for Gawhar Shad in the 15th century in Herat (Photo by Shaista Wahab)

The widowed Gawhar Shad was murdered in 1447, while in her 80s, by a contender for the throne. However, under the last Timurid ruler, Husayn Bayqarah (r. 1470–1506), Herat underwent an even greater renaissance of scholarship, science, calligraphy, music, and the arts, graced by such illustrious figures as the great mystical Persian poet Abdurrahman Jami, the revered miniaturist painter Behzad, a native of Herat and head of its academy for decades, and the historian Mishkwand. The Timurid Renaissance is considered the last great era of classic Persian culture; it was enriched by Chinese influences. Once again, as in the time of the Avesta and in the Samanid and Ghaznavid eras, Afghanistan was a key center of Persian culture. A vigorous literature in the Jagatai-Turk language emerged as well.

The Timurid Empire barely impacted southern Afghanistan. In 1451, Ghilzai Pashtuns from the southeast were able to impose themselves as rulers of the Sultanate of Delhi, as the Lodi dynasty.

After the Timurids lost power, Transoxiana came under the control of a new Uzbek dynasty, the Shaybani, which briefly captured Herat but was unable to hold on to any territories south of their homeland. From that point until the present, the Oxus River (now Amu Darya) has remained an international border, uncrossed by any major army until the ill-fated Soviet invasion in 1979. By the end of the 15th century, all the major ethnic and language groups of today's Afghanistan were already in place in the country. Additional peaceful influxes of migrants later occurred, such as Persians under the Safavids and Central Asians fleeing the Soviet Union, and some internal migration took place as well, but the basic mix was there.

Mughals and Safavids

While the country was never again to face incursions of steppe horsemen greedy for plunder, the era of Mongol and Turkish rule was not yet complete. In 1504, a 19-year-old Turkish-speaking Mongol, Zahiruddin Muhammad (better known as Babur, "the tiger") captured Kabul (at the invitation of its citizens suffering from a local tyrant). A descendant of Genghis (through his mother) and Timur (through his father), the young man had already been warring for years to add Samarkand to his inherited khanate in Ferghana, to no avail. Further failures to the north turned his attention south of the Hindu Kush. It took Babur years to subdue the Pashtuns up to Kandahar. He then launched a number of raids into India, eventually leading to his defeat of the Ghilzai Afghan rulers of Delhi in 1526, in part thanks to his Turkish cannons. At his death, four years later, he controlled most of northern India as well as nearly all of Afghanistan.

Babur was a poet (in Persian and Turkish) and writer; his autobiography, compiled over a 40-year period, is considered a classic of the genre and a major source of information about the period. He wrote of his Timurid predecessors, of the various Afghan tribes, of the flora and fauna of Afghanistan and India, and of his beloved Kabul, which remained his summer capital and which he enhanced with famous gardens. His tomb is in one of his gardens.

Babur, founder of the Mughal Empire, is buried in the Bagh-e Babur (Babur Garden) in Kabul, his beloved summer capital. (Photo by Shaista Wahab)

BABUR'S KABUL

Following is description of Kabul from Babur's autobiograpy, *Baburnama:*

> [The city was] an excellent and profitable market for commodities. Every year seven, eight or ten thousand horses arrive in Kabul. From Hindustan every year fifteen, twenty thousand pieces of cloth are brought by caravans. The commodities of Hindustan are slaves, white cloths, sugar candy, refined and common sugar, drugs and spices. There are many merchants who are not satisfied with getting three or four hundred per cent (Ewans 2002, 27).

The Mughal Empire that Babur founded, which ruled nearly all of India as well as most of Afghanistan, survived at least nominally for more than 300 years. The administrative groundwork for this remarkable achievement was laid by one of Babur's generals, the Afghan native Sher Khan, who seized power from Babur's son in 1537 and ruled for eight years. Not long after, Babur's grandson Akbar began his nearly 50-year rule (1556–1605). He expanded the empire geographically and standardized its administration, often retaining defeated non-Muslim local rulers as his representatives. Much of this structure remained in place under later British rule until the establishment of Indian independence in 1947.

Despite his own illiteracy, Akbar was a great arts patron, favoring the Persian culture, which retained its dominant role throughout the Mughal era. He also tolerated all religions. In 1582, he proclaimed a new syncretic monotheistic religion called Din-i-Ilahi, Divine Faith, combining aspects of Islam, Hinduism, Zoroastrianism, and Christianity. The last of the great Mughal sultans, Aurangzeb (r. 1658–1707), ignored this precedent and fatally weakened Mughal rule by persecuting Hindus and stirring up massive revolts.

Kabul and most of Pashtunistan remained nominally part of the Mughal Empire until its effective demise, although the tribes' loyalty was usually bought rather than forced. During this time, the Uzbeks of Samarkand ruled Balkh and the north (leaving many monumental remains in Timurid style), while the west of Afghanistan came under the dominion of the Iranian Safavid dynasty (1502–1736), which captured Herat around 1506. Kandahar alternated between Safavid and Mughal rule, depending on the fluctuating balance of power.

The intermittent fighting between the three empires encouraged the survival of localism in Afghanistan, as hundreds of small tribal and clan units maintained relative independence or shifted allegiance when it suited their needs. The trend of revolt and of Afghan adventurism in Persia and India accelerated in tandem with the decline of the Mughals. Furthermore, the gradual spread of hand-held firearms made the mountaineers more formidable than ever. Wealthy medieval conquerors, whether from the steppes or civilized empires, had been able to outfit their knights and even horses with elaborate armor turned out by their skilled artisans. Bullets eliminated that advantage.

The Safavid dynasty, founded by Kurdish descendants of Sufi religious leaders, established the current borders of Iran and Shiism as the country's unifying creed. The reign of Shah Abbas I (1588–1629) was the dynasty's high point, as evidenced by remarkable architectural achievements in Isfahan, the capital city. The era of Abbas saw an expansion of European interest in the region, after a century of modest trade, and religious and colonial incursions by Portugal. Abbas received support from western Europeans, who pushed him to open an eastern front against the Ottoman Turks who had been expanding in the Mediterranean and the Balkans. English warships helped Abbas seize the strategic Portuguese colony at Hormuz at the mouth of the Persian Gulf.

Stirrings of Nationalism

Afghan resistance to the Mughals was in part inspired by the work of the poet-warrior-philosopher Khushal Khan Khattak (1613–90), who celebrated his struggles (against rival tribes as well as the Mughals) in Pashto poetry. Head of the Khattak tribe based near Peshawar (modern Pakistan), he was imprisoned by Aurangzeb in Delhi; upon his release, he called on the Pashtuns to unite and resist the wiles and bribes of the Mughals. He summed up his life in his gravestone inscription, "I have taken up the sword to defend the pride of the Afghan, I am Khushal Khattak, the honorable man of the age." (Afghan Network iNteractive) A definitive body of Pashto writings emerged for the first time, no doubt helping to sustain a new national consciousness.

Similar national feelings inspired the most successful Afghan leader of his day, Mir Wais Khan, the wealthy head of the Hotaki branch of the Ghilzai Pashtuns. The Ghilzai had generally supported the Safavids, however, they rebelled when the Safavid sultan Husayn I (1694–1722) tried to forcibly impose Shiite Islam on the tribes. Mir Wais took Kandahar in 1709 and slaughtered the hated local Safavid governor.

The Ghilzai (who may have had Turkish ancestors) were then, as now, rivals to the Abdali (later called Durrani), the other major Pashtun tribe in Afghanistan. Mir Wais's victory encouraged his Abdali enemies, who dominated Herat, to declare that region independent of Persia as well in 1717.

Not long after Mir Wais's death in 1715 his son Mahmud seized control and in 1722 marched on Isfahan, apparently intent on establishing a new Persian dynasty of his own. He captured the city after a brutal siege. Afghan rule, so often successful in India, proved a disaster in Iran. The reigns of Mahmud and his cousin and successor Ashraf (r. 1725–30) were notorious for conspiracy and bloodshed and plunged the country into chaos and warfare.

While Mahmud and his Ghilzai Pashtuns were preoccupied trying to rule Persia from their capital at Isfahan, the Abdalis managed to establish firm control in Afghanistan from Herat to Kandahar. Other Abdalis served in the armies of the bandit and adventurer Nadir, who led the Persian resistance to the Ghilzai shahs. Nadir Shah (r. 1736–47) assumed the Persian throne himself in 1736 and proceeded to build a short-lived empire in the region with strong help from his Abdali and Ghilzai Afghan troops. He asserted his power over Afghanistan, destroying old Kandahar after a year-long siege and laying down a new city in the process, though he never won sustained allegiance from the Afghan tribes.

Nadir campaigned in India long enough to loot a major part of the fabled Mughal treasury and then swung north, where he was murdered by some of his own officers in 1747. The 25-year-old Abdali Pashtun commander of his bodyguards, Ahmad, who was also Nadir's treasurer, made off with much of the Mughal royal hoard, including the famous Koh-i-Noor diamond. Ahmad then led the guard, a ready-made army of 4,000 battle-tested cavalrymen, back to Kandahar.

Ahmad had been fighting for Nadir since he was 16 years old, but as the titular leader of the small but prestigious Sadozai clan of Abdali Pashtuns, he still had powerful connections in Kandahar. Nadir's murder had fortuitously freed the city of Persian rule, and it was now in need of a local leader. In a departure from long traditions of disunity, a *jirga,* or assembly, of all nine Abdali clans met near Kandahar in 1747 to choose a *padshah* (paramount khan, or king). After nine days of deliberation, the choice fell on Ahmad Shah.

Though the Barakzai clan was larger than the Sadozai, its leader, Hajji Jamal Shah, withdrew in Ahmad's favor. According to tradition, the decision was forced by a well-known dervish, or holy man, who spoke in Ahmad's favor and then placed two sheaves of wheat in his turban as an act of coronation. The wheat is depicted in Afghanistan's flag.

KOH-I-NOOR DIAMOND

The Koh-i-Noor, meaning "mountain of light" in Persian, was originally a 280-carat oval cut diamond, probably mined somewhere in India. According to legend, it had passed between various Indian rulers for centuries until it fell into the hands of the Mughal emperor Babur, who described it in the *Baburnama*.

After a detour through Persia, where Nadir Shah gave it its name, and through Afghanistan, where its glory helped legitimize the rule of Ahmad Shah, the "father" of Afghanistan, it found its way back to India. Timur Shah's son Shuja Shah took the stone with him when he was forced from power, only to have it extorted from him by Ranjit Singh, the Sikh ruler of Punjab, in 1813. When the British East India Company later defeated the Sikhs and annexed the Punjab in 1849, it sent the diamond to Great Britain as a gift for Queen Victoria, for whom it was recut to a more modest 106 carats. Given the stone's unlucky history, no English king has worn it, but it was set into the crowns of several queens and is part of the United Kingdom's Crown Jewels.

After a prophetic dream, Ahmad Shah adopted the sobriquet Durr-i-Durran (Pearl of Pearls), and the Abdali were thenceforth known as the Durrani Pashtuns. They provided the rulers of Afghanistan from that point up until 1978.

Blessed with a charismatic personality, more than ample funds, and his 4,000-strong cavalry, Ahmad soon won the acceptance of the Ghilzai Pashtuns as well as the Durrani; the Ghilzai never regained the glory they had won in India and Iran. Ahmad cemented his rule by dividing some of the spoils he had seized in Persia, which had been supplemented by another stroke of good luck. A day before he arrived in Kandahar, a caravan reached the city bearing rich additional booty from India destined for Nadir Shah. As Nadir was dead, Ahmad seized the loot and engaged the services of the Qizilbash mercenaries who were guarding it. The Qizilbash, Persian Shiites, thereafter acted as the Durrani shah's personal guard and administrators; their descendants still constituted a small but prominent administrative caste in Afghan cities as late as the 1970s.

From this point in his life, the new ruler was known as Ahmad Shah Durrani. To later Afghans, he is often known as Ahmad Shah Baba, the father of Afghanistan, and its first king (though the term was not used at the time).

4

THE BIRTH OF MODERN
AFGHANISTAN (1747-1901)

Ahmad Shah's most lasting achievement was to unite all of present-day Afghanistan under native rule, although it took more than a century for that unity to become stabilized and widely accepted by the population and outside powers. In the short term, however, he managed something more—a large territorial empire that gave the Afghans their last years of glory on the world stage.

The Durrani Empire

When Ahmad began to amass power and territory, there was no other power on the scene to stand in his way. The Muslim Mughal state in India had entered the downward phase of its history, characterized by a lethargic ruling class and communal and religious strife. To the west, Persia's cities were decimated by war; after centuries of destruction and rebuilding, some, like Isfahan, would never regain their old size and importance. In the north, in Central Asia, commerce and civilization had peaked as well; the Silk Road was being almost completely supplanted by maritime trade in the Indian Ocean conducted by Europeans, Arabs, and Americans. And firearms, by now widely spread throughout the world, had canceled out the advantage that marauding horsemen from the steppes had enjoyed for millennia.

The only large viable state in the Muslim world was that of the Ottoman Turks, whose territories were a safe distance from Afghanistan. Britain and Russia, the powers that would eventually fill the vacuum in South Asia and bring the Afghan state back down to size, were then only laying the groundwork for their future Asian empires.

Ahmad's first task after being selected paramount Durrani Pashtun chief in 1747 was to expand his narrow base from Kandahar, which remained the Afghan capital for the remainder of his life. He quickly captured Ghazni from the Ghilzai Pashtuns and received Kabul from its Qizilbash rulers the same year without a struggle.

Turning his attention east, he next took Peshawar, the gateway to the prosperous Indus Valley domains of the Mughals. Despite a minor defeat in 1748 at the hands of the Mughal general Mir Mannu, Ahmad was able the following year to extort title to a large chunk of Mughal India from its weak shah (also named Ahmad) by threatening to sack his capital, Delhi. The Mughal Ahmad ceded Sindh at the mouth of the Indus and all of his territories west of the Indus River to the Afghan ruler.

Ahmad thus succeeded in uniting all the Pashtuns, who had begun to develop a national consciousness, under his rule. Unfortunately for their cause, they were unable to hold on to this achievement. The eastern and southern Pashtuns were eventually separated from the Afghan kingdom, to be ruled successively by the Sikhs and the British, and then to be incorporated into the 20th-century state of Pakistan.

Ahmad, his forces swelled to 25,000 by the adherence of the eastern Pashtun tribes, then marched toward the west. He laid siege to Herat, and after nine months wrested it from Persian control. Pushing deeper into Persian-ruled territory, he campaigned for two years in Khorasan, adding that territory to his empire, including the important city of Mashad.

Herat and even Persia had experienced Pashtun rule in the past, but the shah's next target, in 1749, was new territory for him and his tribes: the Turkmen, Uzbek, Tajik, and Hazara lands between the Hindu Kush and the Amu Darya. Unlike Ahmad Shah's more distant conquests in Persia and India, these lands have remained under Pashtun rule ever since; their integration into the Afghan nation-state has remained problematic for much of that time.

Ahmad's remaining campaigns were all in India, where he worked to consolidate and expand his rule, soon to include Kashmir and the Punjab, including the city of Lahore. He captured Delhi in 1757 but allowed the Mughal sultan to hold on to the throne under the watchful eye of Ahmad's second son, Timur Shah, whom he placed there as his agent. The repeated campaigns in India more than paid for themselves, through confiscated treasures and yearly tributes, which Ahmad liberally distributed to his followers back home.

While the Delhi sultan had accepted Afghan control over much of his empire, his non-Muslim subjects had other ideas. Adherents of the Sikh religion were gaining strength in Punjab; they were unhappy with Muslim rule whether from Delhi or Kandahar. In addition, the militant Hindu Marathas who controlled western and central India began to push north into Mughal territory; they defeated Timur Shah with Sikh help in 1757.

In response, Ahmad proclaimed a holy war to resist the Hindus and Sikhs. The call attracted wide Pashtun and Baluchi support, which may have helped him cement control at home. In 1761, two vast armies (each 80,000–100,000 strong, the Hindus assisted by French mercenaries) faced off at Panipat, scene of many fateful battles in Indian history. Ahmad won what appeared to be a decisive victory, slaughtering hordes of soldiers and camp followers. The battle became significant to later Indian historians, who believed that the fighting and huge losses undermined India's capacity to resist the British, who just a few years later consolidated control in Bihar and Bengal farther down the Ganges and began to build a genuine empire in India.

The Sikhs rose up against the Afghans later in 1761. Repeated Afghan campaigns up until 1769 succeeded in destroying Sikh temples and slaughtering thousands of adherents, but they failed to dislodge the Sikhs from control of Punjab.

While Ahmad was preoccupied with his Indian realm, at the other end of his kingdom, the emir of Bukhara was trying to assert suzerainty over the khanates north of the Hindu Kush. Toward the end of his life, Ahmad worked out an agreement with the emir to divide their spheres of influence along the Amu Darya, which is still Afghanistan's northern border. The emir of Bukhara sealed the agreement with the gift of a *kherqa,* a cloak said to have been worn by Muhammad. Ahmad built a mosque in Kandahar to house the relic; in 1994, it was put on display by Taliban leader Mullah Omar when he first conquered the city.

In 1772, suffering from cancer that may have resulted from an old nose wound, Ahmad retired to the mountains east of Kandahar; he was soon dead at the age of 50. Ahmad Shah had succeeded as none before to unite the Pashtuns, largely by force of personality and diplomatic skills. His personal modesty, accessibility, and genuine religious feeling won him a popular following, but he lacked the administrative interest that might have turned a tribal confederacy into a true nation-state.

Had he lived to an older age, the commander might have been able to defend the empire he had carved out. His son and chosen successor Timur (r. 1772–93) was not up to the task.

The Sadozai Shahs

Timur Shah was serving as governor of Herat when his father died. His older brother Sulaiman Mirza briefly contested the throne, but

AHMAD'S PATRIOTIC VERSE

Hearts are filled with the blood of thy love.
For thy sake youth lay down thy lives.
I come to thee and my heart is freed from all cares,
Away from you the worries of my heart horrify me like snakes.
Although I add a great many lands to my realm.
I will never forget your beautiful orchards.
I forget the throne of Delhi when I remember.
The mountain peaks of my beautiful Pashtunkhwa.
They'll cut to pieces the enemy's life stuff,
If the Pashtuns wield their swords.
The time of Farid and Hamid will come again.
When I charge in every direction.
If the whole world be on one side and you on the other.
I'd much prefer your brown arid plains.
Ahmad Shah will never fail to hold you dear.
Though he may seize the lands of the whole world.

— *Pashto poem by Ahmad Shah Durrani translated by M. Hashim Rahimi.*
(Benawa 1981, 120)

Sulaiman's supporters melted away when Timur reached Kandahar. Sulaiman fled, but his father-in-law, Shah Wali Khan, was executed along with his two sons for having backed Sulaiman.

In the face of popular resentment against these and other actions, Timur, in, 1775, relocated his capital to Kabul, on the fringes of Pashtunistan and closer to his Indus Valley territories (and his winter capital at Peshawar). His reliance on 12,000 Qizilbash cavalry to keep the Pashtuns in check gave him a reputation as pro-Persian and pro-Shiite, especially after mercenaries rescued Timur in 1791, toward the end of his reign, by suppressing an uprising of the eastern Pashtun tribes. At the conclusion of that revolt, Timur had its leaders tortured to death, even after they swore an oath on the Qur'an to remain loyal. This sacrilegious act further blackened the ruler's reputation among his contemporaries and most later Afghans.

Many of his father's conquests rebelled against Timur. By 1781, he had lost Khorasan on the west and Sindh to the south. However, within the country his rule was at least nominally respected, often due to the help of Payinda Khan, the head of the Barakzai clan of the

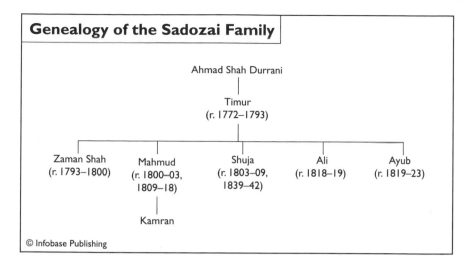

Genealogy of the Sadozai Family

Ahmad Shah Durrani

Timur
(r. 1772–1793)

Zaman Shah
(r. 1793–1800)

Mahmud
(r. 1800–03,
1809–18)

Shuja
(r. 1803–09,
1839–42)

Ali
(r. 1818–19)

Ayub
(r. 1819–23)

Kamran

© Infobase Publishing

Durrani tribes. On the whole, his internal reign was peaceful and just. He himself preferred architecture and gardens to military adventures, and he was reported to respect the rights of foreign merchants in Kabul.

Ahmad had arranged many diplomatic marriages for Timur; the wives and concubines obligingly gave him many sons, 23 of them still alive at the time of Timur's death in 1793. Their power struggles dominated the country's life for the remaining 25 years of Sadozai Durrani rule. Five of the brothers eventually had their chance to rule at Kabul, for seven different terms, but control of Kabul did not always assure much influence in the rest of the country. The Herat and Kandahar regions sometimes enjoyed de facto independence under one or another of the brothers. Shifting alliances pitted family members against one another, with fluctuating support from the Barakzai Durrani and other Pashtun tribes; many of the contenders were murdered, blinded, or swallowed up in dungeons.

Zaman Shah, the first of Timur's sons to rule (1793–1800), managed to win Payinda Khan's backing and reunite the country. He even concluded a peace with the newly powerful Uzbek emir of Bukhara, who reaffirmed Duranni control south of the Amu Darya. But Zaman was less lucky in India: Two campaigns against the Sikhs in 1797 and 1798 were unsuccessful. There, Zaman was defeated by the man he had installed as governor in Lahore, Ranjit Singh (r. 1799–1839).

Zaman's defeat disheartened Indian Muslims looking for another savior from the west and deprived the Afghan treasury of its chief source of revenue. Nevertheless, the very attempt to reassert control frightened the growing British interests in India. They feared a revival of Ahmad Shah's empire; as a precaution they stationed troops in Oudh (Ayodha) midway up the Ganges River. From this point on, no Afghan leader could afford to ignore Britain as an up-and-coming power in South Asia.

Zaman eventually fell afoul of the Barakzai clan by killing their chief Payinda Muhammad Khan; the khan's followers took revenge by blinding and exiling Zaman, but they were still not ready to desert the family of the great Ahmad Khan. The Barakzai threw their support behind Zaman's brothers Mahmud (r. 1800–03 and 1809–18) and Shuja (r. 1803–09 and 1839–42). The brothers were unsuccessful, however, in protecting the country's internal integrity in the face of repeated local uprisings.

In 1809, Shuja Shah became the first Afghan ruler to receive a formal British mission. On June 7, in Peshawar, the two parties signed a treaty of friendship in which they promised a united front against any aggression by a feared Franco-Persian alliance. The meeting proved personally useful to Shuja when he was deposed shortly afterward by Mahmud; he went to live with Zaman under British protection in the Punjab. Years later, the British reinstated Shuja as their client at Kabul for a three-year reign during the first Anglo-Afghan War.

FIRST BRITISH IMPRESSIONS OF AFGHANISTAN

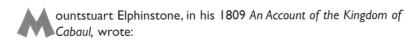ountstuart Elphinstone, in his 1809 *An Account of the Kingdom of Cabaul,* wrote:

> There is reason to fear that the societies into which the nation is divided, possess within themselves a principle of repulsion and disunion, too strong to be overcome, except by such a force as, while it united the whole into one solid body, would crush and obliterate the features of every one of the parts. . . .
> The internal government of the tribes answers its end so well, that the utmost disorders of the royal government never derange its operations, nor disturb the lives of the people. A number of organized and high-spirited republics are ready to defend their rugged country against a tyrant; and are able to defy the feeble efforts of a party in a civil war (Ewans 2002, 41).

Genealogy of the Barakzai Family

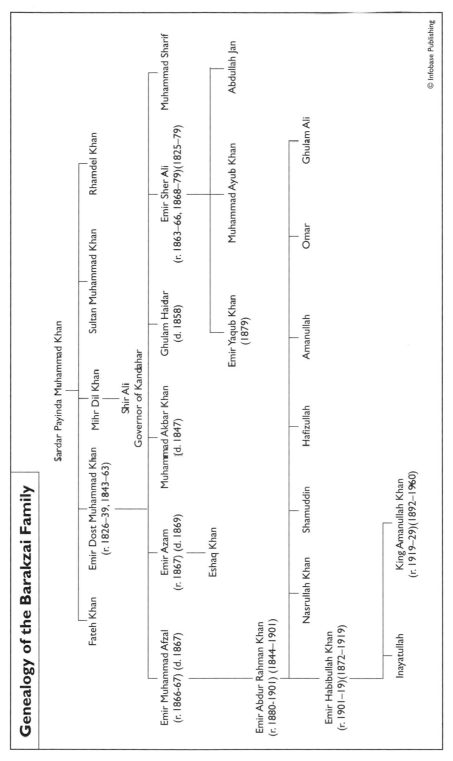

© Infobase Publishing

In 1818, faced with a Persian attempt to take Herat, Mahmud Shah sent his brilliant Barakzai ally, Fateh Khan, Payinda's son, to repel the invaders. Fateh's success was his undoing. Jealous of his power, Mahmud's son Kamran arrested and blinded Fateh on the pretext of a minor insult—Fateh's brother Dost Muhammad had mistreated Kamran's sister during a search for treasure in the harem at Herat.

Back in Kabul, Mahmud and Kamran personally tortured and murdered Fateh. This provoked a general Barakzai uprising, with Dost Muhammad taking the lead. Mahmud fled to Herat, where he and then Kamran ruled under Persian protection until 1842. The brief terms on the Kabul throne of two other sons of Timur, Ali (r. 1818–19) and Ayub (r. 1819–23), only illustrate the general anarchy of the country and the final decline of the Sadozai line. By then, nothing was left of the Durrani Empire in India, and even the Amu Darya border could not hold as Balkh became an independent principality.

The Europeans

For a thousand years, Afghanistan and its neighbors had been living in a cultural environment created during the sudden expansion of Islam in the seventh and eighth centuries. Every twist and turn in dynastic fortune, every new development in commerce or the arts, even the migration of new peoples into the region, could be integrated more or less into this wider, stable context. Nonbelievers were either converted to the faith or kept in a subordinate status.

But well before 1800, the vast Muslim world had begun to lose the initiative in the face of the expanding civilization of Christian Europe. The land borders between the two cultures slowly changed in Europe's favor, first in Iberia and Russia, later in the Balkans. More important, European states gradually gained control of the seas, which gave them a lock on Old World commerce and on the riches of the New World.

European power in South Asia dates back to the year 1498, when armed Portuguese fleets first rounded the Cape of Good Hope and sailed on to India. For nearly a hundred years, Portuguese admirals, merchants, adventurers, missionaries, and colonists were virtually unchallenged as they built up a trading empire, backed by armed might and anchored by colonies around the coastlines of the Indian Ocean. Their direct influence never penetrated far inland, however, and Afghans hardly needed to pay attention to these developments.

By the next century, Portuguese profits and glory had attracted competition from Spain, France, the Netherlands, and Britain. On December

1, 1600, Queen Elizabeth I granted a royal charter, or trading monopoly, to the merchants of the East India Company. This government-sponsored but privately owned enterprise, though founded and conducted for the purpose of making money and bringing wealth back to England, gradually laid the foundations for the British Empire in the East. In India, its first "factory," or trading station, was founded in 1615 at Surat on the west-central coast, with the approval of the Mughal emperor Jahangir (r. 1605–27). Within a century, major British outposts developed at Bombay, Madras, and Calcutta. The company defended its interests using local troops called sepoys under the command of British officers. In the 17th century, Mughal power kept the British and other European factories in check, but after the death of Aurangzeb in 1707, the western European powers all began to expand their influence and combat one another's interests through alliances among the many independent or autonomous states of India.

Imperial rivalries between the European states led to the Seven Years' War of 1756–63, perhaps the first global war worthy of the name. As in the New World, Great Britain triumphed over France in India and won control of the Indian Ocean. Under Commander Robert Clive, the East India Company began consolidating and expanding the lands under its direct control, and it soon became the dominant influence at the Mughal court in Delhi.

After some disastrous episodes of misrule by the company, the British Parliament assumed greater control in 1773. Governor-generals sent by the Crown improved administration, fought local enemies such as the powerful Maratha confederation in the south, and became the de facto rulers of most of India by the early 19th century. Thanks to superior military and medical technology, the latest administrative techniques, excellent political and diplomatic skills, and a measure of curiosity and respect for local cultures that few conquerors had previously shown, a few thousand Englishmen were able to dominate a continent. Only the intervening power of the Sikh state in Punjab under Ranjit Singh gave Afghanistan the luxury of ignoring British power for a few more years. Perhaps the Sikh buffer state also afforded the British protection from the Afghans, whose fierce military prowess had given them an outsized role in previous Indian history.

For a while, France seemed a more imminent threat to the Durrani state, owing to the imperial ambitions of Napoleon I (1769–1821). A Franco-Persian treaty, directed primarily against Russia, was signed in 1807. French envoys and officers may have encouraged the Qajar shahs of Persia to advance toward Afghanistan as a possible first step toward India via the time-honored northwest invasion route, or so the British believed. But the French were unable to help Persia fend off Russian advances in the Caucasus, and after a string of Russian victories there, French ambitions in India became moot.

Russia, as an Asian land power, emerged as a far more dangerous and persistent threat to Afghanistan and, by extension, to British India. Russia's famous quest for a warm water seaport, stymied by the continued power of the Ottoman Empire, drove its imperial ambitions in Central Asia throughout the 19th century. Czarist rule had reached the north coast of the Caspian Sea before 1600, but it stopped there for generations, until Russia began its southward push in the early 19th century. By the Treaty of Gulistan, in 1813, Persia ceded all naval power in the Caspian to the Russians. Despite a British attempt to counteract Russian incursions via its own Persian treaty in 1814, Russian influence in Tehran, the Persian capital, continued to increase, and the Russians continued to advance, annexing Armenia in 1828. Farther east, Russia annexed the Kazakh steppes in the 1820s and eyed the decaying Central Asian khanates that lay just north of the Durrani realms.

Dost Muhammad

The bloodshed and chaos that engulfed Afghanistan during the last years of the Sadozai shahs finally spurred the numerically larger Barakzai clan of the Durrani Pashtuns to seize power in their own right. Under such capable rulers as Dost Muhammad (r. 1826–39 and 1843–63) and later Abdur Rahman (r. 1880–1901), they were able to turn a tribal confederation into a relatively cohesive state.

The surviving sons of Payinda Khan (the brothers of Fateh Khan) eventually all agreed that the Barakzai clan should seize the Durrani succession, but they disagreed as to which of the brothers should rule supreme. Each cohort of full brothers formed a separate faction, generally supported by their mother's tribe—for example, the Ghilzais in the case of the brothers who ruled in Kandahar.

For eight years, the country remained divided into squabbling principalities, and outlying territories such as Baluchistan and Kashmir were lost for good, thereby cutting off the major source of revenue to the Afghan state. Dost Muhammad, Payinda's youngest son and Fateh's lieutenant, was allotted Ghazni, to which he added Kohistan, north of Kabul, all the while building support in Kabul with the help of his mother's Qizilbash tribesmen and his natural charm, diplomacy, and lack of pretense. He won full control of Kabul in 1826 and proclaimed himself emir. The other brothers accepted him as first among equals, but they continued to rule independently throughout the south; Dost could not keep the emir of Bukhara from seizing Balkh. During his first period of rule, Dost Muhammad was barely more than a local feudal lord.

Dost apparently learned to read and write at this point and made efforts to govern justly and peacefully (as attested by the British envoy Alexander Burnes), but he was never averse to force and treachery, killing many of his opponents. He also never established a modern administration so that his rule, which eventually covered all of modern Afghanistan, remained more personal than national.

In foreign affairs, Dost's reign was marked by the first stages of the conflict known as the "Great Game," the century-long clash between the expanding Russian and British Empires, which dominated Afghan history as long as both empires survived, and perhaps even after. Ironically, the Great Game may have also guaranteed the country's independence as a buffer state.

In the early 1830s, the British feared that a weak, divided Afghanistan was an invitation to Russian intervention. They became convinced that their old client Shah Shuja, grandson of the legendary Ahmad Shah Durrani, would make a more popular and reliable ruler than Dost Muhammad. They financed Shuja's 1834 attempt to regain the throne. Dost rallied the Barakzais to defeat Shuja outside Kandahar, but while they fought, the Sikhs under Ranjit Singh used the opportunity to seize Peshawar, where they placed another brother of Dost, Muhammad Khan, as governor. The loss was grating, as Peshawar and its region were indisputably part of the Pashtun homeland.

In 1834, Dost's forces, led by his son Muhammad Akbar (d. 1847), won another victory, this time against the Sikhs, but they stopped short of recovering Peshawar. Two years later, Dost petitioned the new Indian governor-general, Lord Auckland, to use his good offices with his Sikh allies to return Peshawar. This fateful request initiated two years of ultimately fruitless negotiations (conducted for the British by Alexander Burnes), in which Dost hoped to regain Peshawar and the British hoped to bring Afghanistan into their sphere of influence.

While these talks were going on, Persian shah Muhammad Mirza (1810–48), supported by Russian advisers and officers, marched on Herat in November 1837. The city, still ruled by Mahmud Shah's son Kamran, held out during an eight-month siege, which allowed enough time for the concerned British to take countermeasures against what they saw as a Russian threat to India. A British Indian force landed on Kharg Island in the Persian Gulf in June 1838, and the shah retreated under a direct verbal threat from the British envoy.

Perhaps hoping to improve his hand with the British, who were balking at any pressure on the Sikh ruler Ranjit Singh, Dost Muhammad agreed to receive a shadowy Russian emissary named Captain or Lieutenant Vitkevich, while the Persian-Russian siege of Herat was still under way. Dost's brothers in Kandahar were already offering their allegiance to Shah Mirza. This only inflamed Lord Auckland, who had insisted that Dost rebuff any Russian or Persian envoy. Burnes preferred Dost to Shuja Shah but was unable to sway Auckland; he left Kabul in April 1838. The stage was set for the First Anglo-Afghan War.

War with British India

Even the Persian shah's withdrawal from Herat did not succeed in calming the British. They themselves had come to the subcontinent from the sea, but they knew that every previous conqueror had poured into India through the northwest passes of Afghanistan. Only a strong government in Kabul under British protection, they believed, could keep back the Russians, the French, or any other land invaders. Such a state could also facilitate British commercial penetration into Central Asia.

In June 1838, Auckland engineered a three-way treaty with Ranjit Singh and Shah Shuja, under which Shuja would be placed on the throne in Kabul, Peshawar, and the border regions would be formally ceded to the Sikhs, and the British would get to project their power to the very limits of historic India. Britain agreed to supply the funds to make the other parties happy. They also set about bribing various Pashtun chiefs, whose assurances of support proved to be meaningless.

The initial plan was to rely on Muslim recruits from the armies of Ranjit Singh, but the latter proved reluctant to commit his forces to the invasion and even refused to allow passage through Peshawar and the Khyber Pass. The British accepted his decision, perhaps worried that the Sikhs might otherwise annex Afghanistan and become a threat to British India in their own right. The company decided to raise an invasion force of its own, the Army of the Indus. It consisted of 21,000 troops, including British and Indian units and several thousand mercenaries hired by Shuja. Some 38,000 camp followers and 30,000 camels were attached in support.

On October 1, Auckland issued what became known as the Simla Manifesto. It detailed the supposed provocations of Dost Muhammad and announced the East India Company's explicit intentions to invade his domains and install the "legitimate" Afghan ruler, Shah Shuja. Auckland even named the permanent British agents who would advise Shuja once he was on the throne. Auckland's moves, backed in principle by the government in London, were soon attacked as rash, unnecessary, and unjust by a groundswell of Indian and British public opinion. But the die had been cast; the army marched from Firozpur on the Indus in December and reached Quetta on the border of Durrani territory in March, after fighting off Baluchi tribesmen along the way.

Kandahar was taken without a fight in April (local chiefs were bought off, and Dost's brothers fled). Ghazni fell after a major battle in July, in which *ghazis*, fierce religious warriors, made their first appearance. The rapid fall to British general John Keane of that supposedly impregnable mountain stronghold (walls 60 feet thick and 150 feet high), convinced most Afghans that resistance was pointless, even though the walls had been breached thanks to treachery from within. By August 6, the combined British-Indian force reached Kabul. Deserted by most of his supporters, Dost fled north to Bamiyan and then Bukhara, while Shuja Shah and his British backers entered the city the following day.

Unfortunately for the British, Shuja's popularity did not appear to be as great as they had been led to believe, nor were the revenues he could command as ruler sufficient to finance an adequate military force. The British now understood that they would need to keep a substantial garrison in the country to safeguard their dramatic achievements, although they well knew that the locals resented the presence of so many foreign infidels (Hindus and Christians). Much of the army was sent back to India, but one division was left in Kandahar and two brigades in Kabul.

The news late in 1839 that a Russian force of 5,000 men had invaded the Khanate of Khiva south of the Aral Sea reinforced the conviction of the British commander in Kabul, Sir William Macnaghten, that a British forward force would have to stay in Afghanistan—even though the Russian move was itself largely a response to the British invasion. In any case, a bitterly cold winter forced the Russians to withdraw without a single battle.

Shuja desperately needed the British troops, but he refused to allow them to be quartered in Kabul's historic Bala Hissar fort, which he instead requisitioned to house his large household and harem. He feared that the commanding situation of the fort above the town would provoke even more resentment among the population, whom he still hoped to win over. Instead, the brigades, their followers, and the British and Indian families who were now sent for were encamped at an exposed, indefensible cantonment outside town.

The pieces had fallen in place for one of the bloodiest disasters in British imperial lore. Retold and embellished by generations of Afghans, the events of the war would contribute as much as any other factor to the national sense of invincibility and, perhaps, the national resistance to the modern values the foreigners represented.

The British Retreat

Though the Kandahar garrison soon had to face persistent attacks from Ghilzai forces (and from Baluchis on the supply line to the south), Kabul remained quiescent in 1840. Resentment of the British, in part for their public drinking and open socializing between men and women, had not yet reached a boiling point. Macnaghten found himself treated by supplicants as the real ruler, while Shuja remained isolated in his palace.

Dost Muhammad returned from Bukhara in September to raise the flag of rebellion but soon after admitted defeat. The former emir surrendered and was sent to live in Shuja Shah's vacated house in India. Other rebellions in the southwest in the summer of 1841, by both Durrani and Ghilzai Pashtun, were easily put down.

During two years of rule Shuja failed to win any genuine support or to demonstrate any governing capacity. When budgetary cuts in London led to a withdrawal of payments to the tribal chiefs, the Ghilzai closed the route to Peshawar, and the shah's authority melted away. The deterrent power of British troops did not last very long; on November 2, 1841, a mob attacked Burnes's residence on a narrow street in Kabul and killed the officer and his brother; neither Shuja's guard nor the main British force were able even to reach the site.

Bloody uprisings were now reported around the country, and the garrison at Kabul was effectively cut off in November, even from the city itself. Dost's son Muhammad Akbar took command of the resistance. With few options left, Macnaghten tried to play off the various Afghan factions with bribes and contradictory promises; he was murdered during negotiations on December 23, probably by Muhammad Akbar himself. The British, under the inadequate and possibly senile leadership of General William Elphinstone, decided to withdraw without any further delay, under a promise from the Ghilzai of safe passage.

Unwilling to wait for an armed escort and supplies, as promised by Muhammad Akbar, on January 6, 1842, Elphinstone led 4,500 troops and 12,000 civilian camp followers, including many women and children, out of the cantonment, weak from hunger and inadequately dressed for the bitter cold of the passes. Those who did not die of the cold were no match for the irregular forces that attacked them all along the route, including Ghilzai and other tribesmen. A hundred or so British were taken prisoner, and about 2,000 sepoys or camp followers managed to escape back to Kabul. Of the 14,000 others, only one wounded Englishman, a handful of sepoys, and some 20 Afghan supporters of Shuja Shah reached Jalalabad a week later. Shuja himself managed to hold out for a few months but was murdered in Kabul in April, the first time he ventured out of the Bala Hissar.

A new British government in London replaced Auckland in February and forbade any further attempts to dictate or even arbitrate internal power arrangements in Afghanistan. The besieged garrisons at Kandahar and Jalalabad were reinforced from India and in September fought their way against disorganized resistance (including attacks by *ghazis*) to Kabul, where the British prisoners were redeemed.

Along the way, in Ghazni, the British removed the wooden doors from the tomb of Mahmud of Ghazni, who is said to have taken them from the Hindu temple of Somnath. They thus claimed to right a historic wrong, which antagonized Muslim feelings in India without impressing the Hindus. A few calculated acts of bloody revenge were taken against formerly rebellious towns and villages. The ancient bazaar of Kabul, where Macnaghten's mutilated body had been displayed, was blown up in October amid looting and rape. On October 12, the combined forces left Kabul for India.

The Anglo-Afghan War had seriously depleted the company's armies and discouraged enlistment, and its cost of up to £20 million had strained the treasury.

Muhammad Akbar, son of Dost Muhammad, rose against the British occupation of Afghanistan and the installation of Shuja Shah by the British in 1841. (Photo by Shaista Wahab)

The dramatic blow to British prestige is considered to be a contributing cause of the Indian war for independence of 1857. As Afghanistan's first exposure to modern Europeans, the unexpected and unprovoked war had helped implant both hatred and contempt, a dangerous combination.

The British retreat left anarchy in its wake until the resourceful Dost Muhammad returned to Kabul from exile in January 1843 to begin a second, 20-year reign, which he devoted to reassembling the pieces of Afghanistan, perhaps aided by a sense of unity forged during the recent war. In the first decade, several of his sons conquered and ruled the Uzbek and Turkmen regions north of the Hindu Kush in his name. He even retook Peshawar briefly in 1848, while the Sikhs were fighting their last stand against the British, but he abandoned the city after the final British victory the following year. In 1855, he added Kandahar to his dominions, and he finally annexed Herat after a 10-month siege in May 1863, two weeks before his death.

During the same period, the East India Company was also consolidating its power, on a larger scale. The conquest of Sindh (1843), of Kashmir and the Punjab during the Anglo-Sikh Wars (1846, 1849), and of Baluchistan (1859), meant that British India now brushed up against the southern and eastern Pashtun zones. The mountain tribes jealously guarded their autonomy, and a cycle of raids and counter-raids began that were to continue for generations. But the British did succeed in keeping the Kabul authorities out of fully half of Pashtunistan.

Faced with the new power reality, Dost signed two treaties of friendship with the British, in 1855 and 1857, establishing regular ties, but he refused to allow them to station English envoys in Kabul, a longstanding demand. Instead, an Indian Muslim was allowed to represent the company there, a situation that continued for 20 years. The 1857 treaty provided a subsidy for a regular Afghan army as a buffer against the Persians, who had briefly occupied Herat in 1856. Dost refrained from intervening across the border during the 1857 Indian Rebellion, when the beleaguered British might have acceded to his territorial demands. Against the urging of several advisers and chiefs, he chose to concentrate instead on unifying what now came to be seen as the core Afghan lands.

Sher Ali and National Consolidation

Dost designated one of his younger sons, Sher Ali (1825–79; r. 1863–66 and 1868–79), to be his successor, perhaps because Sher Ali had put down six separate Ghilzai uprisings as governor of Ghazni. Nevertheless, as soon as the father died, the same interfamily rivalries and civil wars that had marked Dost's first years in power confronted Sher Ali.

This time, the fighting lasted about five years. At first successful in fighting off his siblings, Sher Ali was eventually defeated by the combined efforts of two older half brothers, one of whom, Muhammad Afzal (d. 1867), took the throne in Kabul in 1866. Sher Ali never gave up the title of emir, and he soon regained the substance as well by a stroke of luck—Afzal's death and a falling out between Afzal's powerful son Abdur Rahman and his surviving full brother, Azam Khan.

Times had changed, even in Afghanistan, and Sher Ali began to behave like a modern ruler. He built up a standing army of 50,000 professionals and conscripts, dressed in uniforms, a novelty for the country. His job became easier when British arms and a regular subsidy were extended to him in 1869 once his throne was secure. Turkish support also materialized after a mission to Kabul in 1876, which unsuccessfully tried to enlist Afghanistan in a joint anti-Russian front. Turkish assistance continued in the 20th century, under both the Ottomans and the later Turkish republic. To a degree, the standing army freed Kabul from dependence on fickle tribal chiefs.

Sher Ali also laid the groundwork for a modern administration, with a Council of Elders to advise him, several ministries, a postal service, and a rudimentary monetary system. He reformed the land tax; levies had been paid in cash and produce but were now paid all in cash (though still never enough to support an ambitious government). The first modern school in the country was set up under government auspices; it included instruction in English and military subjects. The emir also published the first Afghan newspaper, *Shams-al-Nahar* (Morning sun), and established a few light industries, some in support of the army.

Though Sher Ali still had to fight within the country during his second reign (partly against his rebellious eldest son, Yaqub Khan), his biggest problems stemmed from the continuing British-Russian rivalry. He deftly juggled the two powers and other players such as Persia and Turkey, managing to preserve his country's autonomy for another decade.

Russian and British Moves and Countermoves

While British India expanded northward, Russia was aggressively pushing south into Central Asia. In 1864, it annexed all the lands between the Caspian and Aral Seas; east of the Aral Sea, it pushed its border down to the Syr Darya. Tashkent was taken the following year, and

Samarkand in 1868. That same year the khan of Bukhara accepted the Czar as overlord, which brought Russian imperial control down to the Amu Darya, on the border of Afghan territory.

The British disagreed among themselves as to how to interpret and respond to the Russian advances; their policy depended largely on which party was in power in London. For his part, Sher Ali was consistent; he explained his position at the March 1869 Ambala conference of Indian princes, which was convened by Viceroy Lord Mayo to discuss this and other pressing issues. The Afghan ruler was quite willing to ally himself with Britain and work with it to resist any Russian aggression. But he refused to accept any British-born envoys in Kabul, in deference to Afghan public opinion, still smarting from the wounds of the First Anglo-Afghan War. He also wanted Britain to formally recognize his dynasty, and accept his son Abdullah Jan as his successor.

Still following a noninterventionist policy, the British at Ambala refused to make any commitment to Sher Ali's royal line or to give any military guarantees. Instead, in 1872, Britain signed an accord with Russia recognizing Afghanistan as an "intermediary zone" between the two powers, with its northern border at the Amu Darya. The British contended that this pact freed them from the need for any formal guarantees to Sher Ali. The latter considered Lord Mayo a personal friend and was satisfied with informal understandings, but the mutual trust between the two governments wore thin after Mayo was assassinated in 1872 and after British mediators settled a border dispute with Persia unfairly, from the Afghan point of view (the Persians were also displeased).

The Simla Conference of 1873, attended by Sher Ali's vizier, Sayyid Nur Muhammad Shah, marked a real deterioration in relations between the two countries. The British renewed a request to station military observers on the northern Afghan borders, while still refusing to offer any guarantees to the emir personally or to his country.

The situation did not improve when Benjamin Disraeli became prime minister in 1874 and decided to reinstate a "forward policy" in Afghanistan, which aimed to project British power as far as possible, rather than relying on the buffer state concept. In protest, the liberal viceroy Lord Northbrook resigned, leaving Sher Ali exposed on both flanks with no firm ally. The southern Pashtun city of Quetta, just south over the passes from the Kandahar region, was formally occupied by the British in 1876 and converted to a military base.

The forceful new viceroy, Lord Lytton, revived the longstanding demand that Sher Ali accept a resident British agent in Kabul; in the current climate, this seemed like the short road to reducing the country to a protectorate, as Sher Ali implied in his reply to this demand. The emir informed the British that he had rejected parallel demands made in letters from General Kaufman, Russian commander in Central Asia (the Russians were communicating with the emir via a Muslim envoy stationed in the country in 1875). Though he strained to keep the Russians at arm's length, he continued to correspond with them over the next two years, over British protests.

Second Anglo-Afghan War

In 1877, Russia sent a massive army into the Turkish Balkans, posing as protector of the area's Christian populations. After a string of victories, the Russian force approached Constantinople, a holy city for the Eastern Orthodox and an age-old target of Russian imperial ambitions.

For the British, this was a red line, and they sent a fleet through the Dardanelles. After a six-month military standoff, the great powers came to a compromise in Europe at the Congress of Berlin; but while the outcome was still in doubt, Kaufman made plans for a diversionary invasion into India, gathering a 40,000-man army in Turkestan. Not wanting to fight his way through Afghanistan before he even saw Indian soil, he ordered a 250-man delegation under General Stolietov to ride to Kabul to extort Sher Ali's support.

The emir tried to bar the Russians, but they made their way to his capital. On July 22, 1878, unaware that peace had been signed the previous day, they met with Sher Ali and offered him a defensive and offensive military alliance. Russia would station soldiers in Afghanistan and extend its road and telegraph systems into the country. The emir apparently consented to the demands, but we will never know whether he would have carried them out, since most of the Russian delegates left Kabul as soon as they learned that peace had been achieved in Europe.

The invasion plan was now moot. Nevertheless, Lytton was outraged that the Russians had gained admittance where his envoys had been so long excluded. He demanded that a British mission be admitted to Kabul.

On August 18, Sher Ali's son Abdullah Jan died, and the emir requested time for proper mourning before replying to Lytton's letter. Unimpressed and unwilling to wait, the impatient viceroy sent a small force to the Khyber Pass, where it was turned back by the local Afghan governor with a threat of force. The bereaved emir failed to apologize to Lytton's satisfaction for this "insult," though his final message did surrender on the envoy issue. On November 22, the viceroy ordered

British forces to breach the border at three places, possibly in violation of orders from London. By January, they had overcome stiff local resistance and occupied Kandahar, Jalalabad, and the Kurram Valley south of Kabul.

The British forces, supported by rail and telegraph links right up to their side of the border, were equipped with far more advanced weapons than the Afghans, which had not been the case 40 years earlier. Gatling machine guns saw their first use during the campaign. The British (and their loyal Sikh recruits) were also more familiar now with Pashtun fighting tactics and were perhaps motivated by a desire to avenge the tragic losses of the First Anglo-Afghan War. Sher Ali's recruits proved less loyal to the emir than to their tribal chiefs, and his army failed to mount an organized defense.

Sher Ali now turned to his erstwhile Russian suitors, but Russia was no longer interested in a fight with the British. The emir installed his son Yaqub Khan as regent and headed for the northern border, determined to proceed to St. Petersburg to plead his case directly to the Czar. But the Russians refused him passage. He turned back and died near Balkh on February 21, 1879.

The new emir, Yaqub, lacking unified support from his countrymen, was compelled to sign the unequal Gandamak Treaty on May 26. The British agreed to withdraw from Jalalabad and Kandahar but kept the territories they had taken at the southern approaches to the Khyber and other passes (which to this day remain on the Pakistan side of the border). In a provision that is still regarded with shame by Afghans, Yaqub committed future emirs to "conduct all relations with foreign states in accordance with the advice and wishes of the British Government." In addition, the British finally got their permanent missions in Kabul and other areas; in return, they agreed to pay the emir a stipend of £60,000 a year and promised to defend the country against unprovoked foreign attacks.

Stalemate

History soon began to repeat itself. Envoy Sir Louis Cavagnari took up residence in the Bala Hissar in Kabul in July and began advising the emir. On September 3, he and his entire escort of 75 men were killed there by Afghan soldiers and Kabul citizens, despite Yaqub's attempt to stop the fighting.

In response, General Frederick Roberts, commander of the central British column, took his army to Kabul and entered on October 12.

Yaqub had already fled the city, and he soon left for exile in India; Roberts took over, imposed martial law, and ruled as effective emir for the next several months.

Under orders from Lytton, Roberts's first priority was to avenge Cavagnari's death, through mass arrests and executions. Most of those hanged were nationalists or opponents of Yaqub who had not actually taken part in the fight at Bala Hissar. Roberts admitted to 87 executions, but British and Afghans on the scene claimed much higher numbers, to the dismay of public opinion in London.

This time, Afghans had a ready-made historic model of resistance, and rebellion broke out almost immediately. Yaqub Khan's mother handed over her jewels to finance the resistance. Capable commanders emerged from among a broad range of tribes and ethnic groups, including the fiery Ghilzai mullah Mir Din Muhammad, known as Mushk-i-Alam (Perfume of the Universe), who called for a jihad, and General Muhammad Jan from the province of Wardak, south of Kabul. A large *lashkar,* or tribal army, marched on Kabul, and the British once more found themselves besieged in a cantonment outside the city limits. From Kabul, Muhammad Jan offered the British safe conduct to India in return for the restoration of Yaqub Khan; in the meantime, some of his 40,000 men proceeded to loot the city, wrecking its Hindu and Qizilbash neighborhoods.

Mindful of the past safe-conduct promises of 1842, the British rejected Muhammad Jan's offer and bunkered down for a siege. The Afghans launched their major attack on December 23. This time, however, the British were better prepared than their predecessors had been in the previous war. Well supplied, quartered, and led, they were able to inflict some 3,000 casualties on their opponents while suffering few of their own, and they soon retook the city of Kabul. Before long, disunity broke out in the Afghan ranks; many chiefs took advantage of an amnesty offer from Roberts, and other tribesmen returned to their homes. Some fighters retreated to Ghazni, where a National Party of resistance to the foreigners took shape.

Though they had not yet defeated the British in open battle, the resistance was able to mobilize enough strength to harass the occupying forces; *ghazis* played an increasingly important role. The British knew they had to find a credible yet cooperative local ruler who would allow them to withdraw their troops. In February 1880, just such an individual marched into the country from the north. Abdur Rahman Khan, a nephew of Sher Ali born in 1844, had been living in exile in Samarkand and Tashkent, supported by a rich pension from General Kaufman, after losing out in an earlier power struggle. He now began gathering support from the northern khans, and in the presence of a tribal council proclaimed himself emir at Charikar, north of Kabul, on July 20, 1880.

Although Abdur Rahman wore a Russian uniform and had reportedly been promised Russian arms, the British saw him as their best option. In retrospect, it was a shrewd gamble; Abdur Rahman's years of exile under Russian auspices had made him wary of Russian intentions and more than willing to work with the British. The cabinet in London approved the choice as early as March, and envoys sent north from Kabul to meet with the emir were impressed with his character and intelligence. British recognition helped him win further recruits from around the country.

In the vacuum left by Yaqub's abdication, the previous October, British policy had been to detach Kandahar and Herat from the Afghan state, despite the commitments made at Gandamak. Until a new settlement could be negotiated and accepted by at least some Afghans, the fighting continued. This gave the Afghans just enough time to record another legendary blow to British imperial prestige, parallel to the retreat from Kabul in the previous war.

One of Sher Ali's sons, Muhammad Ayub Khan, marched an army from his power base in Herat toward Kandahar and on July 27 routed a British force at Maiwand outside the city in open battle. Spurred on, according to legend, by a local heroine, Malalai, waving her veil as a battle flag, they killed nearly 1,000 out of 2,500 British and Indian troops. The British survivors retreated to Kandahar, where they expelled the civilian population and prepared for a siege. Hearing of the loss, Roberts led 10,000 troops in a rapid march from Kabul and routed Ayub's army on September 1.

Meanwhile, in Kabul, the British reached a political settlement with Abdur Rahman. They agreed to forego a permanent mission in Kabul and to refrain from intervening in internal affairs, while Abdur Rahman accepted the loss of Kandahar and agreed to avoid relations with any other foreign country; in any case, the Russians had shown themselves unwilling to intervene. Even before Roberts's victory at Kandahar, the remaining British troops left Kabul for India.

A new British government was elected in April by a public opposed to the forward policy of Disraeli. The new cabinet ordered a withdrawal from Kandahar in April 1881, and the man they had imposed as governor, Wali Sher Ali, was retired on pension to Karachi. The era of British expansion in India had come to an end. Besides, the romantic image of the fierce Afghan fighter, as later developed by the wildly popular British writer Rudyard Kipling, made any future British government loath to stir up that particular hornet's nest.

Abdur Rahman

Emir Abdur Rahman Khan took the throne in Kabul and began a 21-year reign that put the country on a stable foundation. Though constrained by the terms of his agreement with the British, he was able to navigate skillfully between the two imperial powers and protect most of his territories within borders that became universally recognized.

Abdur Rahman secured domestic peace as well, thus depriving outsiders of any pretext to intervene; he ruthlessly curbed the power of local chiefs and mullahs. But his methods included a cruel intolerance to any opposition, let alone rebellion, punished by torture and sometimes mass execution, giving him the name of "Iron Emir." Individuals were denied the right to move around the country or to travel abroad without government approval. Combined with his policy of cultural and economic isolation, these practices probably kept the country poorer and weaker than it might have been and created problems for his successors.

The new emir inherited a state of anarchy and a depressed economy; his cities were damaged and partly depopulated. As with most new Afghan rulers, his first priority was to deal with internal opponents eager to test his power. Three months after the British withdrew from Kandahar in 1881, Abdur Rahman's cousin Muhammad Ayub Khan captured the city from its loyal garrison. Though the new emir lacked a sizable army, he rallied the Ghilzai tribesmen and defeated Ayub outside the city. At the same time, a force of loyal northerners took Herat, forcing Ayub into exile in India.

Abdur Rahman never faced another comparable threat, but some 40 other rebellions broke out over the years, and he moved steadily and systematically to subdue the various ethnic regions under his rule. Most notably, the Ghilzai rose in 1886, the Uzbek in 1888, and the Hazara in 1891–93. The emir's conscript army, financed and largely armed by the British, successfully dealt with all three rebellions. In 1895, Abdur Rahman imposed the *hasht nafari* (one in eight) conscription system. Drawings were held on the village level; those who drew the lot for the army either served or paid for a substitute; the seven who escaped conscription, or their families, were taxed to support the recruit.

The emir typically followed up his military victories with ruthless revenge against insurgents. He revived the old tactic of resettlement, not used widely in well over a century, moving some 10,000 leading Ghilzai families to non-Pashtun areas in the north. In such potentially hostile neighborhoods, they became loyal supporters of the emir.

The Hazaras in the northwest mountain country were treated far more cruelly. When these Shiites refused to surrender their cherished autonomy, Abdur Rahman proclaimed a jihad and offered *ghazi* status to anyone who enlisted in the fight. The Hazaras were completely repressed as a political-ethnic group, and much of their land was given to others, whom they were forced to serve as slaves. Others were sold as slaves in Kabul. Thousands fled to Mashad in Persia and Quetta in India.

Abdur Rahman proclaimed another jihad in 1885, this time against Kafiristan in the mountainous northeast. He forcibly converted its pagan inhabitants, who had been fiercely independent since the time of Alexander the Great, and renamed their homeland Nuristan. Their brethren across the border in Pakistan have until the present avoided forced conversion.

Abdur Rahman continued and deepened some of Sher Ali's administrative reforms. Perhaps most lasting, he divided the country into provinces, districts, and subdistricts that often ignored ethnic and tribal lines. He chose governors who were not natives of the provinces they administered; loyal to himself alone and supported by army units, they were responsible for collecting taxes and maintaining order. A national police force used spies and informers to guarantee the governors' loyalty. In some cases, the governors and other officials sold off land that had been owned in common by clans or tribes, which undermined the age-old tribal organization, previously the most effective level of government.

In Kabul, a new administration with several ministries was built around a corps of the emir's own relatives, hostage-sons of prominent regional families, and *ghulam-bachas,* or royal slaves, from non-Pashtun areas. He kept his sons in Kabul, where they could not build up local power bases as other sons had done before. Departments were set up to handle the treasury, trade, justice, public works, posts, education, and medicine.

Although he established a national *loya jirga,* an assembly of chiefs, notables, and mullahs, Abdur Rahman limited their power to approving various initiatives. He also appointed the Supreme Council consisting mostly of department heads, which met on a regular basis to discuss policy and advise the emir.

An emir's authority traditionally depended on the approval of the *jirga.* In contrast, Abdur Rahman claimed divine sanction for his rule and called himself "king." As a successful conqueror of infidels, he monopolized the right to call a jihad. After his conquest and conversion of Nurestan, the mullahs dubbed him Zia al-Millat-i wa al-Din (Light of the Nation and Religion).

Mindful of the lingering power of local mullahs, Abdur Rahman declared himself the imam, or spiritual leader, of the Afghan millat, the subcommunity within the Muslim *umma*, or nation. He thus exploited the notion of divine sanction, as evidenced by his successful jihads, to bring the mullahs under his control. In his autobiography, he called these local clerics "ignorant priests" who taught "contrary to the principles and teachings of Muhammad" (Ewans 2002, 101). To rectify the situation, he set up qualifying exams and paid the mullahs according to the results from the funds of the charitable *waqfs,* which he brought under government control. Abdur Rahman established a standardized system of courts ruling according to sharia, or Muslim law, as interpreted by himself as imam.

The king also fought with some success to bring the local and tribal chiefs under control of the governors. In his autobiography, he wrote, "every priest, mullah and chief of every tribe and village considered himself an independent king. . . . The tyranny and cruelty of these men were unbearable" (Ewans 2002, 101). He tore down many independent castles and built his own forts along major commercial roads. He also made use of such traditional tactics as political marriages, bribery, hostage taking, and exploiting intertribal hostilities.

To protect the country's independence, Abdur Rahman refused to allow any railroads or telegraph lines to penetrate over his borders, and he kept the number of official foreign experts to a minimum. The British agent in Kabul was not allowed to meet with his country's nationals there.

On his own account, the king did import a small number of physicians, engineers (especially for mining and irrigation), geologists, and printers. Some foreign machinery for light manufactures was also accepted. Internal commerce benefited from greater security. But modern education was probably more limited than in Sher Ali's reign, and literacy remained very low.

Demarcation of Borders

By the end of his reign, Abdur Rahman had helped put an end to British and Russian territorial ambitions at his country's expense, but not before both powers had absorbed significant chunks of Afghan real estate. In 1884, in the face of further Russian consolidation of its Central Asian territories, Britain and Russia agreed to a joint commission to demarcate the northern Afghan border. Local Russian forces nevertheless continued their movement south, and in March 1885 overcame the northernmost Afghan outpost, at the Panjdeh Oasis. Russian forces might well have continued on to the Hindu Kush, perhaps their natural border with India, but Britain warned that a further advance toward Herat would mean war, and patriotic fever swept both countries. War was averted when Abdur Rahman, then on a state visit to India, coolly accepted the Russian fait accompli. The two powers began two years of strenuous negotiations and agreed on the final northwest border in the summer of 1887, thanks in part to the emir's unfailing restraint and tact in his dealings with both sides. In 1888, the western border with Persia was finalized. The northeast border was drawn in 1891 and 1895, when the emir was forced to accept a long finger of thinly-populated land at great elevation extending to China, in order to keep British India from touching Russian territory.

Afghan losses to the south and east were far more consequential. Ever since the 1850s, when British rule had reached the Pashtun neighborhood, conflicts with local tribesmen became commonplace over such issues as Pashtun raids into the Indus Valley or British interference in intratribal affairs. A cooling of the diplomatic climate between Afghanistan and another new viceroy after 1888 led to increased, bloody clashes. Abdur Rahman tried to appeal directly to London but in vain. In 1893, Indian foreign secretary Mortimer Durand was sent to Kabul, and the general lines of the border were agreed upon (including Afghan acquiescence to the lack of an ocean outlet). It took another four or five years to mark the line on the ground. In 1895, the king was finally invited by Queen Victoria to visit her capital; ailing, he sent his son Nasrullah.

In many places, the final Durand Line lacked any ethnic or topographic basis, bisecting many villages and blocking age-old seasonal migration routes for the large *kuchi,* or nomad, population. More seriously, it cut off a large portion of the Pashtun population from any hope of unity with their brethren who ruled Afghanistan. Those left south of the line, inspired by several militant mullahs and probably encouraged by Abdur Rahman's agents, staged a widespread rebellion that took the British two years to suppress.

To win approval for the Durand Line, the British agreed to raise Abdur Rahman's annual subsidy from 1.2 to 1.8 million rupees, although the emir may not have had any choice in the matter. Abdur

Emir Abdur Rahman Khan's mausoleum in Kabul's Zarnegar Park. He died in 1901. (Photo by Shaista Wahab)

Rahman later claimed that the Durand Line was meant to be a delineation of effective control, not of ultimate sovereignty. Nevertheless, many Afghans have never forgiven him for signing the accord.

Abdur Rahman died on October 1, 1901, in Kabul. His eldest son and designated successor, Habibullah Khan (born in Tashkent or Samarkand during his father's exile), was immediately acknowledged as ruler, both within and outside the country, proof of the old emir's success in pacifying his country, controlling his family, and winning foreign respect.

5

TWENTIETH-CENTURY MONARCHY (1901–1973)

After a century of European imperial encroachment, Afghanistan achieved political independence early in the 20th century. As the country emerged from isolation, it began to deal with the social and economic changes that were occurring everywhere in the world. Nevertheless, the slow progress of modernization and the widespread opposition to government reform programs meant that the lives of the majority of Afghans were still bound to traditional patterns at the time the monarchy was abolished in 1973.

Habibullah Khan

His throne secure from the start of his reign in 1901, Habibullah Khan (1872–1919), was able to devote most of his time to pursuing policy aims; he easily overcame opposition from his father's high-born widow, Bibi Halima (his own mother had been a slave). Though only a portion of the tribal chiefs backed him, the national standing army built up by his father, Abdur Rahman, remained loyal throughout his reign, thanks in part to the rigorous efforts of his full brother, Nasrullah Khan.

Lacking his father's harsh authoritarian instincts and inheriting a state already harshly pacified, Habibullah gave the local khans and chiefs more latitude in local governance, eased up on military conscription, and allowed a greater role for those clergy (allied with Nasrullah) who acknowledged his divine legitimacy. The incipient national bureaucracy established by his centralizing father thus became open to infiltration by traditional, localized power bases.

When local *maliks*, the village chiefs chosen by male heads of households, were coopted into government roles, they were often able to stonewall unpopular decrees, whether out of loyalty to community values or in return for bribes. Regional governors or district officials might now be chosen from among the local khans, major landowners or elected tribal chiefs. Such officials often used state funds and patronage to reinforce traditional power structures. Policies laid down by the increasingly Westernized national bureaucracy had to penetrate these insulating layers before they could be put into effect.

Habibullah allowed many prominent exiles to return to the country and politically repressed notables to become active. The Musahiban family, descendants of Sultan Muhammad Khan of Peshawar, brother of Dost Muhammad, began a long and influential political career under Habibullah. The emir made Nadir Khan (1883–1933), oldest of the five Musahiban brothers, commander in chief; the Musahiban line would later

Emir Habibullah Khan (r. 1901–19) pursued a course of modernization in Afghanistan and careful neutrality in foreign policy. (Photo by Shaista Wahab)

ascend to the throne. Another important family outside the immediate royal circle was the Charkhis, sons of the previous commander Ghulam Haider Charkhi. Their rivalry with the Musahiban would much later prove fatal to them.

Perhaps the most important of the returning exiles was Mahmoud Beg Tarzi (1865–1933), a descendant of Rhamdel Khan of Peshawar, another brother of Dost Muhammad. Tarzi was a nationalist poet, intellectual, and policy adviser who became the key proponent of modernization in early 20th-century Afghanistan; he was also influential among nationalists in India, Central Asia, and other Muslim countries. He had spent years in Syria (then part of Ottoman Turkey; *beg* is the Turkish equivalent of *khan*) with his exiled father, where he married a Syrian wife. There and in travels in Europe and around the Middle East, he met and worked with such prominent reformists as the pan-Islamist Jamal al-Din al-Afghani (1838–97), himself an exile from Kabul.

Once in Afghanistan, Tarzi strove to apply the reformist principles of the Young Turk movement that was beginning to transform Turkey. In his independent bimonthly newspaper *Siraj-ul-Akhbar* (Torch of the news), published from 1911 with Habibullah's permission, he propounded

ACHIEVEMENTS OF MAHMOUD BEG TARZI

The following lists some of the major achievements of the Afghan intellectual and adviser Mahmoud Beg Tarzi, as enumerated in an article appearing in the online publication afghanmagazine.com.

- Established the foundation of journalism by publishing *Siraj al-Akbtar [Siraj-ul-Akhbar,* "Torch of the news"]. . . . Published biweekly from October 1911 to January 1919, it played an important role in the development of an Afghan modernist movement, serving as a forum for a small, enlightened group of Young Afghans, who provided the ethical justification and basic tenets of Afghan nationalism and modernism.
- Published *Siraj al-Atfal* (Children's lamp), the first Afghan publication aimed at a juvenile audience.
- Worked on strengthening the style of Dari and Pashto prose through writing, editing, translations, and modernization of the Afghan press.
- Translated into Dari many of the major works of European authors.
- Effectively guided the second movement of the young constitutionalists called Mashroota Khowha . . . nourishing such devoted liberal patriots as Padshah (King) Amanullah.
- After national independence from the British in 1919, as minister of foreign affairs, established Afghan embassies in London, Paris, and other capitals of the world.
- Showed abundant interest in women's rights and the feminist movement by opening schools for women and printing the *Arshad-el-Naswan,* which was a woman's magazine run by his daughter Shahbanoo (Queen) Soroya and a niece.

(Atta and Haidari, September 1997)

pan-Islamism and condemned British imperialism. He also criticized the stubborn religious traditionalism of Afghanistan as a bar to progress, arguing that economic and social change could be achieved within the overall framework of the country's social and religious structure, on the model of Japan's successful modernization. Tarzi tutored two of Habibullah's sons, Amanullah and Inayatullah, who each married one of Tarzi's daughters. When Amanullah married Soraya, he sent his one previous wife to live with his mother; during his reign as king,

Amanullah effectively had only one wife, following the example set by the monogamist Tarzi.

Habibullah instituted some legal reforms, abolishing the harshest punishments and eliminating his father's spy network. He presided over an era of internal trade growth, aided by new roads (he was an automobile enthusiast), several factories built with foreign technical assistance, and improved communications; telephone lines were strung between Kabul and Jalalabad in 1910. An American engineer was brought in to build a hydroelectric plant, whose output was used to light the emir's palaces and major public buildings.

Habibullah had a modern hospital built and founded several important schools on European lines, including the famous Habibia School, a military academy and a teacher training institute. Many of the country's urban elite began to acquire Western values, but such cultural changes were completely absent in the rural areas where most of the population lived. Even the emir was ambivalent about reform, often denouncing the social and religious criticisms printed in Tarzi's newspaper.

A Careful Neutrality

In 1904, the Persian border, laid down in general terms in 1872, was finally demarcated on the ground, although agreement on sharing Helmand River waters evaded the parties. Shortly after assuming power, Habibullah faced a challenge from Viceroy Curzon, who sought greater influence in Afghanistan in exchange for continuing the subsidies provided for in the Anglo-Afghan treaty of 1880. Curzon, concerned that the Russians were once again seeking representation in the country, insisted that the treaty had expired with the death of Abdur Rahman and needed to be renegotiated. Habibullah, to great domestic acclaim, responded that if that were the case, he was no longer bound to channel all foreign affairs through Britain, and he ordered the appointment of envoys to 24 countries. After four years of dispatches and negotiations, London agreed simply to reaffirm the earlier treaty and replaced Curzon with a more liberal viceroy. In 1906, with relations thus improved, and his domestic prestige at its peak, Habibullah paid an extended visit to India, where he was impressed with the economic and technological progress he saw there; he gave greater support to Tarzi's initiatives on his return.

In 1907, Britain once more riled Afghan opinion by signing a convention with Russia that reaffirmed their bilateral status quo: Britain would handle Russia's affairs within Afghanistan and pledged not to occupy or annex any territory there and not to intervene in internal affairs. Habibullah was expected to add his signature, although the country had not even been consulted during 15 months of talks. He refused, but the insulting request inflamed what became known as the War Party in the country, which included nearly all prominent figures within and outside the royal family, whether reformers or traditionalists. Nasrullah proceeded to encourage armed attacks by trans–Durand Line tribes over the next two years, in opposition to renewed British efforts to tame the frontier. The emir refrained from endorsing the calls for jihad of several mullahs, but he allowed fighters to cross the border.

When Turkey, in October 1914, entered World War I on the side of its German ally, the caliph in Istanbul proclaimed a jihad against the allies, most of whom had been chipping away at the Muslim world for centuries. The call, endorsed by many Muslim activists in British India, also found support in Afghanistan. Habibullah was naturally loath to begin hostilities against the two powers that practically surrounded his country, with no likely support on the ground from the Central Powers, but he gave free rein to anti-British opinion, and he continued the policy of limited military support for the eastern tribes and mullahs against Britain.

The emir pledged his support to a German-Turkish mission that arrived in Kabul in September 1915, provided he was given an unrealistically high level of financial and military assistance. In its absence, he reaffirmed Afghan neutrality in 1916 and accepted an increased subsidy from a grateful Britain. The overthrow of the czar in 1917 was seen by the War Party as a perfect opportunity for Afghanistan to redeem its Islamic mission against Britain, but Habibullah refused to give in.

In consideration, upon the war's end, the emir expected Britain to affirm Afghanistan's full independence in foreign policy. Britain, preoccupied with a renewed northern threat posed by the Russian civil war, hesitated, until its steadfast ally Habibullah was assassinated on a hunting trip on February 20, 1919. The pro-Turkish circles in Afghanistan may have had the strongest motive, but popular opinion laid the blame on Britain. The new emir, Amanullah, executed a couple of suspects of his own and threw his uncle Nasrullah, who had been with Habibullah when he died, in jail, where he apparently died two years later.

Amanullah Khan

The enthusiasm for revolution and reform that swept over much of the world following World War I found its echo in Afghanistan. Amanullah

(1892–1960; r. 1919–29) won the country its independence from British control and launched 10 years of political and economic reforms, until a violent traditionalist reaction forced him to abdicate in 1929.

The third son of emir Habibullah, Amanullah was stationed in Kabul at the time of the assassination, where he was in charge of the treasury and the army. Using both resources, he overcame a challenge from Nasrullah within a few days and was crowned on February 27. Unlike many previous successors, he had a clear idea of his goals from the start—to build an independent, modernizing state in the manner of his fellow Muslim reformer Kemal Atatürk of Turkey (joined as a model a few years later by Reza Shah Pahlavi of Persia).

Amanullah's first priority was to fulfill his father's goal of complete independence, which he proclaimed to a durbar, or assembly, in Kabul. When Viceroy Chelmsford replied ambiguously to his letter declaring independence, the emir called for a jihad and sent troops to the border, catching the British by surprise. The army took the village of Torkham near the Khyber Pass on May 3, and army commander Nadir Khan overran several British posts in the central sector. The British also moved forces toward the frontier, and the Third Anglo-Afghan War, or the Afghan War of Independence, ensued, preceded by an uprising among a few of the border tribes.

At the time, India was racked by anti-British violence, proindependence sentiment, famine, and influenza. The Indian army had been decimated by the fighting in Europe, and what British units remained in India were demoralized and in the process of demobilization. Russia, absorbed in civil war, posed no immediate threat to his rear, and Amanullah seemed to hold all the cards. He may have had dreams of recovering all the Pashtun territories and perhaps areas beyond that in Muslim India. However, his army's performance was spotty, and British officials and commanders in the region used all their political and military skills to forestall a general uprising on the frontier; they also launched a small counterattack between Quetta and Kandahar and sent a few airplanes to bomb Kabul and Jalalabad.

When the hoped-for Indian uprising failed to materialize, Amanullah expressed his desire for a peaceful settlement, which suited the exhausted British (some troops had refused to move to the front). The viceroy agreed to a cease-fire on June 3, 1919, and in July, he sent a negotiating team to Rawalpindi, which signed an armistice agreement that reaffirmed the Durand Line and eliminated British subsidies to the emir. Amanuallah was credited with victory, at home and abroad, when

King Amanullah Khan (fourth from right), seen here in European dress with his cabinet, strove to bring Afghanistan into the 20th century with a multitude of reforms. Resistance to these eventually led to his abdication and exile in 1929. (Courtesy Library of Congress)

the British attached a letter to the agreement stating that his country was "officially free and independent in its internal and external affairs." A final treaty, providing for the exchange of ambassadors, was not signed until November 1921; by then the emir and his foreign minister, Tarzi, had long been pursuing an independent foreign policy.

Mutual suspicion and dislike between Amanullah and the British continued throughout his reign, as did outbursts of British-tribal violence on the Indian side of the border, sometimes encouraged and financed by the Afghans. In return for such misdeeds, in British eyes, as harboring Indian nationalists in Kabul, the British restricted the free flow of goods into Afghanistan. Perhaps the greatest cause for British concern in the 1920s, however, was the Soviet Russian presence in Afghanistan.

At the very start of his regime, Amanullah had turned to Russia, for decades the obvious counterweight against the British. In the wake of the czarist breakdown, the Afghans had made some efforts to recover Panjdeh and Merv, territories earlier seized by the czar. Soviet leader

Vladimir Lenin, overwhelmed with civil war and diplomatic isolation, sent an envoy to Kabul in September 1919 to resolve this dispute and offer support against the British. In exchange, he wanted help in suppressing Muslim resistance in the old czarist colonies of Central Asia, whom he had no intentions of freeing, despite earlier promises. Lenin hoped at least to win some legitimacy by being recognized by a nationalist Muslim ruler. Worrying the British, who favored his opponents in the Russian civil war, was an added bonus.

The emir sent his own envoys to St. Petersburg in October, led by Tajik general Muhammad Wali Khan, and formal ties were set up. In reward, Lenin sent 13 airplanes with pilots and a number of technical assistants, which formed the basis of a new air force. The two countries signed the Treaty of Friendship in May 1921, in which the Soviets promised cash, technology, and military equipment. Soviet technicians laid several trunk telephone lines in the 1920s.

Amanullah eventually grew leery of Soviet intentions, in light of the brutal suppression of Islam and traditional culture in the Muslim Soviet areas. The autonomous khanates of Khiva and Bukhara were abolished in 1924, and Muslim resistance fighters were crushed (though some continued to fight into the 1930s). Afghan forces withdrew from Panjdeh and Merv without a fight. The only help the emir could safely provide to his fellow Muslims to the north was to allow some volunteer fighters to cross into Soviet territory and to accept hundreds of thousands of Turkmen, Uzbek, Tajik, and Kirghiz tribesmen fleeing the other way, thereby greatly increasing the non-Pashtun proportion of his country's population (as well as its exports of *qaraqul* pelts and handwoven rugs). Once Soviet rule was firmly established down to the border, a nonaggression treaty was signed between the two countries in 1926, and air service was established between Kabul and Tashkent. Russian consuls were stationed in Mazar-e Sharif and Herat, with their British counterparts covering Kandahar and Jalalabad.

In 1921, Muhammad Wali Khan led an Afghan mission to Europe and Turkey and set up relations with several countries; treaties were quickly signed with Turkey, France, and Italy providing training for Afghan military personnel. Tarzi, as the first ambassador to France, developed cultural relations between the two countries; a French-language high school (Lycée Istiqlal) was set up in Kabul, and scholarships provided for university study in France. Tarzi also signed a landmark 30-year protocol for joint archaeological work, renewed in 1952. French archaeologists played a major role in the 20th-century effort to shed light on Afghanistan's rich historical heritage. In addition,

Tarzi managed to purchase French arms and ammunition for the army and then enlist French diplomatic support when the British tried to keep the arms from leaving the port of Bombay.

Constitution and Social Reform

The country's independence secured, Amanullah was anxious to strengthen the new state through reform and modernization. Rejecting Tarzi's advice to go slow, he tried to revise the political, educational, judicial, and even gender politics of the country in one generation. This became almost an obsession in the last several months of his reign. Similar policies were implemented successfully in that era in more developed Muslim states such as Turkey and Persia; but Afghanistan proved an unready or unwilling subject.

Atatürk reportedly advised Amanullah that a loyal, powerful army was needed to make reform stick, but the emir's moves in that direction proved counterproductive. Turkish advisers counseled him to retire several older officers and introduce a military service lottery (enabled by his new universal identity cards), which would eliminate the role of village chiefs in recruitment. War minister (and later king) Nadir Khan resigned in protest of these changes. When Amanullah also cut pay and troop levels, he further alienated the one force that might have protected his revolutionary reign. Reduced pay was supposed to be accompanied by free food and shelter, along modern Turkish lines, but corruption and inefficiency absorbed much of the funding, and troops were often hungry and cold.

On April 9, 1923, Amanullah proclaimed the country's first constitution, a basically secular document (non-Muslims had equal rights) with himself as absolute *pashah,* or king, now to be a hereditary position. Written in Pashto, with official translations into Dari and other languages, the document provided for an appointed cabinet or state council and a partially elected consultative body; more radically, it curtailed the power of religious judges. The constitution explicitly guaranteed rights for women, a reaffirmation of earlier royal decrees, and abolished slavery and forced labor. The king also instituted an independent court system and issued new civil, commercial, and penal codes (the latter outlawed blood money, the Islamic option of monetary payments by a murderer to his victim's survivors in lieu of execution).

In the financial realm, the government decreed a reformed, bureaucratic tax system that bypassed the traditional role of regional and local chiefs, and it conducted a livestock census and a land survey to ensure that all property was fairly taxed. Amanullah introduced a national budget in 1922, partly to reduce corruption and nepotism, and he abolished many obsolete sinecures. By eliminating subsidies to royal relatives and tribal chiefs alike, he saved money but also gave up one of the key tools that his predecessors had used for centuries to consolidate and maintain support.

Perhaps the most far-reaching reforms were in education—or would have been had they been widely enforced. Universal education was established as a principle, for nomads as well as the settled population and for girls as well as boys. New primary and high schools were set up, including a French, a German, and two English academies, with the aim of training a new Afghan elite. Queen Soraya herself dedicated the first girls' school; coeducational schools were founded as well. Soraya also founded the first Afghan women's magazine, *Irshad-Niswan* (Guide for women), in 1921. All the new schools taught secular and vocational subjects; some hired teachers from India and Europe.

Other reforms attempted under Amanullah included the adoption of the solar calendar (as opposed to the Muslim lunar calendar), a uniform coinage denominated in afghani in 1927 to encourage trade and industry, and antismuggling campaigns. The king launched a major construction program, centered in his new capital at Darul Aman (abode of peace) a few miles from Kabul, where European architects helped build a palace, parliament, triumphal arches, a theater, a trolley line, cafés, and private villas. Little remains intact of these projects after the wars of the late 20th century.

Amanullah's reforms won support among intellectuals and many other urban residents but antagonized traditionalists and most of the rural population. Many of the changes offended traditional social and religious sensibilities; perhaps more important, they threatened the power of the religious and tribal leaders who formed the framework of governmental, social, and legal life in much of the country.

A major rebellion by the Mangal Pashtun tribe flared up in 1924 in the Khost region, under the leadership of the fiery Mullah-i-Lang (the lame mullah) and other religious figures; Amanullah saw a British hand in the uprising as well. It took the army—and extensive tribal levies—nine months to suppress the rebellion, at great cost to lives and the budget. A rebel march on Kabul was stopped only with the use of two bombers piloted by infidel Germans.

The king had the Mullah-i-Lang and 50 of his supporters executed, but he also called a *loya jirga* to discuss the events. Under conservative pressure, he was forced to modify some of his reforms, backtracking on women's rights and restoring some powers to the mullahs. These steps seemed to win acquiescence if not approval from his opponents, and peace was maintained over the next few years, allowing some of the reforms slowly to take root.

Radicalism and Rebellion

Against the advice of intimates concerned about tribal and religious disaffection, Amanullah and Soraya embarked on an eight-month tour of India, Persia, Egypt, Turkey, the Soviet Union, and European capitals in December 1927. The royal couple were a sensation and picked up diplomatic dividends for their country along the way. But newspaper photos of the sophisticated queen in Western clothing, unveiled and with bare arms, were circulated throughout Afghanistan, where they were considered scandalous and an outrage against national values.

Returning to the country with a keener sense of its backwardness, Amanullah launched a renewed reform campaign, ignoring all cautionary protests from his supporters. Tarzi urged that British aid be brought in alongside increased Russian assistance, to mollify Britain, and he sought top priority for military and administrative reform.

Instead, Amanullah summoned another *loya jirga*. All attendees were required to shave off their beards, cut their hair, and appear in formal Western attire, which some had to acquire secondhand at great expense. When they assembled, the king announced that he would shortly issue a new, more liberal constitution. He proposed to impose monogamy on government employees, to expand education for women, to require men and women in Kabul (and tribesmen visiting the capital) to wear Western clothing, to abolish child marriage, and to discourage the *chadri* (veil) and purdah (the isolation of women at home). He also planned to raise taxes, extend conscription from two to three years, and further curtail the power of religious leaders.

When the *loya jirga* rejected many of these proposals, the king summoned a smaller *jirga* of his supporters that provided the necessary approval. In a dramatic gesture at that occasion, Queen Soraya removed her veil and revealed her face to the attendees, most of whom surely recognized her from the photographs.

Not surprisingly, many Afghans believed the rumors that now began circulating that the king had abandoned Islam for Catholicism, perhaps having lost his senses after eating pork and drinking alcohol in Europe. The king responded to frenzied criticism with repression, executing the chief religious judge of Kabul and other mullahs and jailing the Hazrat Sahib of Shor Bazaar, the most respected cleric in the country.

Violence was by now almost inevitable. The Shinwari tribe near Khyber was the first to rise, possibly as a tax protest. In November 1928, they sacked Jalalabad, destroying the royal palace and the British legation. In the north in December, resistance coalesced around a popular Tajik bandit named Habibullah and nicknamed Bacha-i-Saqao (son of the water carrier, apparently a genuine biographic reference). Bacha overran a large government fort without a fight and raided Kabul.

The king now tried to reverse course, rescinding reforms and freeing prisoners, but it was too late. He abdicated in January 1929 in favor of his half brother Inayatullah, who reigned for three days before he himself was quickly evacuated along with the rest of the royal family with the help of the British envoy. Amanullah, after one last attempt to rally loyal forces in Kandahar, fled to India and then to Italy. He died in exile in Zurich in 1960.

Tarzi and many others claimed, without direct evidence, that the British had supported the rebellion. Delhi would have had its reasons, given Amanullah's anti-British rhetoric and his ties with the Soviets. British officers certainly discouraged the Pashtun tribes on the Indian side of the border from entering the fray, which might conceivably have saved the king, and Britain had also been ungenerous with financial aid. On the other hand, evidence shows that British envoy Sir Francis Humphreys tried to convince the king to mollify his opponents when such a course might have saved him.

Revolution and Restoration

With the sudden collapse of the army and monarchy, Bacha-i-Saqao moved his irregular forces into Kabul on January 17 and installed a government of friends and relatives, with the support of various religious figures. Other followers seized control in Herat, Mazar-e Sharif, and Kandahar.

A Soviet-aided resistance in the north under the ambassador to Moscow, Ghulam Nabi Charkhi, failed to win much support beyond mercenaries hired on both sides of the Soviet border. The Pashtun tribes, some of whom had initially backed Bacha, mostly bided their time until an appropriate contender (and not a Tajik upstart) would appear; long experience had taught them how to live free of control from the capital.

An illiterate native of a small village north of Kabul called Kalakan, Bacha (who preferred to be called Habibullah Khan) and his colleagues ruled the capital as an enemy city, killing off Amanullah's officials, relatives, and followers, as well as other wealthy individuals. Extortion and robbery prevailed. The new government immediately cancelled all of Amanullah's reforms, handing education and the courts back to religious authorities, closing many schools, and reimposing the *chadri* and purdah. Girls who had just the previous year begun to study in Turkey were recalled. Libraries were destroyed and rare manuscripts burned.

The five Musahiban brothers, prominent descendants of Sultan Muhammad Khan, brother of Dost Muhammad, soon rallied their forces as obvious candidates to restore the Durrani monarchy. The eldest, former army commander Nadir Khan, quickly returned from exile in France, entered the country via British India, and with three of his brothers began to assemble a tribal *lashkar* in Khost in March, rejecting overtures from both Bacha and supporters of Amanullah. A lack of funds held the brothers back until October 10, when a force under Shah Wali Khan took Kabul with tribal fighters quietly recruited on the British side of the frontier. On the face of it, Britain tried to appear neutral; overt support would have antagonized the Pashtuns and invited Soviet intervention. Bacha and his top supporters were lured back to the city and executed, probably in violation of a safe-conduct guarantee, and the city was subjected to another round of plunder.

Nadir Shah

The victorious chiefs acclaimed Nadir Khan as the new ruler on October 16. A full *loya jirga* later endorsed the choice in September 1930, naming him Nadir Shah (r. 1929–33).

The king possessed the military and administrative experience and enough determination to piece the country back together by 1931. He used a combination of force, as when he brutally suppressed a Tajik uprising in 1930, and bribery, his method of convincing the Shinwari Pashtun to abandon their uprising the same year. His army, which numbered 40,000 men by 1933, was adequate to the tasks he set. In April 1930, for example, when a Soviet force crossed the border in pursuit of an Uzbek rebel, Ibrahim Beg, the army drove the rebels back to the Soviet Union, where Beg was promptly executed. Tribal and religious leaders, in turn, were able to gain back all they had lost under Amanullah's reforms, most of which Nadir formally abolished.

The king issued a new constitution in 1931, based largely on Amanullah's document of 1923, but with one crucial difference: It gave official status to the laws of the Hanafi school of Sunni Islam. The

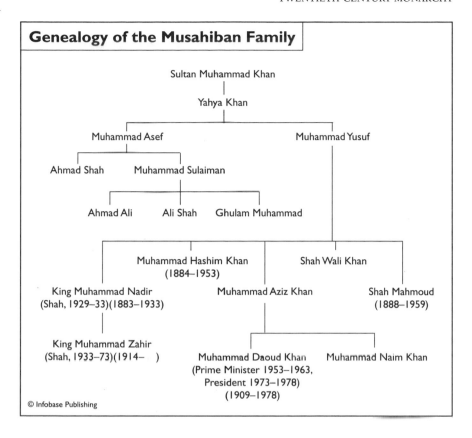

Genealogy of the Musahiban Family

Sultan Muhammad Khan

Yahya Khan

Muhammad Asef — Muhammad Yusuf

Ahmad Shah — Muhammad Sulaiman

Ahmad Ali — Ali Shah — Ghulam Muhammad

Muhammad Hashim Khan (1884–1953) — Shah Wali Khan

King Muhammad Nadir (Shah, 1929–33)(1883–1933) — Muhammad Aziz Khan — Shah Mahmoud (1888–1959)

King Muhammad Zahir (Shah, 1933–73)(1914–) — Muhammad Daoud Khan (Prime Minister 1953–1963, President 1973–1978) (1909–1978) — Muhammad Naim Khan

© Infobase Publishing

bicameral parliament was to be partly elected and partly appointed by the king; 105 members of parliament were to be chosen for a National Council to advise the king. Nothing in the constitution prevented the royal family from ruling at its own discretion. In practice, the National Council gave tribal and religious leaders a voice in the government but also allowed the king to keep tabs on any simmering discontent.

Nadir did pursue modernization where possible; he reopened many schools and built new ones (though he subjected them to a clerical board of censorship). He founded a literary academy and a medical faculty (1932), which later evolved into Kabul University. He completed a modern road from Kabul to the north through the Shibar Pass, built several irrigation dams, and drained northern swamps to promote cotton cultivation.

Nadir enlisted the talents of several leading businessmen to help improve economic planning and stabilize finance and to promote investment in favored projects. In cooperation with Abdul Majid

Zabuli, the country's most prominent merchant and entrepreneur, the government founded a bank in 1931 with both public and private sector participation. It was renamed the Bank-i-Melli (Afghan National Bank) in 1932. It was used for government financing and currency management and to fund development projects. Nadir continued Amanullah's efforts to engage foreign countries in trade and investment; cotton, fruit, and *qaraqul* became important exports. Revenues from taxes on trade became high enough to relieve internal taxes. A thriving private sector emerged along modern lines for the first time.

In foreign affairs, Nadir pursued a carefully balanced policy, dismissing some of Amanullah's Soviet technicians on the one hand but refusing entry to their British counterparts on the other. One of Nadir's brothers was named ambassador to Moscow, another, to London. The anti-British rhetoric of Amanullah's reign disappeared, as did Amanullah's occasional aid and comfort to tribal rebels on the Indian side of the Durand Line. Consequently, the opposition charged that Nadir was a puppet of the old British enemy. After all, the British had allowed him and his brothers to return to the country from their side of the border, and once he was on the throne, they gave him a gift of 10,000 rifles, ammunition, and £175,000, sorely needed in light of the empty treasury. Nadir may also have secretly sought British guarantees against Soviet aggression.

Rule by the Musahiban Brothers

On November 8, 1933, a young student named Abdul Khaliq assassinated Nadir Shah, apparently as the result of a long-standing feud between the Musahiban and the Charkhi family, supporters of Amanullah. Ghulam Nabi Charkhi (perhaps Abdul's father; others believe that Abdul may have been a servant of Ghulam Nabi's family) had been executed a year before on suspicion of fomenting rebellion, and a cycle of assassinations of major figures, including the king's brother Muhammad Aziz, and executions had followed. Most of the assassins were graduates of the Nejat school, a hotbed of anti-British and nationalist sentiment.

In subsequent years, revolutionary circles educated at the state schools in Kabul and other cities merged to form a small but influential movement of educated Afghans from wealthy backgrounds who were alienated from both the court and government in Kabul and the traditional religious and political leadership in the tribes. It was a forerunner of the more ethnically and economically diverse radical movements that emerged at the University of Kabul in the 1950s and 1960s, which ranged in ideology from marxist to radical Islamist.

Historical precedent suggested that one of Nadir's powerful brothers might succeed him, either Prime Minister Muhammad Hashim (1884–1953) or Minister of War Shah Mahmoud (1888–1959), commander of the army in Kabul. But they both deferred to Nadir's 19-year-old son Muhammad Zahir (1914–   ), who was proclaimed king the same day, November 8, 1933.

After the assassination, the two brothers quickly reasserted their family's control, perhaps more strongly than before. They executed 18 alleged conspirators and arrested hundreds of others; no serious domestic opposition would trouble the government for more than a decade. In 1939, a localized rebellion did break out in the Khost region, led by Shami Pir (the "Syrian Saint"), a relative of Queen Soraya. It collapsed when the British, plagued with low-level resistance on their own side of the border, paid the Pir a substantial sum to leave the region.

Muhammad Zahir, educated in France and Afghanistan, had been groomed for the throne by his father. Nevertheless, though he reigned for 40 years, for most of that time, he was content to leave effective power in the hands of his uncles—Hashim remained prime minister until 1946, when Mahmoud replaced him—and his cousin Muhammad Daoud, who replaced Mahmoud as prime minister in 1953. Lacking the dynamism of so many of his relatives, Zahir was eventually ousted in a republican coup in 1973, but he survived in exile long enough to become an admired symbol of his country during years of civil war and oppression. He returned amid wide acclaim in 2002 to live out his life as a private citizen in the old royal palace in Kabul. He was the last ruler of the 226-year Durrani Pashtun dynasty.

King Muhammad Zahir ruled for 40 years before he was overthrown by his cousin Muhammad Daoud in 1973. He returned from exile in Rome in 2002 to help the government of Hamid Karzai. (Afghanistan News 6, no. 73 [September 1963], Royal Afghan Embassy in London)

Under Zahir, domestic policies continued along the path of slow modernization set by Nadir. More schools were built, although the vast majority of the population remained illiterate throughout this era. The Bank-i-Melli continued to initiate new companies, called *shirkats,* to pursue new economic activities on a monopoly basis, with heavy participation by the government and the royal family. A new state bank was incorporated in 1938, the Da Afghanistan Bank; it opened offices in India, Britain, and Germany.

Foreign Entanglements

For a century, Afghanistan had been caught in a vise between Russian and British imperialism, but a shrinking world gave the country more options in the 1930s. Afghanistan joined the League of Nations in 1934. The same year, it established diplomatic relations with the United States. The two countries had begun diplomatic contacts and exchanges as early as 1922; in 1936, they signed a treaty of friendship, and a small American presence appeared in the fields of education, trade, and oil exploration. A permanent U.S. envoy was not assigned until 1942; the United States did not view the country as having great economic or strategic value. In 1937, Afghanistan signed the Sa'adabad Treaty of Friendship with Iran, Iraq, and Turkey, which had more symbolic than practical import.

More important, the pro-German sympathies that had spread during World War I now intensified, and Afghanistan eagerly accepted assistance from Germany and its Axis allies Italy and Japan. While the country still refused to admit permanent Russian trade missions, no such reluctance was shown to Germany. Regular weekly air service between Berlin and Kabul began in 1937; the route was later extended to China. German companies set up offices in the capital and built a few factories, and mining experts began exploring mineral resources in the sensitive border province of Paktia, opposite the troubled Tribal Agencies of British India. German anthropologists conducted surveys in Nurestan, raising British Indian suspicions. German technicians also supervised the construction of several bridges and dams for irrigation and electricity generation, which, however, nearly all collapsed in subsequent spring floods. Students were sent to study in Japan.

Nazi envoys used racist propaganda to further their inroads, with some success. They convinced some educated Afghans that they were the "original Aryans" and discouraged the previously widespread belief that the Pashtun were one of the biblical Lost Tribes of Israel. In

FLIRTATION WITH NAZI GERMANY

In the early years of World War II (1939–45), elements within the Afghan government contemplated an alliance with Nazi Germany as a counterbalance against their traditional opponents—British India and Soviet Russia. They probably had at least some support from King Zahir. After the German defeat of France in June 1940, negotiations intensified.

The influential Afghan minister of national economy, Abdul Majid, who had helped establish the country's banking system, told the Germans his government was prepared to give active support for an anti-British revolt among the Pashtuns on the Indian side of the Durand Line. This would divert British resources from the war against Germany, while also righting what most Afghans considered a historic injustice.

The German ambassador in Kabul notified his government that he expected Afghanistan to join the Axis, in return for deliveries of planes and tanks, mediation with the Soviets (then still allied with Germany), and support for an Afghan territorial outlet to the sea. The two countries also discussed joint assistance to the anti-British coup in Iraq. German agents in Afghanistan, operating under cover of business and research activity, contacted anti-British forces along the border and helped conduct several damaging raids into India, although some of them were captured or killed by British and even Afghan troops.

The German invasion of the Soviet Union in June 1941 effectively put an end to the flirtation, as Afghanistan was now surrounded by Allied forces.

Afghanistan, as in Iran and the Arab world, Germany presented itself to Muslims as a model for modernization independent of the old imperial powers, a path that also avoided the atheistic and antitraditional elements of communism.

On August 17, 1940, Zahir issued a *farman,* or decree, of strict neutrality between the opposing powers in World War II. Britain remained concerned about Germany's influence; the country had extended a 27 million Deutschmark credit for arms purchases in 1936, and German agents were reportedly considering a coup to restore the anti-British Amanullah, then living in Fascist Italy, to the throne. Germans also worked to promote violence on the Indian border.

Germany's invasion of the Soviet Union in June 1941 changed the equation. In August that year, Britain and Russia jointly invaded and occupied Iran and removed its shah, who had refused to expel German agents. In October, the two powers made a similar demand to Afghanistan. Prime Minister Hashim responded by expelling all nondiplomatic personnel of all the belligerent nations, in effect giving in while placating domestic opinion, which had been outraged by the demand. He then convened a *loya jirga,* which reaffirmed strict neutrality. In the end, the country benefited from substantially increased agricultural sales to British India during the war and from increased exports of wool to the United States; it also established diplomatic ties with China, the other major Allied power.

In 1946, with Germany defeated, Britain about to leave India, and Russia devastated by war, the new prime minister, Shah Mahmoud, turned to the victorious United States as a likely partner for development. He launched the ambitious Helmand Valley Project to expand agricultural production in the country's southwest, hoping to build on earlier Afghan, German, and Japanese irrigation work. The plan was expected to yield a huge increase in agricultural production and spark industry through hydroelectric power.

Unfortunately, the project, run in 1946–53 in cooperation with the San Francisco engineering firm Morrison-Knudsen, achieved only some of its goals, despite eventual financing from the U.S. Export-Import Bank. There were decidedly mixed ecological and social results. Failure to consider the impact on the local population, insufficient Afghan engineering and administrative resources, inadequate funding and research, and other factors turned the Helmand Valley Project into one of the earliest examples of the overambitious and underachieving foreign aid programs of the cold war era. The project, however, did succeed in training large numbers of Afghan mechanics and other skilled workers.

The ambiguous results of the Helmand project did not encourage any greater American interest in the country. The United States refused to sell the country arms, despite requests dating back to 1948 and a personal request by Shah Mahmoud during his 1951 visit to the country (a request drawn up by war minister and later prime minister Muhammad Daoud). Washington feared that Afghanistan might use the arms in the festering border struggle against Pakistan, an important U.S. ally. Furthermore, any arms the United States might send would hardly protect the country against intervention by the Soviet Union which by now had emerged as a superpower.

Experiment in Liberalization

Prime Minister Hashim Khan's authoritarian tactics and personality had helped stabilize the country following the turmoil of the Amanullah era and kept it safely neutral during World War II. Nevertheless, the royal family decided in 1946 to replace Hashim with his more liberal younger brother Shah Mahmoud, probably as an attempt to satisfy the desire for genuine self-government, which, as the educated Afghan public knew, was sweeping the postwar world.

On taking office, Shah Mahmoud immediately freed political prisoners, gave freer rein to the press, and opened up the political process to new forces. Some 40 to 50 members of the 120-member "Liberal Parliament" elected in 1949 were reformers. They took their constitutional duties seriously and began questioning government ministers about policy and ministerial budgets, although most ministers, unused to such scrutiny and fearful of corruption charges, managed to avoid the questions.

The reformers were able to pass laws guaranteeing freedom of press, and several opposition newspapers appeared in 1951 and 1952, written in Persian and Pashto; however, none of their circulations exceeded 1,500. These newspapers (generally biweeklies) were unrelenting in their criticism of conservative religious leaders and of the royal family. They demanded that the government be put under genuine parliamentary control. Some particularly militant writers of letters to the editor were arrested.

Dissidents and reformers began to organize political groups. The National Democratic Party was formed, as was a student union at Kabul University, whose 20 or 30 members conducted unrestricted political debates; European and American high school teachers also encouraged student activism. In 1947, the Wikh-i-Zalmayan, or Awakened Youth, movement emerged, originally in Kandahar; it attracted members of a variety of dissident groups and called for legal rights for women, parliamentary government, free political parties, and other reforms.

The government tried to form a party of its own, with little success, though it succeeded in keeping most civil servants from joining the liberal groups. Government resistance to the popular demands seemed to provoke the small liberal milieu into greater militancy, while the more vitriolic tone of the press and among university students (who staged plays critical of the monarchy and Islam) scared some moderates into the government's arms.

In 1951, the government closed the student union; several student leaders fled to Pakistan. The following year, in preparation for the 1952 elections, all nongovernment newspapers were closed, and a couple of dozen leaders of the Awakened Youth were arrested, effectively shutting down that group. Many of the imprisoned liberals recanted their views and were allowed eventually to serve in the government. King Zahir freed those still in jail in 1963, at the start of his own reform movement.

The new parliament of 1952 was much more representative of the traditional elites, and therefore, of the majority of the rural population; another reform experiment had been reversed. Nevertheless, the brief experiment had great repercussions for the future of Afghanistan. The generation that came of age at the time formed the core of future radical movements, and of the Communist regimes that took over after 1978. Nur Muhammad Taraki (1917–79), Babrak Karmal (1929–96), and Hafizullah Amin (1929–79) were all involved in the reform activity of the late 1940s and early 1950s.

Pashtunistan

Thus, the Mahmoud government, ushered in with high hopes, had little to show for its efforts to achieve economic development or political reform. Success in foreign policy proved similarly elusive, especially in the Pashtunistan affair that preoccupied the country's leaders for some six years.

Since 1893, Afghanistan had been forced to recognize the Durand Line as its effective southern and eastern boundary. No government, however, ever accepted it as the permanent international border with British India, as it left perhaps half of all Pashtuns outside the Pashtun-dominated Afghan state. The approaching independence of India appeared to be the best, and perhaps the final, opportunity to rectify what Afghanistan had always seen as a historic injustice.

In British India, the Pashtun regions made up the North-West Frontier Province, which was divided into the "Settled Districts," self-governing since the 1930s, and several mountainous Tribal Agencies. In each of the latter, a British agent, backed up by army units, tried to keep the overall peace while leaving the tribes functionally autonomous. In the 1920s and 1930s, the Indian National Congress of Mohandas Gandhi was very active in the North-West Frontier Province; as the country moved toward partition into a Muslim state (Pakistan) and a majority Hindu state (India), the North-West provincial legislature actually voted to join India, perhaps in exchange for a promise of autonomy. But Britain put the question to a popular vote, and in July 1947, the Settled Districts voted in a referendum to join Pakistan. Consultative *jirgas* held in the Tribal Agencies came to the same decision.

During this political process, Afghanistan tried to pressure the British Indian government to offer the Pashtuns the additional choices of joining Afghanistan, becoming an independent state (Pashtunistan), or deferring the decision to a later date (as India's Princely States were allowed to do). When Pakistan became independent and assumed control of the province in 1947, Afghanistan was the only country to vote against its admission to the United Nations, which Afghanistan had joined the previous year. The Afghans based their position on the principles of self-determination; their opponents feared that their real goal was to annex the North-West Frontier Province and possibly even Baluchistan, which would give their country access to the sea.

Relations between the two Muslim states continued to deteriorate, as a proindependence "Red Shirt" movement became prominent in the province in 1947. Pakistan imposed delays on shipments of goods to Afghanistan (which caused further problems for the Helmand Valley Project). In July 1949, after a Pakistani aircraft bombed a village a mile into Afghanistan, a *loya jirga* in Kabul repudiated all historic treaties with the British and recognized Pashtunistan as an independent country; a tribal assembly on the other side of the border proclaimed the militant fakir of Ipi, Mirza Ali Khan, as president of the new state. In 1950 and 1951, militant Afghan tribesmen crossed the border to aid the rebels, leading Pakistan to sever diplomatic ties with Afghanistan for several months and withhold oil shipments.

The Soviet Union was eager to step into the breach. It signed a far-reaching barter agreement with Afghanistan in 1950, trading wool and cotton for oil and allowing the transshipment of goods through its territory; bilateral trade soon doubled. Under the agreement, the Soviets built oil storage facilities and began prospecting for oil and gas in the country's north. A permanent Soviet trade office opened in Kabul.

Afghan leaders were privately concerned about the advance of Soviet power in Europe, Stalinist repression in Central Asia, the ominous migration of large numbers of ethnic Russians to the region during and after World War II, and the parallel flight of local Muslims. The Soviets even sent provocateurs into Afghanistan in the late 1940s, who were turned in to the Afghan government by anticommunist Uzbeks, Tajiks, and Turkmens. But these concerns were not enough to keep them from taking advantage of persistent Soviet overtures in the absence of any real alternative.

The First Daoud Era

A generational crisis within the royal family brought King Zahir's cousin Muhammad Daoud Khan (1909–78) to power as prime minister in 1953, probably with the support of the king himself and with the acquiescence of Mahmoud and the older generation. The two younger men, Zahir and Daoud, had both been educated in the West. After their fathers were assassinated in the turmoil of the late 1920s, they were jointly tutored in politics and government (together with Daoud's brother and later foreign minister Muhammad Naim) by their uncle, Prime Minister Hashim. Now in their 40s, Zahir and especially Daoud wanted to assume their birthright as rulers of the country.

Daoud's dynamic 10-year term brought significant economic and social changes to the country, although political reform was never high on his list, and he did not hesitate to repress serious opposition. In fact, he successfully used the army to suppress intertribal fighting in Paktia Province in 1959 and to enforce at least some land tax collections on the Durrani Pashtuns of the Kandahar region.

Daoud did not at first introduce major policy changes. He continued to pay Pashtun tribes on both sides of the border and disseminate anti-Pakistan propaganda, but with no discernible results. He also continued to pursue U.S. economic support for the sluggish Helmand Valley Project.

The new government reorganized the administration of the project and officially inaugurated two major dams in the mid-1950s. Crop production increased dramatically with the availability of year-round water; however, within a few years, inadequate water distribution and control, poor drainage, salinity, silting of channels, and the uncontrolled spread of weeds had cut in half the initial bumper crops. Some nomads were successfully settled in a number of new villages, although the original plan for mixed tribal and ethnic populations had to be dropped when conflicts developed. In 1961, experts from the U.S. Bureau of Reclamation began to assist the project, now primarily under Afghan leadership, and many of the problems were corrected.

A renewed attempt to obtain American arms failed in late 1954, for reasons that are still debated. According to one theory, Afghanistan refused to accede to a U.S. request for a formal political alliance, such as joining the Central Treaty Organization along with its Muslim neighbors Iran and Pakistan. Another, conflicting theory claims that the Afghans might have joined the alliance but only in exchange for explicit guarantees against a Soviet military reaction, which the United States was not prepared to extend at that time.

Daoud turned to the Soviet bloc, first buying $3 million worth of arms from Czechoslovakia in 1955 and then obtaining a $32.5 arms loan from the Soviets to buy T34 tanks and MiG-17 and other aircraft. The Soviet Union began training the Afghan military, both locally and within the USSR.

Trade and development agreements were also signed with the Soviet bloc beginning in 1954, covering oil pipelines, cement plants, and other infrastructure investments. Some of the projects failed, but the Soviets staged a propaganda victory by paving Kabul's streets, a project that the United States had earlier refused to finance. Thus, the Soviets were well placed to take advantage of a renewed crisis with Pakistan in 1955. For internal reasons, Pakistan decided to merge all its provinces into one, thus eliminating the North-West Frontier Province (an act that was later rescinded). Afghans responded with anti-Pakistan riots and flag burnings in several cities, leading to a suspension of relations and renewed Pakistani trade barriers. Once again, Soviet ties became economically crucial, and the two countries renewed their earlier barter and transit agreements. (All in all, the Soviet Union provided more than $1 billion in military aid and $1.25 billion in economic aid in the decades preceding 1979, in contrast to less than half a billion dollars from the United States.)

At the height of the dispute, Soviet leaders Nikita Khrushchev and Nikolai Alexandrovich Bulganin visited Kabul on the way home from a triumphal visit to India and came out explicitly in support of the Afghan position. They announced a gift of a hospital and a fleet of buses, as well as a long-term $100 million loan. The loan was used to finance an air base at Bagram north of Kabul, hydroelectric plants, and a new road to the Soviet border that would tunnel under the Salang Pass. With the fresh loan, the Afghans in 1956 launched a five-year economic plan along Soviet statist lines, designed by Finance Minister Abdul Malik, who had studied in Turkey under the similarly statist ruler Kemal Atatürk.

Fearful that Afghanistan was moving into the Soviet bloc, the United States responded in 1955 with additional assistance. This included some military training and $25 million in arms but focused primarily on reform of the educational systems and aid to higher education, which in turn spurred Russia to set up a technical college. The United States also conducted road-building projects of its own, linking the major cities to Pakistan and Iran; helped set up Ariana, the national airline; and built a major international airport at Kandahar. All these transportation improvements facilitated a significant rise in tourism.

Eventually, the two superpowers learned to tolerate each other's presence in Afghanistan and even cooperated on various road, power, irrigation, and food processing projects. In total, aid from both sides (more from the Soviet Union than from the United States) covered 80 percent of the country's development budget. In 1957, King Zahir visited Moscow; in 1959, President Eisenhower visited Kabul. Daoud's nonaligned stance, called *bi-tarafi,* or "without sides" in Farsi, seemed to be accepted by both powers.

In one of Daoud's few genuinely revolutionary moves, he ordered the wives and daughters of the royal family and other prominent figures to appear unveiled at the August 1959 ceremony marking the 40th year of independence, just 30 years after King Amanullah had tried to do the same. The passage of time and Daoud's much stronger military position made all the difference. When a large number of mullahs objected but could not provide Daoud with explicit Islamic justification of the *chadri* and purdah, 50 of them were jailed as heretics. The mullahs were soon released but only after they acknowledged the policy that every family would decide for itself whether to impose *chadri* and purdah.

In the previous few years, the government, under the advice of legal experts with secular as well as Islamic educations, had appointed women as singers and staffers for Radio Afghanistan, as receptionists and hostesses for Ariana Airlines, as factory workers in a pottery factory and a telephone exchange, and even, in 1958, as a delegate to the United Nations. In 1961, women were admitted to all the faculties of Kabul University. By the 1970s, unveiled women were an accepted part of the workforce in government and many private offices.

Perhaps Daoud's greatest success was in expanding the educational system, with financial and technical help from abroad. He set up primary schools in many villages, high schools in provincial cities, and boarding schools in Kabul for provincial students. United Nations figures, although probably exaggerated, showed dramatic progress, with elementary enrollment quadrupling from 1951 to 1965, when 360,000 (mostly boys) attended; the number grew further to 940,000 in 1978, at the time of the Communist coup. Secondary schools enrolled less than 5,000 students in 1951, 45,000 in 1965, and more than 100,000 in 1978; higher education jumped from 461 in 1951 to 3,400 in 1965 and more than 20,000 in 1978. This was an impressive achievement in a population of perhaps 15 million.

A New Pakistan Crisis

For all his domestic successes, it was Daoud's inability to accept the status quo on the Pakistan border that led to his downfall and the end of his first period in power.

In both 1960 and 1961, Daoud sent combined army-tribal forces across the border to intervene in local disputes within Pakistan. The first incursion was repelled by Pashtun tribesmen on the other side; the second, with the help of Pakistani air force and army, which suffered substantial casualties. In August 1961, the powerful new Pakistani president, Ayub Khan, himself a Pashtun, closed his country's consulates in Afghanistan.

In retaliation, the Daoud government suspended all relations and closed the border between the two countries; some 200,000 seasonal *kuchis* (nomads) were prevented from following their traditional routes across the Durand Line. The 18-month closure (with one emergency eight-week reprieve) caused serious economic dislocations to Afghanistan, including huge trade losses and a drastic drop in crucial customs income, despite attempts by both the United States and the Soviet Union to open alternate transit routes. When combined with overspending on development projects, the affair led to shortages, inflation, and the evaporation of foreign reserves.

By this time, King Zahir, who had been playing a more active leadership role in recent years, and the royal family were ready for a change. They were mindful of recent bloody republican revolutions in Iraq (1958) and Yemen (1962) and worried about Daoud's increasing dependence on the Soviets. Besides, the very population that benefited from Daoud's successes in education, economic growth, and women's rights were no longer happy with authoritarian rule. Long consultations ensued within the power elite, with the participation of eminent non-royal advisers and even non-Pashtun cabinet ministers. On March 9, 1963, King Zahir accepted Daoud's resignation, and the era of constitutional monarchy began.

The New Democracy Period

King Zahir named a caretaker prime minister, the German-educated physicist Muhammad Yousuf, who in a radio address a few days later promised greater freedom in politics and a more liberal economy. By the end of May, the new government reestablished full trade and diplomatic ties with Pakistan; while no formal agreement was ever reached, the border dispute never again heated up to such a dangerous boil.

Yousuf quickly established his reformist credentials; on March 28, he appointed a seven-man committee (including the prominent liberal Muhammad Siddiq Farhang) to draft a new constitution, and on March 31, he ordered an investigation of the country's primitive penal system, in which torture was routinely used by police (often untrained army recruits) to extract confessions.

Ultimately, Zahir's 10 years of effective rule, popularly called the New Democracy period, did not bear fruit in a stable, democratic government, nor did it consistently respect basic freedoms of speech, the press, and political organization. A vibrant political life did emerge, however, in which large segments of the population came to participate. But the immature system had no way to resolve conflicts between newly conscious social, economic, and ideological groups, an ominous sign for the future.

In September 1964, a *loya jirga* assembled to consider the draft of the new constitution, which had been explained in detail in Radio Afghanistan broadcasts. There were only four women among the 452 *jirga* members, but the delegates were in other respects genuinely representative of the ethnic, religious, social, and political diversity of the country—including the fact that most were illiterate. Its two weeks of deliberations proved to be a model of serious, reasonable debate; many of the illiterate members were eloquent orators experienced in local councils and tribal *jirgas*.

The discussion largely served to rally support for otherwise controversial measures, such as the use of the word *Afghan* to represent all citizens and not just Pashtuns. Religious objections to the role of secular law and an independent nonreligious judiciary were overcome, as drafters pointed to the provision that sharia would be the default law in the absence of any contradictory legislation, and as delegates recounted glaring inequities and corruption perpetrated by some of the impoverished and ignorant rural *qazis* (Islamic judges). Members succeeded in adding a clause prohibiting forced resettlement of populations; they also added an anti-Daoud ban on open political activity by members of the royal family.

The constitution as finally approved provided for a two-chamber *shura,* or parliament, with a fully elected Wolesi Jirga, or lower house, and a Meshrano Jirga, or upper house, one-third appointed by the king and two-thirds chosen by the provinces. All basic rights were guaranteed, for men and women and even for non-Muslims. But the *shura's* powers were mostly negative; it could reject the ministers appointed by the king and could reject ministerial bills. The document provided for political parties, but the legislation to set them up was never passed.

The first *shura* was elected in August–September 1965 and took office in October; only a minority of eligible voters actually participated, especially in rural areas. The elections were relatively unimpeded by the government and produced a lower house encompassing many independent provincial notables and landlords and a sizable component of liberals and even radicals, including four members of the People's Democratic Party of Afghanistan (PDPA), the new Communist Party. When Yousuf tried to present his government, many of whom had been ministers in the past, he was interrupted by vociferous student protesters in- and outside the chamber, and the session had to be adjourned. Later that day, three people died when police fired at protesters outside Yousuf's home, leading to a political crisis and Yousuf's resignation in favor of Education Minister Muhammad Hashim Maiwandwal, who was able to calm the students. Maiwandwal, who founded the moderately socialist Progressive Democratic Party, took seriously ill in October 1967 and was replaced as prime minister by former diplomat Nur Ahmed Etemadi.

Radicalization

The outsized political role of students, which had begun during the earlier reformist era under Shah Mahmoud, was one indication of the growing power in political life of the educated class. In 1964, the various faculties of the University of Kabul were united in one campus built with American aid money, with dormitories for some 1,200 students. Earlier students had been assured of jobs in the government and development bureaucracy, but the much larger numbers of students now enrolled, many from poor or middle-class backgrounds, faced a reality of stagnant government budgets and the lack of a large private sector.

In addition, by this period, thousands of students had returned from studying abroad, many from the West and some 6,600 from the Soviet Union. Politics was one of the few outlets for students and graduates; lacking much connection with the traditional world of their parents, many turned to radical ideologies, whether Islamist or communist. Returning home to work or teach, some graduates spread these ideologies to provincial centers.

Student demonstrations became more frequent as the decade progressed, sometimes in support of industrial strikes, especially during and following the worldwide revolutionary year of 1968. Fights erupted between leftists and militant Muslims (who won student elections in 1970), with occasional fatalities. Following student strikes and protests against government educational policies, the university was closed for six months in 1970.

The growing strength of the Left among the educated classes had little impact in the countryside. In the 1969 elections, the conservative rural elites, secular and religious, increased their representation in the *shura,* and most liberals and radicals were voted out of office (though Babruk Karmal and Hafizullah Amin kept their seats). A Muslim backlash against women's rights and occasional antireligious expressions in the press gained strength. In 1970, a purportedly antireligious newspaper poem provoked riots in Kabul and disturbances in the provinces that were suppressed through arrests, expulsions, and army action. That same year, Muslim radicals were jailed after 5,000 women protested a spate of acid attacks against women who appeared without veils.

Communists and Islamists Organize

In January 1965, Nur Muhammad Taraki, a longtime critic of the government, assembled some 30 members of various marxist study groups at his home to found the PDPA. All those present were pro-Soviet Marxist-Leninists, and the party was organized along Stalinist principles. Two of the founding members, Taraki and Babrak Karmal, later served as presidents after the Communist coup of 1978.

Almost certainly financed by Soviet payments, the party was able to attract support among students, and four of its members won election to the 1965 *shura.* When a 1966 law allowed greater press freedom, Taraki, in April, founded the country's first explicitly leftist newspaper, *Khalq* (The people), which, however, was shut down by the government after only six issues. Karmal was more successful with his own, more cautious newspaper, *Parcham* (Banner), which survived for about a year in 1968 and 1969.

By 1967, the PDPA had split into two major factions, each claiming to be the genuine PDPA, led respectively by Taraki and Karmal. Taraki's party, generally known as the Khalq, drew support primarily from rural Pashtuns; it advocated a dogmatic communist line and supported the Pashtunistan cause. Karmal's Parcham faction drew most of its support from middle-class urbanites and was more ethnically diverse; it followed a pragmatic policy that sought alliances with nonmarxist groups and a more gradual road to communism. The four PDPA candidates who were elected to the *shura* in 1965 were all associates of Karmal, including his close companion Anahita Ratebzad. Smaller splinter marxist groups were formed on purely ethnic and regional lines, Tajik and Panjshiri. A Maoist, pro-Chinese party also emerged, led by members of the Mahmoodi family. Unlike the other marxist parties, the latter group actually worked to organize Kabul factory workers, most of them ethnic Hazaras, and led most of the labor strikes of that era. Middle-of-the-road parties also appeared, such as Maiwandwal's social democratic group.

In 1965, a group of professors and teachers led by Gholam Muhammad Nyazi, head of the Kabul theology faculty, established the clandestine Jamiat-i-Islami, the Society of Islam. The members had been educated in state madrassas (religious schools) and universities, and, in the case of Nyazi, at the venerable Al-Azhar University in Cairo. Their ultimate goal was a modern Islamic state purified of Western cultural influences and guided strictly by Muslim law. They were uninterested in Pashtun nationalism and had little use for the uneducated ulemas and mullahs who were bound by rural Afghan traditionalism, which was not necessarily based on rigorous adherence to Muslim law.

The Jamiat's main impact was through its sponsorship of the Organization of Muslim Youth, which in a few years won control of student government at Kabul University. Like the PDPA, the Jamiat soon split into two. Tajik leaders Burhanuddin Rabbani and Ahmad Shah Massoud opposed any immediate revolutionary activity, preferring slow conversion of the army and bureaucracy to an Islamic perspective, while Ghilzai Pashtun Gulbuddin Hekmatyar supported popular uprisings as a means to power.

Economic Troubles, Political Stalemate

By the early 1970s, the government was facing growing deficits, largely due to a slowdown in foreign aid from the major powers. Corporate taxes and customs receipts had kept pace with the slowly growing private sector, but land and livestock taxes had plummeted, in part due to the parliamentary power of provincial landlords.

Foreign aid had succeeded in laying down the vital infrastructure for a modern economy, but maintenance of these projects required technical and financial resources that were in short supply. To the shame of the educated population, the country remained at the bottom of international rankings in education and health care. Corruption still seemed to plague the government.

The final straw for Zahir's fragile experiment was a widespread famine in 1969–72. Perhaps 100,000 died while American wheat shipments were squandered through the corruption or inefficiency of the relief effort, which was run by the king's son-in-law and chief adviser, General Abdul Wali. Large flocks of sheep died, and thousands of peasants lost their land to creditors. The government and parliament seemed unable to mobilize the country, in large part because the king, on Wali's recommendation, refused to sign the law regularizing political parties, forseen in the 1964 constitution. Furthermore, the municipal and regional elections required by the constitution never took place.

In 1972, the king named a dynamic new prime minister, Musa Shafiq, who tried to jump-start progress on some of the outstanding issues. He even managed to reach agreement with Iran on the Helmand River water rights dispute. However, former prime minister Daoud, kept on the sidelines for 10 years, saw an opportunity for a comeback of his authoritarian approach. On July 17, 1973, while King Zahir was visiting Europe, Daoud staged a coup and proclaimed a revolutionary republic, with himself as president and prime minister. The second Daoud era had begun. It would prove far more tumultuous than the royal cousin's first decade in power and have much more tragic outcomes.

6

A COUP AND A REVOLUTION
(1973–1978)

With the nearly bloodless coup of 1973, Muhammad Daoud Khan officially abolished the monarchy and proclaimed a republic, the first in Afghan history. From a traditional perspective, the event was merely the last of a series of turnovers within the Durrani dynasty, with one ambitious cousin replacing another, and hardly a political revolution. But in practice, Daoud presided over five years of stunning growth in the size and influence of revolutionary circles. Whatever the royal president's intentions, these circles were intent on transforming every aspect of their country's culture and society and soon got their chance to try.

The 1973 Coup

Daoud had been planning the coup for at least a year, in cooperation with both moderate and leftist opposition activists. Young military officers trained in the Soviet Union actually carried out the takeover, leading a few hundred troops to seize key positions in Kabul. Wide sections of the public welcomed the new regime, including army leaders grateful for the massive arms and training assistance Daoud had won from the Soviets during his earlier tenure; Pashtun nationalists who expected the nationalistic Daoud to revive the campaign for Pashtunistan or for a revised border with Pakistan; reformers who remembered Daoud's firm stand in favor of making the veil optional; and leftists who had been quietly conspiring with the new president for some time.

The Parcham faction of the PDPA, led by Karmal (whose father was a general closely tied to Daoud), may have played a role in the takeover; it had won numerous supporters in the army. The Communists had agitated ceaselessly against Zahir, who in turn had refused to legalize political parties. They now expected major political benefits from the coup;

a few Parcham sympathizers were appointed to top roles and many more to lower positions in the new government, and the faction was able to recruit widely in the first months after the coup.

However, Daoud did not prove as pliable as the Communists may have hoped. He soon placed personal associates in key army positions and shunted many young Parcham officers to the provinces. He eased the two leftist ministers out of the cabinet on grounds of inefficiency and rejected a Khalq offer to replace them with more capable cadres of its own. Known anticommunists were gradually brought into the government as well.

Other critics of King Zahir were also soon disheartened. In September, former prime minister and moderate reformer Muhammad Hashim Maiwandwal, who had returned from abroad after the coup, was charged with involvement in a takeover attempt and arrested along with 44 other politicians and military officers, including Zahir's last reforming prime minister, Musa Shafiq. Maiwandwal died in prison in October, reportedly under torture, while Parcham was still running the Interior Ministry, leading observers to believe that the popular leader was deliberately eliminated as a potential rival to the PDPA.

One-Man Rule

In an August 23, 1973, address to the nation to justify his coup, Daoud pointed to the lack of economic progress during the previous decade, including an actual decline in planned capital investments. The following March he set up a trade development program under the Ministry of Commerce to promote trade, facilitate industrial growth, stimulate the development of the nation's products, and stabilize consumer prices.

In keeping with the approach then prevailing in the developing world, Daoud favored a centrally directed economy planned around major industrial projects. As in the past, this would necessarily entail massive foreign aid, which had been declining for several years. The most likely source would be the Soviet Union, with the United States playing an auxiliary role; but Daoud, like Nadir Shah in the 1930s, tried to reach out beyond the two great powers that hemmed in his country.

In 1974, Afghanistan reached a $2 billion 10-year accord with Iran on economic assistance (though very little money was ever expended) and explored possible aid from Saudi Arabia, Iraq, and Kuwait, where large numbers of Afghans were beginning to work and send home earnings. Agricultural production was barely keeping up with population

Removed from power in 1963, Muhammad Daoud (right) returned to office in 1973, ousting the man who had earlier ousted him, his cousin King Muhammad Zahir (left). Here, they are shown in 1961. (*Afghanistan: Ancient Land with Modern Ways*, Ministry of Planning of the Royal Government of Afghanistan, 1961)

growth, despite some modest land reform. Trade revenues suffered from increasingly unfavorable terms with the Soviets.

President Daoud tried to use his expansive powers to chart a course independent of the many groups that had supported him at the start. He served as his own prime minister the entire five years of his rule. In 1976, he organized the National Revolutionary Party to mobilize wider support. In January 1977, he convened a *loya jirga* to approve a new constitution; it provided for a one-party state with a strongman president and a mixed economy with state ownership of natural resources and basic industries.

Any hopes of political liberalization foundered as independent newspapers appeared and were shut in quick succession. A cycle of conspiracies, arrests, and executions set in. After sporadic Islamist uprisings, sponsored by Pakistan in retaliation for Daoud's support of Pashtun separatists, the Afghan president arrested Islamist leader Muhammad Nyazi and hundreds of his associates. Many of them were executed; those who escaped arrest fled to Pakistan and began organizing resistance movements, which would later come into their own fighting the

Communist regime and the Soviet army. Gulbuddin Hekmatyar founded the Hezb-i-Islami (Islamic Party), and Burhanuddin Rabbani headed the Jamiat-i-Islami.

Estrangement from the Soviet Union

The Soviet Union welcomed Daoud's coup, which they almost certainly knew about in advance. The Soviets were unhappy with Zahir's relatively liberal regime and friendly ties with the United States and had worked closely with Daoud in his days as prime minister to build up the army. The Soviets supported Daoud's well-known militancy against Pakistan, a U.S. ally, and most of all, they hoped to exploit Daoud's ties with Karmal and the Parcham.

During the new president's visit to Moscow in 1974, he won a debt moratorium and a commitment for $428 million in new economic assistance. This was less than he had hoped for and was accompanied by pressures to work more closely with the Parchamis.

The visit only increased Daoud's wariness about the Soviet embrace. He was happy to accommodate the Soviet Union on peripheral or symbolic matters; during his five-year term, Afghanistan consistently voted with the Soviet-dominated "unaligned bloc" in the United Nations and supported Russia's foreign-policy interests in the Israel-Arab dispute and in other matters. Daoud also agreed to bar any Western economic activity in northern Afghanistan, near the Soviet's heavily fortified "iron curtain" along the Amu Darya frontier (backed up by a 40-mile no-settlement zone).

But the Afghan president consistently sought an American or Western counterweight to Soviet influence. It was his misfortune that U.S. world influence was at a low point following the crushing defeat in Vietnam. At the same time, Soviet foreign policy was moving away from support for friendly, progressive noncommunist regimes and toward the promotion of communist revolution wherever possible. Daoud's persistent attempts to suppress the Left within Afghanistan, including Soviet-trained officers in the army, played into the hands of Soviet hard-liners.

As early as 1974, Daoud turned to India and Egypt to help with military training. Like Afghanistan, both countries relied on Soviet armaments and military doctrine and supported Soviet foreign-policy objectives, but Daoud's replacement of many Soviet military advisers with Muslim personnel, did not sit well with Moscow.

Daoud had wasted no time in reviving the Pashtunistan issue after his coup. He gave sanctuary to Baluchi and Pashtun rebels from Pakistan, which retaliated with bomb blasts in Kabul and Jalalabad and support for Afghan Islamist rebels. This time, however, persistent diplomatic efforts by Iran and the United States, combined with an obvious lack of interest among Pakistan's Pashtuns, defused the issue. Daoud and Pakistan president Zulfikar Ali Bhutto traded official visits in 1976. During Daoud's March 1978 visit to Islamabad, he agreed to stop supporting rebel groups and to expel Pakistani militants in the future. He also made arrangements to train Afghan military personnel in Pakistan.

Daoud's second visit to Moscow, in April 1977, marked a sharp deterioration in his personal ties with Soviet chief Leonid Brezhnev and between their two countries. Daoud reportedly complained about Soviet efforts to reunite the Parcham and Khalq factions of the PDPA. Brezhnev on his side condemned the rightward shift in Daoud's government and demanded that Afghanistan expel the NATO and UN experts working on projects there, some of whom were stationed north of the Hindu Kush. Daoud is said to have rejected the demands in anger and walked out of the meeting. To make matters worse, the Afghan president announced plans to visit Washington, D.C., in the spring of 1978.

Historians disagree about the Soviet role in the Communist coup of April 1978. The Soviets and their embassy in Kabul were in constant, intimate contact with both factions of the PDPA and had been helping to fund their activities for years. Hundreds of Soviet advisers served within Afghan army and air force units; such units actually carried out the coup, which was not a popular "revolution," as was claimed by the new regime.

If plans for a coup had been prepared well in advance, as Hafizullah Amin later claimed, then the Soviet embassy would surely have known about them. However, the events that immediately preceded the coup, including the actions and reactions of the government and PDPA leaders, were not under Soviet control; furthermore, it is not obvious that the Soviets would have expected to benefit from such a coup attempt, especially since its outcome could not be predicted. In the end, the sequence of events precipitated by the takeover proved disastrous, possibly even fatal, for the future of the Soviet Union.

Even with Soviet backing, the coup might have failed had Daoud ever succeeded in laying down a base of support in the army or the public. But moderate reformers, Pashtun nationalists, and Islamists had all been disappointed by his actions. Daoud's new cabinet of March 1977 was composed almost entirely of personal friends and excluded even moderate leftists; over the next 12 months, Daoud appeared to rely increasingly on a small circle of conservative or right-wing advisers, alienating most of the politically active population. As a result, a relatively small number of Communist activists were able to prevail in 1978 (as Daoud had done five years before), despite the opposition of most of the Afghan people to the domestic and foreign policies that the Communists would soon try to implement.

The Saur (April) Revolution

In July 1977, the Khalq and Parcham factions agreed to reunite, following persistent pressure from the Soviet Union and the active intervention of the Communist Parties of Iran and India. The two factions were to appoint 15 members to a new central committee. In the field, however, and especially within the army, each faction continued to operate largely on its own, with one eye on its rival.

The factions had managed to preserve and increase their strength in the face of Daoud's purges and repression. While Daoud had dismissed many army officers belonging to the Parcham faction or transferred them away from Kabul, others had escaped detection; many other Parcham supporters were ensconced in the civilian administration. Furthermore, the Khalq more than made up for the Parcham's losses in the armed forces, thanks to an intensive recruitment campaign led by Hafizullah Amin, who had earlier been successful in organizing students and teachers into the PDPA. Amin, who focused on Pashtun officers, later claimed that the Khalq had been prepared for a coup as early as 1976.

Recruitment was aided by decades of Soviet political indoctrination among the thousands of army and civilian personnel trained in the Soviet bloc or in Soviet-run military and technical academies in Afghanistan, and among the tens of thousands of skilled and unskilled workers on Soviet aid projects. By 1978, Soviet-trained personnel filled a majority of professional and technical positions in the government bureaucracy and comprised fully a third of armed forces officers, including a majority in the air force.

On the other hand, most of the ideological and political leaders of Afghan communism were trained in the West and in Western-run schools in Afghanistan. When the first Communist cabinet was assembled, only the three military officers had been trained in the Soviet Union; of the 16 civilians, 10 had been educated in the United States and two in Western Europe. They could all speak English, but almost none of them spoke Russian.

The incident that precipitated the Communist takeover was the murder of the Parcham ideologist Mir Akbar Khyber by two gunmen on April 17, 1978. The PDPA blamed Daoud for the killing, although others later blamed the Khalq; at the time, public opinion blamed the U.S. Central Intelligence Agency, but PDPA leaders may have genuinely felt their lives under threat from Daoud. The two factions organized a funeral procession in Kabul that became an anti-American and antigovernment demonstration of some 10,000–30,000 people. Nur Muhammad Taraki and Babrak Karmal both delivered incendiary speeches.

On April 25, an alarmed Daoud had the two leaders arrested along with several of their colleagues. Taraki's arrest was a red line for the Khalq; unfortunately for Daoud, his police neglected to take Amin into custody until the following day. Amin, according to his subsequent account, took advantage of the slipup to relay crucial instructions to conspirators in the armored corps, air force, and radio station, in accordance with an elaborate prearranged plan. In any case, Khalq officers may have felt little choice once PDPA leaders were under arrest.

Several hundred men and 50 tanks of the Fourth Armored Corp attacked the Arg (presidential palace) on April 27, where a cabinet meeting was in session. The attack was the signal for other Khalq cadres to take over armories and command centers across the capital; other tanks took over the military and civilian airports. The 2,000-man palace guard (who apparently thought they were fighting against an Islamist coup) and two infantry divisions tried to resist but were crushed.

The rebels were aided by general confusion in the army, which had been ordered to conduct celebrations that day to mark the arrests of the PDPA chiefs. Many non-PDPA officers, unclear of the forces involved but with little reason to support Daoud, played it safe. When Daoud resisted arrest at the palace early on April 28, he and 30 members of his family were killed. Perhaps 1,000 others died in the fighting.

On the night of April 27, while Daoud was still resisting, two officers—Major Aslam Wantanjar, a Khalqi who commanded the Fourth Corps and who had also participated in Daoud's 1973 coup, and air force officer Abdul Qadir, a non-Pashtun Shiite and Parchami—announced the government takeover on the radio. They reported, in Pashto and Dari, respectively, that a military council had taken power and would rule in accord with Islam to benefit the people of Afghanistan. Taraki refrained from reading the communiqué himself for fear of tipping off right-wing officers to the true nature of the coup. The military council lasted for only two days, to be replaced on April 30 by

NUR MUHAMMAD TARAKI

The genial face that stared down at Afghans from billboards and paintings everywhere in 1978–79 belonged to the son of a semi-nomadic Ghilzai Pashtun livestock dealer. He was born in a village in Ghazni Province in 1917, but the family often traveled over the border to the Quetta region in the North-West Frontier Province of British India. His class and ethnic background made him a useful icon for the new Communist regime, though his ideas and values were more those of a detribalized, urban intellectual of the Left.

Taraki's education was relatively modest, including provincial elementary and high schools. It was enough to win him a job with a prominent Kandahari fruit exporting company, which sent him in 1932 on a five-year stint in Bombay. He learned English at night school there; his contacts with Indian Communists seem to have set him on his radical political path.

Upon his return Taraki attended a college of public administration and won a series of government jobs, including positions at Radio Kabul and the Bakhtar News Agency. He was politically active during the thaw of the late 1940s, publishing a reformist biweekly newspaper in 1949. A peripheral member of the liberal Wikh-i-Zalmayan, or Awakened Youth, movement, he resigned as liberalization faltered and took a job as press attaché at the Afghan embassy in Washington, D.C. When recalled to Kabul, he publicly criticized the new Daoud government; with his asylum request denied by the United States, Taraki recanted, returned, and was forgiven by Daoud.

the Revolutionary Council of the People's Democratic Republic of Afghanistan. The new council was essentially the PDPA central committee with the addition of several army officers.

The next day, the council appointed a cabinet headed by the 60-year-old Taraki as president and prime minister, with Karmal, Amin, and Watanjar as deputy prime ministers. Before the month was over, the council gave way to a politburo, and the refashioning of Afghanistan into a Communist state had begun.

The Khalq Triumphs

A fierce power struggle between the two PDPA factions ensued, despite Soviet Communist Party mediation, and the Khalq soon emerged triumphant. On June 27, Amin was named general secretary

Taraki published social realist short stories in the 1940s and a Pashto novel in 1957, *The Journey of Bang,* depicting the tribal Pashtun world in marxist terms. Two more novels and a theoretical treatise followed, but the writer never won much standing in literary circles and was known as a loyal supporter of the Communist line rather than as an independent thinker.

Taraki visited the Soviet Union in the early 1960s; his lack of any obvious means of support in these years (his translation agency was only moderately successful) led many observers to assume he was on the Soviet payroll. His office was a center for circles of radical activists, and in 1965, he founded the People's

Nur Muhammad Taraki, the head of the Revolutionary Council and the first president of the Communist regime, shown here in a propagandist painting created for the one-year anniversary celebrations of the Saur Revolution. (Photo by Shaista Wahab)

Democratic Party of Afghanistan (PDPA); he remained its leader and then the leader of the Khalq faction, after the 1967 split, until the party took power in 1978.

of the politburo, while Taraki began to be referred to in party literature as the "Great Leader" and "Great Teacher." His image soon became unavoidable, installed everywhere and held aloft at organized mass demonstrations.

The factional dispute had policy implications. The politburo explicitly rejected Karmal's longtime goal of a united front alliance with noncommunists, ruling instead that the PDPA would lay down all policies for the state. Party secretaries were named for the provinces with authority over their respective governors, and a structure of district and subdistrict party bosses was eventually set up. Khalq activists were assigned to create movements for peasants, women, and youth.

By July, Amin was the sole deputy prime minister and as head of the new secret police agency, Da Afghanistan de Gato de Satalo Adara

(AGSA, Pashto for Afghan Interests Protection Agency), the key man in the country. The politburo now effectively disposed of Karmal and nine of his top supporters, including future president Muhammad Najibullah (1947–96), by sending them as ambassadors to various foreign capitals where they would have to report to Amin as foreign minister. Karmal apparently tried to organize a countercoup in the days before he left the country. Apprised of his plans, Amin staged mass arrests of key Parchamis in the party and government in August and subsequent months; many were tortured and killed. Karmal and Najibullah became exiles in Prague or Moscow, where they did not have to wait long for another chance at power. In all, the Khalq government executed some 500 Parchamis in the following months.

Most Afghans in Kabul, let alone in the provinces, were at first unsure how to react to the PDPA coup. They had little reason to assume it would change their lives any more than had previous changes in government, peaceful or violent. Apart from supporting a layer of bureaucracy and benefiting from such useful services as education and intercity roads, millions of Afghans continued to live their lives as nomads or in villages that were largely autonomous of the center.

Few mourned the end of 50 years of rule by the Musahiban family, who had presided over a modernization process too rapid for some in the rural areas but inadequate to the needs of the educated class. President Taraki was a rural Ghilzai Pashtun by birth and upbringing, and middle class by education and lifestyle, as such, he was accepted by several weighty constituencies in the country. Never as polished as the other PDPA leaders, he had some initial success convincing groups of tribal elders that the revolution against the Durrani tyrants aimed solely to ensure basic needs to the people; he downplayed socialist ideology and his 40-year attachment to the Soviet Union.

The triumph of the radical Khalq over the more gradualist Parcham by the autumn and the ascension of the ruthless Amin over the more genial Taraki assured that any popular illusions would not last. In June 1978, the government felt secure enough to replace the country's black, red, and green flag with a Soviet-style red one.

The government now quickly imposed a program of radical reform upon an unprepared nation. While the initial steps were in fact far short of classic socialism, they were implemented in a manner almost guaranteed to provoke resistance; beginning with Decree Number 4 (May 15, 1978), they left out the classic opening statement "in the name of God."

NATIONAL FLAGS OF AFGHANISTAN

Afghanistan changed flags more than any other country during the 20th century. The variety of designs and their symbolism provide a thumbnail sketch of the country's political history.

In the late 19th century, Emir Abdur Rahman flew a black flag (a traditional Muslim military banner) with the royal arms in the center in white, a mosque surmounting crossed arms and surrounded by the Durrani symbol of wheat sheaves. This flag continued in use under Abdur Rahman's successors until 1919, but only over the palace and at military bases and customs offices.

The reformist king Amanullah proclaimed the first national flag in 1919 in keeping with the country's newfound independence; the mosque was now surrounded by sunrays modeled on Ottoman standards. After returning from his famous European trip in 1928, the king proclaimed a new flag on European (and Soviet) models, with three vertical bands: black for the past (and resistance against the British), red for the blood of the country's defenders, and green for hope and peace. The red band bore the arms, a gold sunburst over snowcapped mountains, surmounted by a five-pointed star, all enfolded by wheat sheaves that recalled the Durrani symbol—and also Soviet iconography.

Even the brief interregnum of Bacho-i-Saqqao produced its own flag: appropriately, the red, black, and white stripes used by the destructive Mongol invaders of the 13th century. King Nadir Shah revived Amanullah's colors and his three bands but replaced the progressive symbols with Abdur Rahman's more traditional arms centered on the image of a mosque; he also added the Muslim date for 1929, the year of his own accession to the throne. This flag remained in force with only minor changes until 1974.

At that point, President Daoud's republic needed a new flag. Daoud kept the original black, red, and green colors but replaced the royal arms with an eagle, representing the legendary first king of the Aryans, topped with a rising sun symbolizing the new republic; he also changed the date to 1973. A minimalist impression of the mosque could still be seen, barely, on the eagle's chest.

During the Communist era, the Afghanistan flag was changed several times. In the radical Khalq phase after October 1978, the flag was a classic communist design: a red field with a gold emblem on the upper left; Afghanistan's emblem was the word *Khalq* ("the people," the name

(continues)

139

NATIONAL FLAGS OF AFGHANISTAN
(continued)

of the ruling faction within the Communist Party), a star, and the sheaves of wheat. After the Soviet invasion, the three old colors returned, with a new emblem of a book, wreath, and red star above the sunburst; in the center of the emblem, an inconspicuous stylized white mosque in a green field reflected the new regime's attempt to placate the Muslim faithful. The book and star were dropped in 1987.

From 1992 to 1996, the Islamic State of Afghanistan piously replaced the red band with white, added the year 1992, the *shahadat* (There is no God but Allah and Muhammad is his messenger), and the *takbir* (Allah is great) in Arabic script. It also restored the old mosque-arms-sheath motif used for most of the century. In 1996, the Taliban adopted a pure white flag with the *shahadat* and *takbir* in large black script taking up two-thirds of the width.

The flag of the revived Islamic Republic of Afghanistan after 2002 resembles the 1931–73 flag. The date on the flag was changed to 1919, the year of Afghanistan's modern independence.

Revolution by Decree

Khalq leaders understood from the start that a doctrinaire marxist regime would have trouble surviving in a conservative, basically agricultural country, even with the help of the army and the police. To counter the inevitable opposition, the regime tried to win over the rural masses as quickly as possible with a series of revolutionary decrees that they hoped would divorce oppressed villagers from their traditional chiefs.

The program was proclaimed in utopian fashion almost the moment the Khalq faction prevailed. The reforms, had they been carefully fashioned and implemented gradually, might well have given the regime a rural support base. Imposed in autumn 1978 at a breakneck pace, they had the opposite effect. Several Western observers have surmised that the primary initial goal was to destroy the old system in order to replace it later with a purely collectivist agricultural system.

Decree Number 6 (July 12, 1978) cancelled old mortgages on small holdings and other debts and banned high interest rates. It caused the rural credit system to freeze up, as traditional lenders such as landowners, nomads, and local khans simply refused to advance any further loans. Wherever the decree actually took effect (that is, where the police and army were able to impose it), poor peasants were without recourse to obtain seed and fertilizer for the next crop. Decree Number 8 (November 28, 1978), seized all holdings above 14 acres for distribution to tenants, the landless, or small landholders; it resulted mostly in uniting local secular and religious leaders, almost all of them landlords, against the regime. Land registries were primitive, with communal lands sometimes listed in the name of tribal chiefs. In certain areas, landless clans or migrants were given plots, at the expense of the dominant clans. Some of the government representatives who were sent to the provinces to implement the law were beaten or murdered by landlords and by government opponents. A program for peasant cooperatives, which some feared as a prelude to collective farms, lagged behind the breakup of large holdings into tiny plots.

The decrees were carried out at the local level by young urban revolutionaries unfamiliar with rural social realities and tribal loyalties; even worse, there had not been time to set up the necessary bureaucracies to take the place of traditional arrangements for functions such as irrigation maintenance and allocation of water. In consequence, only a minority of peasants rallied to the program, and agricultural production plummeted. In less than two years, the wheat crop dropped 10 percent, while cash crops such as cotton fell by 30 percent.

Even the literacy campaign proved to be a political disaster. The regime recruited and sent thousands of volunteers throughout the country with orders to teach the entire population to read within a year. Previous education programs had involved villagers in building schoolhouses and had used local teachers. Most of the new teachers were students from Kabul and other cities, who were often perceived as arrogant and insufferably disrespectful of the village elders who were forced to sit uncomfortably in their classrooms. Enforced coeducation, with young men teaching adult women in mixed classes, was another shock to local value systems.

Alienated from their new teachers from the start, illiterate premodern adults had little reason to credit even factual lessons in science and world history, let alone the marxist slogans found in every textbook. The study of Russian, the infidel language of a European imperialist power, did not help the program's popularity.

Decree Number 7 (October 17, 1978), concerning women's rights and marriage, was a textbook case of the application of modern European principles with little regard for the traditional social fabric, which had provided its own fragile protections for women. In theory, the restriction on the "bride price," or dowry, was a blow for women's dignity and equality; in practice, it threatened to remove a wife's economic security in case of divorce. It also damaged her social status: In the old system, even a poor husband had to "buy" his wife at a significant price that manifested her worth to both her family, which was losing an important economic producer, and to his, which had to pay out a substantial part of their scarce resources. In addition, high dowries had kept all but the wealthiest men from exercising their Muslim right to four wives.

Similarly, freedom of choice for brides and grooms undermined the careful system of family alliances that protected communal property and social peace, most commonly through the marriage of first cousins. The new minimum age for marriage, 16 for girls and 18 for boys, prevented some parents from ensuring in advance the economic and social future of their children and families. In any case, few of the intended

MARRIAGE CUSTOMS

Most Afghan youth do not date before marriage. They often do not even meet each other, as the matches are arranged by their parents.

Among educated urbanites, young Afghans frequently choose their own mates, but in tribal areas, marriage is still used to strengthen the bond between families. Normally, the boy's family will approach the girl's with a proposal. Any objection by either of the prospective mates must be made at the very start, if at all. If both sets of parents agree in principle, negotiations between the two families begin. They must determine the amount of the girl's dowry (*jahiz*, in Dari) and discuss details of the *shirin-i-khori* (engagement) and *arusi* (wedding).

After the two families agree, the next step is *shirin-i-geriftan* (taking sweets). Female members of the bride's family prepare a tray of sweets and present it to the mother, aunt, or other female members of the groom's family; this visit makes the marriage official. A few days later, the women of the groom's family return the tray laden with money.

Friends are then invited to a *shirin-i-khori* (eating sweets), which is arranged and paid for by the bride's family. The groom's family takes care of the wedding celebration itself, which usually occurs a few months later and can last for three days. At the wedding, the marriage contract, or *nikah-namah,* is signed in front of several witnesses.

beneficiaries welcomed their new freedoms, while devout Muslims and Pashtun traditionalists were horrified.

Repression and Resistance

No doubt to head off opposition to its revolutionary program, the Khalq instituted an immediate program of arrests and executions of potential opponents. It began in the cities with members of the royal family, liberal or Maoist intellectuals, dissident PDPA factions, high-ranking clergy, and the heads of the Sufi orders, including the prestigious Hazrat of Shor Bazaar; 70 male members of his family were killed early in 1979. Professors, businessmen, and government officials who had served under either Zahir or Daoud came under immediate suspicion, and many soon became victims, too. Individuals who might have lent their talents to the regime were replaced with neophytes whose only qualification was Khalq membership; many skilled people left the country. Curfews and severe travel restrictions began to drive away many UN and other foreign personnel as well.

Most of the 100,000 or so people who constituted the elite classes in Afghanistan in 1978 escaped this early wave of repression, but their troubles had only begun. Twenty-four more years of arrests and executions (not least between rival Communist factions), mass flight abroad, resistance to the Soviets, civil war, and, finally, the destruction of most of the city of Kabul eventually reduced these strata to a small remnant of their prerevolutionary numbers.

In June 1979, the 200 young Islamist militants arrested by Daoud in 1975 and still alive were executed in one night. Few records were kept or remain of those executed in the countryside. In February 1980, the new Communist government installed by the Soviet invaders stated that several thousand had been executed in a year and a half of Khalq terror; anticommunist Afghans placed the number at 50,000–100,000.

The famous Pul-e Charkhi prison on the outskirts of Kabul, which was as yet uncompleted and lacked sanitary facilities, became the center of torture and executions. Families of those who were arrested or had disappeared waited outside the prison walls day after day, hoping to receive word about the fate of their lost loved ones. The chief agent of the terror was the AGSA, and its main engine was a network of willing or coerced informers. In mid-1979, Amnesty International estimated that about 12,000 people had been held without trial since the revolution began.

A sign posted by the Taliban in Pul-e Charkhi Polygon, the execution grounds near the notorious prison, refers to those martyred by the Communists and welcomes all Muslim fighters. The picture was taken in 1997. (Photo by Bruce Richardson)

The toll soon climbed as a result of spontaneous rural resistance in every province, especially with the end of the agricultural season in late fall 1978. Well-armed Afghans led by tribal elders attacked many small government posts with heavy casualties, executing all the militants they could find. The government controlled the top echelons of the military, but about half of the 90,000 recruits quickly deserted or joined the rebels. When spring arrived, the fighting did not subside, as it had in earlier civil and foreign wars.

As resistance spread, certain regions fell away entirely from central control, including the Hazarajat, Badakhshan, and Nurestan, which rose in July 1978 and declared a Free Nurestan in March 1979. These minority ethnic regions remained effectively autonomous for years, posing an ongoing challenge to Afghan unity.

A major uprising broke out in Herat in March 1979, where army units under Ismail Khan defected to the rebels and other local units melted away. Troops were brought in from Kandahar and Kabul, and Il-28 bombers were sent to suppress the uprising at the loss of thousands of lives, including that of a hundred murdered Russian advisers

THE AFGHAN SECRET POLICE BETWEEN 1978 AND 1992

The Da Afghanistan de Gato de Satalo Adara, or AGSA (Pashto for Afghan Interests Protection Agency), was created around July 1978. With the help of agents from the East German State Security Department, AGSA built a large network of informers, who were encouraged to report family members, friends, colleagues, students, and teachers suspected of being enemies of the government.

As part of Prime Minister Hafizullah Amin's last desperate attempt to rally support in September 1979, he renamed AGSA as Kargari Astekhabari Mussassah, or KAM (Workers' Intelligence Institute) and promised to rein it in. In fact, the newly named agency, headed by Amin's nephew Asadullah, continued to function as before.

After the Soviet invasion in December 1979, Babrak Karmal replaced KAM with the Khedamati Ittlaati-e Dawlat, or KHAD (State Information Service), which was trained by the Soviet secret service, the KGB. His close associate Najibullah took control of the new agency, gaining the name "Najib the Bull" for his cruelty, as he laid the groundwork for his own takeover in 1986. During its 13 years of operation, KHAD had 30,000 employees and worked some 100,000 informants. In 1984, Amnesty International reported that physical and psychological torture (often in front of family members) had become systematic in KHAD centers in Kabul and elsewhere.

and their families whose heads were paraded around the city on pikes. Khan escaped to become a major leader of the mujahideen, the Islamic guerrilla fighters. Amin responded with further government purges, taking over himself as prime minister.

In Kabul, in June 1979, Hazara workers, known for their labor militancy, staged violent demonstrations against the regime; underground antigovernment news bulletins (called *shab-namah,* or "night letters") became ubiquitous in the capital. A major demonstration there was put down in June with heavy casualties. In August, an armored unit seized the Bala Hissar before it was put down.

Some Ghilzai regions stayed loyal to the Khalq, whose leader was after all the first of their tribesmen to rule the country in centuries, after sometimes bitter submission to the Durranis. The government also won followers in mixed ethnic regions, where some subordinate and landless groups benefited from the reforms, and among the middle and lower levels of the urban bureaucracy.

International Repercussions

The struggle very quickly took on an international component. By the end of 1978, tribal leaders had led some 80,000 Afghans into Pakistan, whose beleaguered president, Zia ul-Haq, was happy to adopt their cause and provide financial aid and encouragement. Eight guerrilla training camps were set up in the North-West Frontier Province. From that early date, moderate and more extreme Islamists competed for support from Pakistan and other foreign sources.

The Soviet Union had been quick to welcome the Saur Revolution and recognize the new regime. In May 1978, Amin visited Moscow and was welcomed as a fraternal Communist leader. The two countries

HAFIZULLAH AMIN

Hafizullah Amin was born in Paghman, near Kabul, in 1921; his father was a minor civil servant. He earned a bachelor's degree in mathematics and physics at Kabul University and then worked as a teacher and principal at boarding high schools for boys. He went to the United States in 1957 to study for an M.A. at the prestigious Teachers College of Columbia University. He returned to the United States in 1962 for Ph.D. studies at Columbia and, while there, also studied at the University of Wisconsin. He apparently learned his marxism in American academic and student activist circles.

His activities in the United States as head of the Union of Afghan Students and his leftist views led to his recall to Afghanistan in 1965, where he soon became a founding member of the PDPA while teaching at a girls' high school. Amin was the only Khalq faction member to win a seat in parliament (the *shura*) in the 1969 elections.

As a teacher and principal, Amin worked hard to win students over to his radical ideas, and he won many converts among the boys and girls. Many of the rural Pashtun boys he recruited continued their studies at the military academy. After Muhammad Daoud's 1973 coup, the PDPA Khalq faction assigned Amin to head recruitment among his former students and others in the officer corps, where his energy and organizational skills won the party many adherents. These were the men who effectively put the PDPA into power in the 1978 "revolution."

signed an accord for 30 new aid projects, and in June, the Soviets also approved $250 million in military support.

In Moscow, in December 1978, Amin and Taraki signed a new Treaty of Friendship and Cooperation with the Soviet Union. The Soviets pledged to provide direct military assistance if requested, over and above the thousands of advisers already stationed within the country's armed forces (some of whom formed coherent units of their own). They kept their promise, sending several hundred additional tanks and much other equipment over the following year, as well as pilots who began flying combat missions against the rebels. Amin insisted on clauses that would place Soviet troops under Afghan control and make their ultimate withdrawal a decision solely for the Afghans, that is, himself. He thus displayed an early independence of the Russians that presaged their eventual split a year later.

The various aid programs entailed the arrival of several thousand Soviet advisers, many of whom became increasingly involved in the actual running of the government and the military. Soviet leaders were thus intimately aware as the months passed that Afghanistan was gradually falling apart.

In April 1979, the Soviet Union sent a new adviser, Vasily Safronchuk, to try to convince Taraki to bring Parchamis and noncommunists into the government. The advice was rejected, reportedly due to objections by Amin. By March, Amin had taken over the prime minister's portfolio from Taraki, who became little more than a figurehead who was widely reported to have succumbed to alcoholism. Yet the Soviets felt obliged to do what they could to keep the revolution alive, on grounds of ideology, prestige, and power politics, especially once the rebels began to receive support from abroad. Safronchuk did succeed in convincing the leaders to stage public visits to mosques and to suspend the land reform program in July 1979.

The United States was initially cautious in its response to the Saur Revolution; President Jimmy Carter apparently wanted to keep his options open and avoid a breakdown in relations. Amin, for his part, also tried to keep bilateral ties intact, perhaps in order to maintain some independence from the Soviets. He made sure to meet with U.S. ambassador Adolf Dubs on a regular basis. Then, in February 1979, Dubs was kidnapped by leftist opponents of the regime, who demanded that the government release their comrades from Khalq jails. The United States asked the government not to try to rescue Dubs by force, fearing that he would not survive the attempt. The government ignored this request and sent a force against the kidnappers; Dubs was killed in the shootout.

The decision to stage a dangerous rescue was widely attributed to both Taraki and Soviet advisers, rather than to Amin himself. The net result was to alienate the United States further from the regime and to cut off the one channel Amin may have had to seek U.S. support. President Carter now slashed aid programs and reduced the U.S. diplomatic presence to the level of chargé d'affaires; several other Western countries followed suit. In the summer, the United States sent its first shipment of arms—a small quantity of old British rifles—to the rebels (Tanner, 232–233), while the CIA began developing ties with rebel groups.

If the implicit threat in the Friendship Treaty of Soviet armed intervention was meant to intimidate Pakistan from aiding the regime's opponents, it did not work. In January 1979, Zia allowed 5,000 rebels under Hekmatyar's Hezb-i-Islami to cross into Afghanistan's Konar Province and attack its capital; the local garrison, under Abdur Rauf, a former Khalq member, came over to the rebels. Soviet helicopter gunships were needed to suppress rebellions in April in Gardez and Jalalabad by Pakistani-supported rebels. In that campaign, army reprisal units lined up and murdered more than 1,000 civilians in the town of Kerala (Ewans 2002, 195). The event was photographed as a deterrent to other resisters, but the victims, who were said to have been shot for refusing to chant revolutionary slogans, soon won the status of martyrs for the rebel cause.

As late as mid-1973, before Daoud's palace coup, Afghanistan was a mostly rural, highly traditional country. For nearly a century it had enjoyed internal stability and external peace, with only minor interruptions. Yet, by the end of 1978, nearly all the country's social, economic, and government relationships had been upended, and the assumption of peace and law had been undermined. The conditions had been created for 22 years of cruel, destructive, unremitting war.

7

SOVIET AFGHANISTAN (1979–1989)

Russian imperialists had long dreamed of a southern border on the Hindu Kush, if not the Arabian Sea, but by the end of the 19th century, they had trimmed back their aspirations in Central Asia and accepted an independent Afghanistan as a buffer state. Their Soviet successors continued that realistic policy.

Russia and the USSR had trouble enough controlling the millions of Muslims living under its rule without swallowing up Afghanistan. Besides, by the 1970s, the Soviets already had their longed-for Indian Ocean warm-water ports in allied countries such as Somalia and Aden and had replaced Britain as the most influential power in India; they did not need Afghanistan as a pathway to either of those goals. From Lenin to Brezhnev, Soviet leaders were pleased to cultivate mutual interests with Durrani royals such as King Amanullah and President Daoud.

After the Saur Revolution of 1978, that option was gone. The Soviets had backed the PDPA leaders who replaced the Durranis, but the catastrophic blunders of the Afghan leadership were threatening to destabilize not only that country but the region as a whole. The likely alternative to PDPA rule was no longer a friendly neighboring potentate such as Daoud but rather a hostile Islamic state. Besides, once Communist rule had been established, if a counterrevolution succeeded, it would be a major setback for the worldwide revolutionary cause.

These considerations aside, it may not be a coincidence that of all the options the Soviet leaders considered using to face these dangers, the one they finally chose turned out to be a revival of czarist practices of a century before to send in the troops and set up a loyal local governor. They made that historic choice in December 1979.

Dissension in the Ranks

After Amin refused to accede to Soviet directives in mid-1979, the USSR started casting around for alternatives. It may have been behind a takeover plot mounted by surviving Parchamis in the spring, and, according to reports that reached the U.S. embassy in the summer, the Soviet Union tried negotiating with the Etemadi brothers, who had served as prime ministers under King Zahir, about setting up a noncommunist government. But the Soviet ace in the hole was Taraki, the "Great Leader" whom Amin was trying to shunt aside.

All year, the two leaders had been locked in a political struggle over key positions in the cabinet and the military. On July 28, Amin succeeded in getting the politburo to call for a "collective leadership," a blow at Taraki, and in filling most top positions with Amin's own loyalists and family members, though a hard core of Taraki supporters remained.

On September 2, Taraki visited Moscow on his way to a nonaligned conference in Havana, for meetings with Brezhnev and, possibly, with Karmal. He returned to Moscow on his way home, possibly because he was warned by his supporters in Kabul that Amin was plotting to kill him. The alarmed Soviets apparently agreed to a preemptive attack on Amin. In return, Taraki agreed to broaden the regime with non-Khalq and noncommunist forces. These plans became more problematic when an attempt to kill Amin, apparently led by Taraki supporter Asadullah Sarwari, was uncovered; it succeeded only in making the dictator more vigilant and paranoid. Sarwari, the bloodiest and most notorious of the Khalq leaders, had once been a supporter of Amin.

On September 14, Taraki summoned Amin to his office. Longtime Soviet ambassador Alexander Puzanov encouraged the suspicious leader to comply. Amin arrived with armed guards, including his top security aide, Syed Daoud Tarun; in the ensuing shootout, Tarun was killed. Amin later returned with a larger force and arrested Taraki, whose supporters, including Sarwari, fled to the Soviet embassy and from there were smuggled into the Soviet Union. On September 16, Amin took over his former colleague's presidential and party leader positions and announced to the country that the ailing chief had resigned. The illness grew worse, according to a September 23 announcement, which prepared the country for Taraki's death on October 9. Most observers believed he was murdered that day, suffocated at the hands of security agents, though some believe he had been dead since the September 14 shootout.

Amin managed to get Puzanov recalled to Moscow, but that provided scant comfort; he feared that at best the Soviets would evacuate their military advisers and leave him to his fate or at worst continue to seek his death. His back against the wall, the Khalq leader spent his last three months in a desperate attempt to win wider support. He included some Muslim clerics in a new constitutional committee and pressured those mullahs under his control to call a jihad against the rebels. He condemned the excesses of AGSA (which he outlined in some detail) but attributed them to Taraki. He renamed the agency and called for a new emphasis on legality in place of his deceased rival's "cult of personality." A special revolutionary court ordered the release of some political prisoners. In early December, Amin set up the National Organization for the Defense of the Revolution as a "coalition" group.

The war was not going well; tribal leaders refused Amin's pleas for support, and a joint government-Soviet offensive in Paktia in October took heavy casualties but failed to dislodge the rebels. By then, more than 200,000 Afghans had fled to Pakistan, where they were being openly trained for rebellion. Amin repeatedly sought a summit with Pakistan's president, Zia ul-Haq, who finally agreed in December—too late to do Amin any good. In Kabul, assassinations were thinning out the leadership, which was forced to repress still another army mutiny in October. Desertions had driven the army down to a third of its

Built in 1922 by King Amanullah, the Darul Aman palace, outside Kabul, was designed by French architects in the style of 18th-century European palaces. President Hafizullah Amin was killed in this palace by the Soviets when they invaded Afghanistan on December 27, 1979. (Photo by Bruce Richardson)

151

strength; it was now being led by a cadre of PDPA-affiliated captains and majors who had replaced nearly all the experienced generals after the coup.

At least two more assassination attempts on Amin took place in December, in one of which he was apparently wounded. Reportedly, the Soviets also tried to sedate and kidnap the president via his cook in order to compel him to resign or join a coalition with Karmal. Amin and a small force of soldiers withdrew to King Amanullah's palace at Darul Aman, outside Kabul.

The Internal Soviet Debate

Starting in the spring of 1979, the Soviets began to face the possibility of direct intervention in Afghanistan. While they were examining the complex military and political implications, the situation in Afghanistan deteriorated, and the balance in the debate shifted clearly to the side of invasion.

Soviet rulers never seriously considered the option of just walking away from the problem. In February 1979, chief ideologist Michael Suslov had said that Afghanistan was one of the "states of socialist orientation" that had recently arisen in former colonial countries around the world in a trend that confirmed the historical inevitability of socialism. Soviet media and international propaganda took up the theme. In March, Foreign Minister Andrei Gromyko told the politburo, "Under no circumstances may we lose Afghanistan."(Rasanayagam 2003, 85). According to the "Brezhnev doctrine," formulated a decade before in the wake of the invasion of Czechoslovakia, every Communist country had the right to intervene wherever socialism was under siege.

Besides, the Soviets began to fear that if Afghanistan were "lost," the United States might try to turn Afghanistan into their new regional base following the fall earlier that year of their client, the shah of Iran. Prior to the killing of U.S. ambassador Dubs in February, Amin (acting as foreign minister) had cultivated cordial ties with him; they met twice a month. KGB boss Yuri Andropov even suspected the American-educated Amin of being a CIA agent, a charge that was being widely disseminated in Soviet-sponsored underground newsletters. The Afghan leader's attempts in the autumn to reach out to Pakistan and the United States could be seen as confirmation of this hunch.

Some Soviets had seen a CIA hand in the uprisings that broke out around the country in 1978. Afghans recognized such tribal rebellions as a common occurrence in their history that did not need outside instigation, but once the rebels took to the field, they did in fact receive support (minimal as yet) from Pakistan and Saudi Arabia, both U.S. allies, and some minor direct help from the United States. After the invasion took place, Brezhnev told *Pravda* that there had been a real threat that Afghanistan would become "an imperialist military bridgehead on our country's southern border" (Brezhnev 1980). In light of the growing U.S. ties with China, Russia's fierce rival, the prospect of another enemy to the south (contiguous to China) was daunting.

But while they believed the United States might be trying to win over Afghanistan through spies, diplomacy, and local rebels, Soviet leaders were confident the United States would not militarily resist a full-fledged Soviet invasion. Only a few years had passed since the country's defeat in Vietnam, and the morale and strength of its armed forces were at an ebb—President Jimmy Carter had even broadcast American "malaise" to the world. The militant students who took U.S. diplomats hostage in Tehran, Iran, in November 1979, inadvertently created a distraction that was likely to keep America out of the Soviets' hair.

The Soviet rulers also had to consider the impact of an Islamist victory in Afghanistan on the tens of millions of Muslims under their direct rule. The latter were already being targeted by the new Islamist Iranian regime of Ayatollah Khomeini; a radical Muslim Afghanistan would be an even greater threat, with its large population of Tajik, Uzbek, Turkmen, and Kirghiz, many of whom had arrived in Afghanistan earlier in the century as refugees from Soviet religious and ethnic persecution; many had relatives and clansmen across the border.

Despite all these considerations, on March 17–19, the Soviet politburo decided against invasion at that time. At the meeting, Andropov argued that the premodern society of Afghanistan was not ready for genuine socialism; it could be imposed by "our bayonets," but that would not serve the Soviet Union's wider interests. The leaders conveyed their decision to Taraki on his visit that month; he asked for more military assistance, but they encouraged him to try to replace Amin instead. They reiterated their decision after another politburo meeting in May, which turned down a request from Taraki and Amin for Soviet helicopter crews, paratroopers, and two emergency divisions. By July, however, they agreed to send a disguised paratrooper battalion and KGB units to protect the Soviet embassy, as well as additional detachments to secure the air base at Bagram.

The continued weakness of the Afghan armed forces despite Soviet aid and advice, the murder of Taraki in September, and the subsequent attempts by Amin to reach out to Pakistan and the United States caused a quick reevaluation. The KGB deputy chief in Kabul, Alexander

Morozov, began advocating invasion, and on October 29, the special Soviet Politburo Committee on Afghanistan endorsed the recommendation. Brezhnev fell into line and, on December 12, gave the go-ahead.

An internal report to the Communist Party Central Committee later that month explained the intervention as support for Babrak Karmal's attempt "to save the motherland and the revolution." The dispatch of the Soviet army, the report claimed, was a response to the Afghan government's earlier requests for "additional military assistance"; it was also "in accordance with the provisions of the Soviet-Afghan treaty of 1978" (Rasanayagam 2003, 90).

Invasion

In April 1979, General Aleksey Yepishev of GLAVPUR, the central political office of the Soviet armed forces, visited Afghanistan at the head of a sizable mission to evaluate the morale and capabilities of the Afghan forces; he reportedly brought back a pessimistic report. Observers noted that Yepishev had conducted a similar survey in Czechoslovakia in 1968 before the Warsaw Pact invasion. In a further parallel to the Czech experience, General Ivan G. Pavlovsky, who had planned and directed the 1968 invasion, arrived in Kabul in August with a larger group of experts; they spent two months traveling around the country under a veil of secrecy, presumably scouting out the invasion route.

Earlier in the year, reservists had been called up to bring military units in Soviet Central Asia to full strength, and two divisions had been moved up to the Afghan border. These initial preparations did not necessarily signal invasion. They could also have served to pressure Amin or to back up a projected coup by his domestic opponents or by exiles such as Karmal. But in November the picture became clear: Bridging equipment was brought forward to the border units on the Amu Darya, and Marshal Sergei L. Sokolov set up his headquarters there at Termez. Warsaw Pact countries in Europe put their forces on an advanced state of readiness.

In a last-ditch effort to preclude a crisis, on November 28, Lieutenant General Viktor S. Paputin, first deputy minister of internal affairs, arrived in Kabul to try to persuade Amin to resign in favor of Karmal; failing in that goal, he may have set up one of the subsequent assassination attempts. On December 17, secret police chief Asadullah Amin was wounded (or poisoned) in one such attempt; the Soviets had him replaced by Sarwari, back from a brief exile in Moscow.

From late November, the troops began to move. A 2,500-man heavily equipped airborne division was gradually flown from the Tajik

Soviet Socialist Republic to Bagram Air Base, and Soviet infantry and armored battalions were moved to Kabul airport. On December 20, another armored unit took over the Salang Tunnel to protect the key land link between Kabul and the Amu Darya border.

Though the Afghan armed forces were led mostly by Communists, Soviet advisers at the unit level used various deceptions to keep their "fraternal" Afghan officers in the dark and to prevent them from resisting. Ammunition, batteries, and fuel were removed from equipment on the pretext of inspection or replacement, and Soviet troop movements were described as training exercises. On December 24, Nikolai Vladimirovich Talyzin, Soviet minister of communication, arrived in Kabul as an official guest of the Afghan government. He proceeded to make final arrangements for disrupting communications within Kabul and between the capital and the provinces.

These careful preparations assured a smooth and relatively painless invasion. On December 25, four motorized divisions crossed over from Turkmenistan and Uzbekistan and started moving south along the two main roads. One column reached Kabul the next day, and the arms of the pincers soon met at Kandahar. Airborne troops landed near Herat, Kandahar, and Jalalabad. By the 27th, there were 50,000 Soviet troops in the country, including 5,000 in Kabul, and they had been moved into position near key facilities. Some of the forces were armed with anti-aircraft missiles, apparently to prepare against resistance by the Afghan air force.

On the 27th, Soviet troops disabled Kabul's telephone infrastructure and seized the radio station. Other forces surrounded the Darul Aman palace where Amin was holed up while special agents disguised in Afghan uniforms penetrated the building. In close fighting that claimed some high-ranking Russians, including General Paputin (though some say he committed suicide for failing in his earlier mission), Amin himself was killed. In doing so, Amin partially redeemed his reputation in the eyes of Afghan nationalists. Those of the 1,800 Afghan guards who survived the fighting were reportedly executed to eliminate witnesses, though a few managed to escape.

The New Regime

On December 27, at 8:45 P.M., Karmal announced on Radio Kabul that he had put an end to the "intolerable violence and torture of the bloody apparatus of Hafizullah Amin" by deposing the "rogue." The statement was actually broadcast from a transmitter in Termez on the Soviet side of the border.

BABRAK KARMAL

Babrak Karmal was born in 1929 into the highest reaches of Afghan society, in dramatic contrast to his PDPA colleague Nur Muhammad Taraki, a fact that partly explains their bitter rivalry. Karmal's father, General Muhammad Hussain Khan, served as governor of Paktia Province.

Karmal's family ties with Afghan royalty and the business elite help explain the Parcham leader's later success in winning the confidence of Muhammad Daoud; they also accord with his political stance, which always favored coalitions with nonmarxist parties and social elements. His easy sociability and confidence, in contrast to Taraki's more withdrawn personality, won him many followers among middle-class and educated urbanites.

Karmal emerged as a student leader in 1951 and an activist in the Wikh-i-Zalmayan (Awakened Youth movement); he apparently became a Soviet-oriented Communist during a three-year prison term he received for those activities. It was there that he took the Pashto name Babrak ("little tiger") Karmal ("workers' friend"). After his release in 1956, he served in the army and obtained a law degree while continuing his political activities to the degree tolerated by the Zahir and Daoud governments. Karmal led one of the marxist study groups that merged into the new People's Democratic Party of Afghanistan (PDPA) in 1965. Elected to the Wolesi Jirga that year, he organized the student demonstration that disrupted its opening session (and that convinced King Zahir to hold off on further liberalization), and he was the chief orator in that chamber for the next several years.

Karmal's ethnic affiliations were a matter of some controversy. His father's family had moved from Kashmir to a Tajik village near Kabul and were usually considered Tajik; his mother was a Ghilzai Pashtun, and at various times he claimed that identity in public, though he is said to have been a Dari speaker. The Parcham faction he led within the PDPA included far more Tajiks and other non-Pashtun ethnics than did the Khalq faction of Nur Muhammad Taraki and Hafizullah Amin. Urbanites of mixed or weak ethnic affiliations also found his circle more welcoming. Once he became president in 1980, he faced rumors from personal and regime opponents that he was in reality a Kashmiri Hindu, as supposedly confirmed by his Indian features.

Karmal opened with an invocation from the Qur'an and implied that the takeover was a domestic Afghan affair, a continuation of the Saur Revolution. He called on all elements of the population to join a "national democratic government"; socialism, he explained, would come in due course but only after society had been gradually transformed. Karmal declared an amnesty and promised to release prisoners held at Pul-e-Charkhi. Refugees were invited to return and reclaim their property. A new provisional constitution was already prepared, he reported, giving pride of place to Islam via a Department of Islamic Affairs (by which he later tried to control the clergy, mosques, and charitable endowments).

Further broadcasts, this time from the Kabul station, named Karmal as president, prime minister, and secretary general of the PDPA and reported that Amin had been "executed" for crimes against the people. On the morning of the 28th, the station announced that the new government had appealed for assistance, including military aid, from the Soviet Union under the 1978 Friendship Treaty, in response to provocations by "foreign enemies." Karmal himself did not appear in the country until January 1, 1980.

From the start, most Afghans considered Karmal to be a Soviet puppet. Indeed, once the Soviets decided to invade and install a new regime, they left little to chance. On December 27, Talyzin invited leading Afghan dignitaries to a reception at the Intercontinental Hotel in Kabul, where, at the end of the festivities, they were all arrested.

From a position of total military control, the Soviet leadership quickly suppressed the independence that Afghanistan had long struggled for and finally won in 1919; after 60 years, Afghanistan's international relations were once more in foreign hands. In Moscow, on January 4, Soviet foreign minister Gromyko briefed his new Afghan counterpart, Shah Muhammad Dost, on the outlines of the new government's foreign-policy line.

In domestic matters, Andropov visited Kabul in early February to outline the program he expected the new leadership to implement. These included a united PDPA with both Khalq and Parcham factions, efforts to improve relations with tribal and religious leaders, a return to normal economic activity, and improvement of the armed forces. He reported back to the Politburo on February 7; the meeting discussed the withdrawal of Soviet troops, which one optimist hoped might occur after one to one-and-a-half years.

Domestic Resistance

The Soviet invasion galvanized the rebellion that had emerged after the Saur Revolution into a genuine, broad-based national resistance movement. It also removed any diplomatic or political constraints against stepped-up military aid to the mujahideen rebels from the United States, Pakistan, and other Muslim countries.

The quick success of the invasion forces in securing the cities and the major intercity routes was a deceptive achievement. British forces had scored similar quick gains at the start of the First Anglo-Afghan War in 1839, only to face eventual defeat three years later in the face of a brutal, grinding resistance. With all the advantages of modern transportation and communication, the Soviets were able to drag out the process for nine years, at enormous cost to both themselves as their Afghan opponents, but with the same ultimate results.

International Reaction

News of the Soviet invasion stunned the world and appalled most of its leaders. U.S. president Jimmy Carter called the attack "an extremely serious threat to peace" and "a violation of the United Nations Charter." He called Brezhnev's explanations in their private communications as "completely inadequate and completely misleading" (Ewans 2002, 207).

Carter warned that the Soviets could not invade a neighbor "with impunity." However, the countermeasures he imposed may have hurt the United States more than the Soviet Union and were not much welcomed by Americans, who were more preoccupied by the Iran hostage crisis. The administration put the SALT (Strategic Arms Limitation Talks) II missile treaty on hold, although ratification by the Senate had been in doubt in any case. More important, it cut back contracted shipments of grain to the USSR from 25 to 8 million tons; American farmers protested the huge loss of revenues, while Argentina and other countries made up the import loss to the Soviets, at a lower price.

The Soviets were similarly able to work around a new U.S. ban on high-technology sales, by buying most of the goods from Europeans and others. A ban on Soviet fishing in U.S. waters may have had a minor impact, but the U.S.-led boycott of the 1980 Moscow Olympic Games (45 countries stayed away) only allowed the Russians to grab up most of the medals, repeating the U.S. experience when the Soviet Union boycotted the 1976 Olympics in Chile. Finally, a U.S. delay in opening new consulates in New York and Kiev was hardly more than a slap on the hand.

After a quick analysis, the Carter administration openly adopted the "strategic" theory, which understood the Soviet invasion as part of a long-term imperialist thrust toward the warm water and oil of the Persian Gulf. The president announced a new "Carter doctrine," under which the United States would respond to an assault on the Persian Gulf with military force; he began to set up a "rapid deployment force" for use in the Gulf. Once the Russians became bogged down in Afghanistan, any further Soviet military advance hardly seemed imminent; nevertheless, the fear of such aggression influenced U.S. policy toward the Soviets throughout the decade. The resulting American pressure may have helped hasten the fall of the Soviet Union after 1989.

The Soviets put their best face on the situation. At the United Nations, on January 14, they used their veto to dispose of a critical non-aligned resolution in the Security Council but could not prevent the General Assembly from handing them a stunning defeat. A resolution for a complete withdrawal of "foreign troops" from Afghanistan passed by a vote of 104 to 18, with 18 abstentions; India was one of the few self-defined nonaligned countries that abstained. More such votes followed year after year; by 1987, the margin was even more lopsided: 123-19, with 11 abstentions. Later in 1980, similar resolutions were approved by the Non-Aligned Movement and the Islamic Conference.

For decades, the USSR had escaped criticism from the newly independent countries of Asia and Africa, despite ruling its vast Asian empire with an iron fist. It might have lost that privileged status over time for a variety of reasons, but the invasion of Afghanistan wiped it out overnight.

Ultimately, a large number of countries, including former allies or supporters of the Soviet Union, were recruited to the anti-Soviet effort in Afghanistan. U.S. national security advisor Zbigniew Brzezinski later confirmed that the CIA had begun providing help to the rebels in July 1979, but after the Soviet invasion, he advocated a more intensive program, encouraging Muslim countries to help with propaganda and covert aid. During a visit by Carter's defense secretary Harold Brown, China agreed to provide significant quantities of assault rifles, grenade launchers, and anti-aircraft weapons via Pakistan for the rebels; it was a cheap and

Mujahideen fighters train with Soviet machine guns at Shaghai camp in 1986. (Photo by Bruce Richardson)

painless way for China to make trouble for its Soviet rival. Eventually, the United States obtained Soviet arms (which were familiar to the Afghans) from several other countries, including Egypt, Saudi Arabia, and India.

The European Community responded by calling for a peace conference to resolve the conflict within Afghanistan and provide guarantees for the country's neutrality. Other than that, most European governments believed that the United States was overreacting, given the relative unimportance of Afghanistan strategically and given that there was nothing anyone could do, practically speaking. It was assumed that a Soviet offensive in the spring would finish off the resistance.

The Regime Reaches Out

With the death of Taraki and Amin and the full support of the Soviet Union, Karmal finally had his chance to implement the united front approach that he had been advocating since the first days of the PDPA.

Perhaps if the Afghan Communist revolution had reached out to noncommunists from the start, in April 1978, and had avoided radical measures, Karmal's strategy might have been able to win enough time for the regime to assert control. However, by the time he was installed by Soviet troops in January 1980, most Afghans were already firmly in the opposition camp. Appeals to the people based on Islam and national unity rang hollow now, when the country's cities were occupied by the troops of an atheist foreign power.

Karmal's efforts to expand the regime's base included several components: initial prisoner releases; inclusion of non-PDPA figures in the government and the creation of a National Fatherland Front to mobilize noncommunist segments of the population, the relaxation of unpopular reforms, a massive reeducation program, rhetorical and financial concessions to Islam, and an appeal to ethnic minorities. Symbolic steps included denouncing the violence of the Amin regime and restoring the national flag.

Amnesty

On January 8, 1980, the regime declared a general amnesty. It soon claimed to have released 8,000 prisoners; opponents claimed the true number was perhaps 3,000–4,000 and consisted mostly of Parchamis. Thousands of others remained behind bars, and many more soon joined them. On January 11, family members who had gathered outside Pul-e-Charkhi invaded the prison when only 120 prisoners emerged; few found their relatives alive. As part of the amnesty, Karmal promised to restore property to returning exiles or to their close relatives. In fact, the flight of Afghans to Pakistan and Iran accelerated dramatically under the Soviets.

National Unity

Karmal's first "national unity" government included three non-PDPA ministers (out of 28), as well as a few Khalqis, but Parchamis were overwhelmingly in control. A new seven-person politburo was announced, to include Karmal, his mistress Anahita Ratebzad, and three other Parchamis as well as the brutal Sarwari and another Khalqi. By May, about 40 percent of the top 200 government positions had been filled by non-PDPA members.

In practice, the political affiliation of government officials and military officers became irrelevant at all but the top levels, as Soviet advisers multiplied in the foreign ministry, the secret police, the armed forces, and most departments. As the fighting escalated and the economy fell apart, those regions (mostly urban) still controlled by the government came to rely on the Soviet Union and its representatives for even the most basic necessities of food and fuel.

On January 2, 1981, Karmal announced the formation of the National Fatherland Front (NFF); its founding congress took place on June 15. Some 15 component organizations, with a total claimed membership of a few hundred thousand, covered the panoply of population groups familiar in their Soviet bloc counterparts—trade unionists (200,000 eventual claimed members), youth (25,000), Pioneers (scouts; 85,000 boys and girls), women, clergy, tribal elders, tribal *jirgas*, university students, peasants, and others. The NFF and most of its components failed to achieve the hoped-for degree of activism.

Backtracking Reform

The Soviets had always been skeptical of the relevance of radical reforms in Afghanistan. Karmal showed himself more than willing to bow to necessity. As early as 1980, the government announced a policy of noninterference in the customs and traditions of those tribes that were willing to keep their peace, particular in sensitive areas near the Pakistan border. Traditional subsidies to clans and their leaders were revived.

In summer 1981, Karmal announced major exemptions to the policy of land reforms. Military officers, progovernment tribal elders, and owners of large mechanized farms would no longer be subject to confiscations. Peasants who voluntarily sent their sons to serve in the armed forces would get priority on any remaining redistribution. The policies were welcomed in those few rural areas still under government control.

Education

Within a few months of the invasion, the Soviets were forced to conclude that the regime and the PDPA had very little popular support and also lacked the resources or skills to increase their support in the near term. This was an old experience for the Russian Communists, and they set about imposing their old solution—to reeducate the younger generations in Soviet beliefs and values.

They established a Young Pioneers program for 10-year-olds, enrolling 40,000 children by 1982, who were trained to spy on classmates and families. Fifteen-year-olds were encouraged to join cells of the Democratic Youth Organization (DYO), which were assigned such tasks as surveillance, guard duty, and propaganda. Selected youth were recruited into the PDPA. In 1987, Najibullah claimed that 30 percent of youth were members of the DYO or the PDPA.

The many war orphans, together with children captured in villages, were placed in Fatherland Training Centers, supervised by KHAD. Some were sent back to infiltrate rebel groups. Thousands of students were sent to study in the Soviet Union—some 4,000 older students a year by 1984, plus 2,000 seven- to 10-year-olds.

The school curricula were rewritten at all levels, and students were required to attend political classes and learn Russian. University enrollment fell to a third of the pre-invasion enrollment of 15,000; the faculties were purged of nonmarxist instructors, who were replaced by activists with political rather than academic qualifications.

The media were also dominated by Soviet products and Soviet advisers. Films were screened to decry Afghanistan's past and present an idealized Soviet Union.

Islam in the Service of the State

Karmal made liberal use of religious rhetoric from his earliest statements as leader, even claiming that the Soviet intervention was "an act of God." Starting in April 1980, the traditional Muslim invocation "in the name of God, the Merciful, the Compassionate" once more appeared at the start of government documents, after an absence of nearly a year. A provisional constitution formally acknowledged the supremacy of Islam.

The government worked hard to create an official Islam, Soviet style, to make religion work in the service of the state. For the first time in Afghan history, a Department of Islamic Affairs was set up under central auspices, with the apparent goal of coopting and reining in the clergy. The department, later a ministry, took control of all endowments and private funds of mosques and religious orders. The money was used to renovate more than 500 mosques around the country and to build new ones, 34 in Kabul alone. The clergy became government employees and were encouraged to join the Council of Religious Scholars and Clergy, a key component of the NFF.

The regime used economic incentives as well, eventually including special allowances and ration coupons for mullahs and ulemas. It even helped subsidize the hajj, the annual pilgrimage to Mecca, and supplied firewood to mosques as economic conditions worsened. Karmal claimed in a 1985 address that the government had handed out thousands of copies of the Qur'an.

The regime organized frequent clergy conferences to communicate its positions, but only so much could be done to win over the existing clergy. After all, local mullahs who had denounced Taraki's relatively modest reforms as violations of sacred tradition could not be expected to trust Soviet puppets, as they saw the government, even when dressed in Islamic garb. Furthermore, religious authority in Afghanistan was as fractured as political authority and, thus, more resistant to any form of central control. Most clergy had only local followers, apart from a few prominent religious dynasties who claimed descent from the prophet Muhammad. The latter had been severely persecuted by the Khalq; the survivors were implacably opposed to the regime. In Central Asia to the north, by contrast, the powerful khanates had long maintained strong hierarchies of clergy; the Soviets had only to suborn some "red mullahs" to win a degree of popular consent.

Instead, the Karmal regime and its Soviet advisers focused on educating a new generation of subservient clergy. A more quiescent Islam was taught in madrassas, religious studies programs in general schools, and at the Kabul University theology faculty. For the general population, the Soviet period saw a reduction in the study of Arabic, the language of Muslim scripture and prayer.

Despite all of Karmal's efforts, the Muslim character of the opposition only intensified. Within a few months of the invasion, a national movement called Allah-u-Akbar (God is great) was coordinating internal resistance, distributing underground literature, and conducting religious processions that chanted antigovernment slogans. In

February 1980, protesters by the thousands in Kabul and other cities violated curfew and climbed to their roofs each night to shout the Muslim call to prayer; observers estimated that most of the urban population participated.

Nationalities Policy

Decree Number 4 of the Saur Revolution, issued in May 1978, had proclaimed Uzbek, Turkmen, Baluchi, and Nuristani to be national languages on a par with Pashto and Dari. The only practical effect at first was an increased exposure of minority cultures in the media.

Under Karmal and his largely non-Pashtun Parcham faction, the policy was expanded, drawing on decades of Soviet experience implementing Stalin's nationalities policy. Provincial schools in the north began to teach in these languages instead of Dari, the medium of instruction in all previous Afghan schools. Books and periodicals published in the corresponding national republics of the Soviet Union were disseminated in Afghanistan, and government propaganda in both countries stressed the common ties between the ethnic groups on both sides of the border.

In Soviet Central Asia, the policy had largely succeeded in replacing dangerous pan-Islamic loyalties with easier-to-manage identities based on ethnic groups confined mostly to Soviet territory. In Afghanistan, the policy was designed to appeal to people chafing at 250 years of Pashtun supremacy, though conversely it could hardly be welcomed by Pashtuns, especially the nationalists of the Khalq faction. In any case, many of the Uzbeks and Turkmens of northern Afghanistan were the children and grandchildren of anti-Soviet resistance fighters; to them, any integration with the Soviet Socialist Republics (SSRs) to the north, economic or cultural, was a hard sell. Apparently, no comparable attempt was made to develop the national culture of the Hazara, an ethnic minority long persecuted despite its Dari dialect; perhaps the regime feared to create a possible opening for Iran's Khomeini regime among this Shiite population.

Ironically, the nationalities issue proved to be a serious problem for the Soviet occupation force. By design, many of the invasion troops consisted of reserve soldiers from the Islamic SSRs; they were closest to the action, and, it was believed, their presence would help win over Afghans, especially those of the north. At the very least, Soviet advisers hoped, a Muslim coloration would lend more credibility to the Red Army's claim to anti-imperialist credentials.

Perhaps it helped in the north, but the Pashtun regions of the south were accustomed to their dominant status within the country and were also cognizant of historic rivalries with the khans of Bokhara and Samarkand. The sudden invasion of their heartland by thousands of such troops was a greater provocation, perhaps, than a blatant Soviet intervention might have been.

Worse yet, the invasion of Afghanistan revealed—and exacerbated—serious ethnic fissures within the Soviet armed forces. Muslim troops often felt divided loyalties, even using their service as an opportunity to explore their ethnic or religious identity in a more authentic context. Slavic troops, naturally, grew suspicious of any fraternization in an unfamiliar language. Violence escalated within the Soviet units, with victims on both sides. By March 1980, the Soviets had begun replacing Central Asians with Slavs.

Factionalism Erupts Again

No matter how desperate the situation of the government, the bitter struggle between Khalq and Parcham continued almost without letup. Subfactions also coalesced around leading figures within the two factions, while Soviet agents reportedly worked to create its own PDPA faction they hoped could impose unity by force.

Karmal managed to consolidate power at the top. In June, with Soviet help, he removed the key Khalq leader Sarwari, who was advocating the withdrawal of Soviet forces, and began a roundup of other Khalq leaders. Thirteen were executed that month, including three ministers.

Factionalism continued to plague the PDPA, although its numbers did rise as membership became a criterion for advancement, as in all Communist countries. In mid-1982, Karmal claimed 70,000 members; observers estimated the true number at 20,000, with at least two-thirds Khalqis. Factional strife occasionally turned bloody; five party members were killed during the Party Congress of March 1982, which Karmal managed to control by dominating the selection process. Khalq and Parcham students at Soviet universities clashed as well.

The ranks of the armed forces (the 30,000 troops that had not deserted by the end of 1980) remained primarily a Khalq preserve. Officers openly signaled their dissatisfaction with Karmal in April 1980 by flying the red flag, and not the restored tricolor, during the parade to mark the second anniversary of the revolution. They resisted various orders from Karmal and his Parchami defense minister and rejected

Parcham officers sent to replace Khalqis transferred to less important posts. Some Khalq officers, refusing to be used as cannon fodder for Parcham or the Soviets, as they put it, went over to the rebels. Hundreds of others were arrested on suspicion of disloyalty, sometimes due to misinformation spread by rebels.

With the Defense Ministry in Parchami hands, the Khalqi interior minister Syed Gulabzoi built up a Khalq-dominated police force that became larger than the army. It included an infantry unit, the Sarandoy, which sometimes fought pitched battles against the KHAD, tightly run by the Parchami Muhammad Najibullah; the KHAD fielded a full division of its own, along with its vast network of agents.

Thus, the array of forces that could have been available to pursue the war against the rebels was shot through with dissension and paranoia. Furthermore, army recruitment from the shrinking pool of available manpower in the Soviet-controlled zones was a constant problem. Partly in response, the regime tried to build up various militias. Government workers were expected to serve guard duty at night, while other civilian units guarded farms and factories. Some tribal militias were in effect enlisted through large payments to the elders, in accordance with old Afghan tradition.

Political Retreat

None of Karmal's new policies had much of an impact on the fortunes of the opposing sides in the war. The measures did not even reach most of the population in the rural and mountain districts, and by the mid-1980s millions of citizens—a third of the population by most estimates—were living in refugee camps in Pakistan and Iran under the control of fiercely anti-Soviet mujahideen leaders.

The war was a constant political and military drain on the Soviet Union, with no end in sight. Despite improved Soviet tactics and a ruthless scorched earth policy, by the mid-1980s the rebels were gaining in numbers, training, and especially weaponry. Besides being a major burden on the Soviet economy, the occupation was damaging Soviet prestige around the world, especially among Muslim countries. A quick successful invasion might have been soon forgiven and might even have increased Soviet clout in the region, but the long, futile struggle against the Afghan people had become an unalloyed liability.

Nevertheless, the USSR was in no position to consider a strategic retreat; its aging leadership was consumed with a succession crisis for nearly all this period. Party chief Leonid Brezhnev died in November 1982 after at least a year of physical incapacity, while his two aging suc-

The Afghan war was costly for the Soviet Union. The mujahideen were able to bring down Soviet aircrafts with sophisticated weapons received from the United States and other countries. This image was taken in Khost in 1991. (Photo by Bruce Richardson)

cessors, Yuri Andropov and Konstantin Chernenko, also spent much of their brief reigns contending with serious illness. Mikhail Gorbachev took over as party chief in the spring of 1985 determined to promote détente with the United States and China, but even if he wanted to pull out of Afghanistan, as yet he lacked sufficient support in the Soviet leadership to do so.

Gorbachev reportedly gave Soviet forces a year to crush the resistance, while pressuring Karmal to depart even further from the language and policies of the revolution. In April 1985, Karmal convened a *loya jirga*, with 1,800 claimed members representing the entire country (perhaps 600 actually attended). An even larger *jirga* was summoned from among the "frontier tribes," including hundreds of representatives from both sides of the Pakistan border. National elections were supposedly held in August 1985, though even in Kabul there was little participation. None of these initiatives won the leader new supporters.

Later in 1985 Karmal brought noncommunists into the government once more, and the following year he charged a new National Reconciliation Commission, including businessmen and religious figures,

167

to draft a new constitution. He encouraged the emergence of quasi-independent workers' organizations.

By now, however, the Soviets viewed Karmal as ineffective and too closely identified with the regime's failures. On May 4, 1986, the brutal but effective boss of KHAD, Muhammad Najibullah, a Parcham loyalist but a Pashtun, took over PDPA leadership with Soviet support and consolidated power over the next few months. Karmal was exiled to Moscow in November; he died there of liver disease 10 years later.

In early 1987, Najibullah announced a unilateral six-month ceasefire, which he later extended for another six months. National Reconciliation Commission committees were set up around the country and ordered to contact resistance groups, exiles, and refugees. Najibullah claimed that several thousand opposition representatives had joined the committees and that local coalition governments had been set up in several places.

MUHAMMAD NAJIBULLAH AHMADZAI

Muhammad Najibullah was born in August 1947 to a fairly prosperous family from the Ahmadzai subtribe of the Ghilzai Pashtun of Paktia Province. His father served as the Afghan consul in Peshawar in the 1960s.

Najibullah attended the prestigious Habibia High School in Kabul, then earned his medical degree at Kabul University in 1975. While still in his teens, he attended the founding session of the PDPA in 1965; when the party split, the upper-middle-class Najibullah was one of the few Pashtuns who joined Karmal's Parcham faction. Tall and heavily built, he served as Karmal's bodyguard until 1973.

Najibullah led the Parchamis at the university, where he often addressed student demonstrations; he was a passionate orator in Pashto, Dari, Urdu, and English. His activism led to two jail terms but also to a place on the Central Committee when the PDPA factions reunited in 1977. His fortunes subsequently followed those of his mentor Karmal, whom he followed into exile late in 1978 and back into the country's top leadership in 1980. They finally parted ways when the Soviets lost confidence in Karmal in 1986 and made Najibullah the fourth, and last, Communist ruler of Afghanistan.

Najibullah summoned a *loya jirga* in November 1987, which approved a new constitution providing for a multiparty democracy. The *jirga* named him president of the new Republic of Afghanistan, dropping the East German–style *Democratic* from the country's name. He staged elections the next year. The Soviets hoped for the best but began to prepare their withdrawal.

Soviet Withdrawal

Soviet leader Gorbachev began searching for a way to extricate his forces from Afghanistan in 1985, but the withdrawal process stretched out much longer than the time it had taken for the Soviets to plan and carry out their invasion in the first place. Rather than a unilateral pullout, which would be seen as a complete defeat at the hands of the United States and Pakistan, the Soviets turned to the United Nations and began a time-consuming diplomatic process.

The United Nations had been calling for a troop withdrawal in a series of lopsided General Assembly resolutions going back to early 1980. In the absence of a positive Soviet response, Secretary General Kurt Waldheim appointed Undersecretary General Javier Pérez de Cuéllar in February 1981 as his personal representative on Afghanistan. Pérez de Cuéllar made several trips to the area and met with representatives of the Afghan and Pakistani governments. The experience proved helpful when he became secretary general in January 1982.

The Office of the Secretary General began working out withdrawal plans from the start of 1982, under the direction of Undersecretary General Diego Cordovez. However, even if the Soviets had been prepared at that early date to leave, which is unlikely, UN efforts were complicated by the diplomatic isolation of the Democratic Republic of Afghanistan (DRA), the Kabul regime. Pakistan did not recognize the government and tried to prevent its representatives from participating in any talks. Eventually, Cordovez expanded the talks to include the Soviets as well as U.S. representatives. Negotiations were complicated by the death of Soviet ruler Andropov, who had seemed willing to reach an agreement, and his replacement by the more hard-line Chernenko. Gorbachev's ascension was the signal for revived diplomatic activity.

In July 1986, Gorbachev announced a symbolic withdrawal of 8,000 troops as a sign that he was serious about a political settlement. By the end of the year, he summoned Najibullah to Moscow and told him of his final decision. The Afghan leader was given time to stabilize internal support and to try to win a pledge of noninterference from Pakistan.

More than a year of desultory talks ensued between the DRA and Pakistan over the withdrawal timetable, until the Soviet leader announced in February 1988 that all troops would leave in a 10-month period starting May 15. With this incentive, internal and external talks accelerated. It was soon agreed that the withdrawal would proceed even in the absence of an internal political solution (which seemed unattainable); the United States and Russia agreed that both would continue to arm their respective allies. On April 14, 1988, Afghanistan and Pakistan signed a bilateral agreement on the principles of noninterference and nonintervention.

The full Geneva Accords were signed the following month, confirming Afghanistan's right to self-determination, the complete withdrawal of Soviet troops by February 15, 1989, and the honorable return of all refugees to Afghanistan. The United States and the Soviet Union were to act as guarantors. The United Nations Good Office Mission in Afghanistan and Pakistan (UNGOMAP) monitored the withdrawal of Soviet troops by land and air through its permanent outposts at the border points of Hayratan and Torghundi and at the Sindand Air Base. The Soviets completed their withdrawal by the scheduled date, leaving Najibullah's government in place in Kabul. After three more years of fighting and negotiations, the president stepped down in favor of the mujahideen and the new Islamic Republic of Afghanistan.

8

AFGHANISTAN IN REBELLION (1978–1992)

In the 20 months between the Saur Revolution of April 1978 and the Soviet invasion of December 1979, violent opposition to the new Communist government and to its revolutionary program broke out here and there in most of the country's provinces. From the start of 1980, however, the struggle took on the character of a national resistance.

Thousands of mullahs all over the country issued calls to jihad. In a country with a long tradition of gun ownership, tens or even hundreds of thousands of men were able to participate. Even an heirloom musket could do some damage to Russian morale, let alone the AK-47s and other Soviet weapons seized from government outposts around the country. All those who responded to the holy call were named mujahideen, "those who wage jihad."

The Saur Revolution had provoked mass tribal uprisings in various provinces, a tactic used successfully in the past to force a change in regime in Kabul. Once tens of thousands of heavily armed Soviet troops were stationed around the country, quick regime change seemed very unlikely. Opponents settled into guerrilla tactics aimed at wearing down the occupiers and depriving the Karmal regime of national and international legitimacy. An unremitting series of sniper attacks, ambushes, and assassinations were carried out by units of 10 to 30 fighters, too small a target for air attack or Soviet sorties. Soviet forces holed away in barracks at airfields and around the cities. All told, the organized mujahideen probably numbered some 150,000 men under arms within the country, but many of them were only part-time soldiers. Many returned to refugee camps in Pakistan and Iran during lulls in the fighting or when their families needed them.

With time, the resistance became institutionalized. A minority of the population, variously estimated at 10 to 20 percent, remained under government control. A much larger number of Afghans lived in autonomous rural areas under constant threat of attack by land or air, or in vast, impoverished refugee camps in Pakistan and Iran. They experienced a very different Afghanistan, characterized by war, carpet bombing, mass flight, and the disruption of agriculture, trade, and time-honored social hierarchies and practices.

Local warlords or militia groups affiliated with Islamic political movements imposed whatever authority existed beyond the village level or within refugee camps. Such localism and factionalism weakened the opposition and complicated political life for years after the Soviets finally withdrew.

Rise of the Mujahideen

Pakistan, like British India before it, was the natural home for those on the political outs in Afghanistan, a place for them to nurse their wounds and plan their return to power. By the time of the Soviet invasion, a host of small political parties had set up shop in Peshawar since the years of the Daoud regime.

The trickle of refugees from the first pitched battles in the summer of 1979 turned into a flood several hundred thousand strong by early the next year, as entire villages and clans crossed over the Durand Line. In desperation at this huge, unmanageable influx, the Pakistani government turned to the political groups in Peshawar to help impose some order, especially for the purpose of distributing relief.

In 1980, the government of Pakistan gave formal recognition to seven political parties headquartered in Peshawar; every individual or group had to register with one of the seven to receive aid. The parties all developed military units as well; eventually, most of the military and financial aid from Pakistan, the United States, Saudi Arabia, and other interested foreign parties was funneled through these seven groups, although smaller factions continued to compete for such support as well. Membership in these groups was fluid, and alliances came and went during the years of struggle. Still other, unaffiliated groups fought from bases within the country.

An attempt to unify the major groups via a *jirga* in May 1980 in Peshawar soon failed. Most of the fighters and refugees were sympathetic to a united front under King Zahir, but they could not overcome fierce resistance of Gulbuddin Hekmatyar and his radical Hezb-i-Islami (Islamic party). Furthermore, according to some observers, Pakistan itself was not really interested in having a strong, united Afghan military force stationed in its North-West Frontier Province, with its often restive Pashtun majority.

KHAD, the Afghan secret police, also worked hard to sow discord within the resistance, with a great deal of success. Apart from the many agents provacateurs who incited internecine fighting with disinformation and targeted atrocities, the KHAD fielded dozens of "false bands" inside the country, who would establish mujahideen credentials and then attack the genuine rebels from the rear. By October 1982, 84 such bands were operating in all parts of the country. A Foreign Intelligence Directorate was set up within KHAD, which succeeded in infiltrating mujahideen groups in Iran and Pakistan and in buying off tribes on both sides of the border with Soviet funds.

The resistance groups based in Pakistan were mostly Sunni Muslim, as was the large majority of the population of both Afghanistan and Pakistan. The Shiite resistance groups were based within Afghanistan, in the central and western regions; they received support from the Shiite government of Iran.

Three of the Peshawar mujahideen groups were considered to have a "traditionalist" orientation. Their goal was simply to expel the infidels from Afghanistan and overthrow the anti-Muslim regime. They had no political program of their own and would have accepted the restoration of the Durrani monarchy.

The other four mujahideen groups based in Pakistan were considered "Islamist." They supported the establishment of a government and society reorganized around Muslim principles and values. That would rule out either a Western-style parliamentary republic as had been tried under Daoud or a hereditary monarchy, which they considered a violation of pure Islam. Though many of them were Pashtuns, they opposed Pashtun nationalism and condemned mullahs and ulemas who ruled according to local Pashtun and other traditions rather than Muslim law.

Pakistan-Based Resistance Groups

The most radical of the Islamist groups was Hezb-i-Islami, led by Hekmatyar, a Ghilzai Pashtun from northern Afghanistan. Impressed by Hekmatyar's fierce determination and organizational skills, top Pakistani civil and military authorities, many of whom were Pashtuns, favored Hekmatyar when handing out arms and money, as at first did the U.S. Central Intelligence Agency and the Saudis. He is said to have received about one-third of all CIA assistance to the rebels, and his was the first group to obtain significant quantities of anti-aircraft Stingers.

GULBUDDIN HEKMATYAR

Born in 1950, Hekmatyar had emerged as a radical Islamist during his student days under the reign of King Zahir, when he argued for popular uprisings to force an immediate Islamic revolution.

Hekmatyar studied first at the military academy and then at the College of Engineering at Kabul University, but he never completed his studies. In 1972, he was arrested and imprisoned for the murder of a student. The following year, he escaped to Pakistan and set up the Hezb-i-Islami. As early as January 1979, Hekmatyar led a force of several thousand rebels across the border into Konar Province, capturing a local government garrison with the help of defecting soldiers.

In all, some 30,000 rebels fought under Hekmatyar. Unlike most of the large mujahideen forces, Hezb-i-Islami did not have a single geographic base in any one region of the country. Along with various local allies, it fought in the regions north of Kabul as well as in the Pashtun south.

After the fall of Najibullah in 1992, Hekmatyar was named prime minister in the interim Islamic republic. Determined to seize full power, he conducted unremitting rocket attacks against Kabul, resulting in thousands of civilian deaths and large-scale destruction. He was forced by the Taliban to flee to Iran in 1996; nevertheless, unlike most of the veteran mujahideen leaders, he opposed the American intervention of 2001 that overthrew the Taliban and installed the government of Hamid Karzai. As late as the elections of 2004, Hezb-i-Islami was said to have some soldiers fighting alongside Taliban and al-Qaeda units against the government.

Hezb-i-Islami, predominantly Pashtun, was tightly organized under a rigid hierarchy. It ran schools and training camps in Pakistan and maintained a strong-armed presence in Nangarhar Province east of Kabul and in Baghlan and Kunduz to the north. However, neither the movement nor its leaders ever developed the practical skills or interest in actual government, which might have tempered their extreme views.

The movement's enthusiasm, if not fanaticism, could be a drawback as well as an asset. The group's bold frontal attack on Kabul in 1990 was a disaster, and much of its energy was dissipated fighting other mujahideen. Eventually, Hezb-i-Islami became heavily involved in the production and sale of opium. Its popular support was limited by Hekmatyar's Islamic purist rejection of many Pashtun traditions, especially that of tribal autonomy. He and most of his followers were "detribalized" Pashtuns from the northern enclaves where many Ghilzai Pashtuns had been banished by Emir Abdur Rahman in the late 19th century.

A breakaway faction that also used the name Hezb-i-Islami was led by Maulana Yunis Khalis, a Khugiani Pashtun mullah born in 1919 in Nangarhar Province near Jalalabad. Khalis, a radical Islamic scholar and former government official, split with Hekmatyar in 1979. He won support from many traditional ulemas in southeastern Afghanistan and also had a following around Kandahar. Among his supporters was Abdul Haq, who commanded resistance forces in and around Kabul. Mullah Mohammed Omar, future head of the Taliban, got his early training in Khalis's organization, and Khalis was later aligned with both the Taliban and al-Qaeda.

Veteran Islamist intellectual and political leader Burhanuddin Rabbani, born in 1940 in Badakhshan, led another of the Islamist mujahideen movements, under the familiar name of the Jamiat-i-Islami (Society of Islam). It drew support mostly from Rabbani's fellow Tajiks and other non-Pashtuns and was more moderate in its Islamic views. It was active near Kandahar, but most of its forces were in the north, under autonomous local commanders.

The most prominent of the Jamiat fighters was Ahmad Shah Massoud. From his powerful base in the Panjshir Valley, not far from Kabul, he posed a constant threat to the key Soviet supply line; his Tajik troops fought off a dozen major Soviet offensives. A charismatic leader and spokesman as well as a brilliant tactician, the young Massoud, born in 1953, kept the regime off balance for years. He was assassinated by an al-Qaeda agent on September 9, 2001, just before the terrorist attacks in New York City and Washington, D.C. that brought American forces into the conflict.

Other prominent commanders in this party were Zabiullah from Balkh Province and Ismail Khan from Herat Province. Zabiullah was killed in 1984 by a land mine; members of Jamiat suspected that Hekmatyar's men had set up the incident. For geographic reasons, the Jamiat received less support from Pakistan than some of the other resistance forces; this was perhaps compensated in part by good relations with Iran.

The fourth of the Islamist groups was the Ittihad-i-Islami Bara-i Azadi Afghanistan (Islamic Union for the Liberation of Afghanistan), headed from 1980 by former professor Abdul Rasul Sayyaf, a Kharruti Pashtun born in 1946. Sayyaf had studied theology at Kabul University, where he was accused of throwing acid in the faces of unveiled women, and then at Al-Azhar University in Cairo, where he established links with the Muslim Brotherhood. He was jailed by Daoud and released in 1979. He drew much of his support from Saudi Arabian Wahhabis (supporters of a fundamentalist Sunni movement), and his group recruited many Arab volunteers. It was not heavily involved in the fighting.

Among the traditionalist groups, the Mahaz-i-Milli-i-Islami (National Islamic Front) was led by Sayyid Ahmad Gailani, a wealthy businessman and member of the old Kabul elite. Gailani, who claimed descent from the Prophet, was the head of the important Qadiriya Sufi order. His party took a relatively liberal, nationalist line, attracting much support among Pashtuns around Kandahar and the south and among the Turkmens along the northwest border. His support for King Zahir alienated many of the Islamists, and he won little support from Pakistan or Arab militants. Despite his moderate credentials, Gailani was unable to win much aid from the Americans.

The Jabha-i-Nijat-i-Milli (National Liberation Front) was led by the moderate scholar Sebghatullah Mujadidi, member of a large, distinguished Islamist family that led the Naqshbandi, the other major Sufi

Sayyid Ahmad Gailani, the leader of the National Islamic Front, a moderate Islamic resistance group, fought against the Soviet occupation of Afghanistan. He became foreign minister in the first postcommunist government. (Photo by Shaista Wahab)

order in Afghanistan. He had spent the Daoud years in exile in Denmark, which saved him from the mass slaughter of the rest of his clan by the Khalq in 1979. As a traditionalist, he was able to attract support from remaining supporters of King Zahir. Like Gailani's group, the Jabha did not attract much Pakistani or Arab support, and its fighters were ineffective.

Mujadidi's lineage won him the position of president of Afghanistan for a brief two months in 1992 after the fall of the DRA. Later, in December 2003, delegates to the constitutional *loya jirga* voted him their chairman.

Another traditionalist group was Harakat-i-Inqilab-i-Islami (Islamic Revolution Movement), led by Maulvi Nabi Muhammadi, a mullah and teacher born in 1921. It attracted a large Sufi following and also drew support from guerrillas in Muhammadi's native Logar Province south of Kabul, in Helmand Province, and in various places in the north. Over time, the group was weakened by its reputation for corruption and involvement in drug trafficking.

Other Resistance Groups

Just as Pakistan sponsored a variety of resistance groups among the Sunni ethnic groups of Afghanistan, Iran provided Shiite mujahideen, mostly from the Hazara ethnic group, with money, arms, and training. At the start of the uprising in 1979, traditional Hazara elites united in a parliament, or *shura*, of the Hazarajat, which tried to provide whatever governmental functions remained in the mountainous region that the Soviets all but ceded to the rebels. But the Hazaras, long excluded from the country's political life, lacked the resources to govern. They broke up into a host of competing factions. Local khans, traditional Shiite religious leaders, Khomeini-style Islamic extremists, and working-class leftists fought one another bitterly. The most important of the eight Hazara parties was the radical Islamic Nasr, short for Sazman-i-Nasr-i-Afghanistan (Victory Organization for Afghanistan), led by Mir Husain Sadeqi.

Fighting among these groups probably caused more casualties and destruction than attacks by Soviet forces did. After the Soviet withdrawal from Afghanistan, most of the groups were pulled together into the Hezb-i-Wahdat-i-Islami Mardum-i-Afghanistan (Islamic Unity Party of the People of Afghanistan) under Iranian sponsorship. Its leader, Abdul Ali Mazari, was later killed by the Taliban. His replacement, Ustad Haji Muhammad Mohaqiq, was a candidate in the 2004 presidential elections as standard-bearer of the Hazaras.

Among the smaller Shiite mujahideen groups was Sheikh Akbari's Sepah-i-Gruh-i-Pasdaran (Guardians of the Revolution), closely tied to the Iranian Pasdaran Party. Another was Shura-i-Ittifaq-i-Inqilab-i-Islami (Association of Islamic Revolutionary Unity), led by Sayyid Beheshti.

The Role of Pakistan

General Muhammad Zia ul-Haq had seized power in Pakistan in July 1977, ousting the elected prime minister, Zulfikar Ali Bhutto, who had appointed Zia army chief the previous year. Ignoring a promise to restore civilian rule, Zia spent the next few years tightening military control and pushing the country in a more Islamist direction. In April 1979, Zia had Bhutto hanged, to a chorus of international criticism.

At first, the Soviet takeover of Afghanistan underlined Zia's international isolation. Only Pakistan's thinly-populated Baluchistan Desert stood between a well-equipped Soviet army and the warm-water ports that Russia had always sought. The country's other neighbor and long-time rival was India, one of the few countries in the world that did not denounce the Soviet invasion. Zia's internal policies had antagonized the public in his Western allies, and his country's continued pursuit of nuclear weapons technology was a major sore point with Pakistan's old allies in Washington.

In the end, though, Zia was able to turn the Soviet threat into an opportunity. Following the advice of Pakistan's Inter-Services Intelligence (ISI), led by the Pashtun general Akhtar Abdur Rahman Khan, he made the decision to throw his country's resources behind the Afghan resistance, thus assuming the roles of defender of Islam and front-line coordinator of the global fight against communism. As long as he played the part to the satisfaction of the United States and the Arab oil potentates, he could count on de facto acquiescence in his undemocratic rule.

Zia did not publicly acknowledge his arms aid to the mujahideen. In any case, most of the arms used by the militias in the early years were brought over by Afghan army deserters or were captured from government outposts. Some of the rest came from China, arranged through American intermediaries, paid for by the Gulf States, and smuggled in by roundabout routes. All the assistance was funneled through the ISI, which reported directly to Zia and operated independently of the armed forces and the foreign ministry; the latter could honestly plead innocence. On the other hand, though, Pakistan's role in training the mujahideen was harder to conceal. Between 1984 and 1987 alone, 80,000 mujahideen passed through training camps run by the ISI. Pakistani hospitals near the border also treated thousands of injured fighters.

By the mid-1980s, several thousand foreign Muslim volunteers had rallied to the jihad, finding their way to the various camps in Pakistan and in some cases actually joining the fighting in Afghanistan. Most of them were Arabs, many of them Sunni militants from Saudi Arabia, but they were joined by recruits from the Balkans, the Caucasus, and Southeast Asia.

The Role of the United States

U.S. president Jimmy Carter was outspoken in his opposition to the Soviet takeover and in his statements of support for Afghanistan's and Pakistan's independence. However, he was not willing or able to offer much in the way of concrete aid.

A public made cautious by defeat in Vietnam was wary of any new involvement in Asia; after all, America's massive participation in Vietnam had begun with low levels of discreet assistance of the kind being suggested in Afghanistan. The United States was already bogged down in the hostage crisis in neighboring Iran and had no desire for any further involvement in the region. In the end, Carter's rhetoric boiled down to about $30 million worth of arms deliveries to the rebel groups in 1980, carefully disguised through third parties. An offer of $400 million in aid to Pakistan was scorned by Zia as inadequate.

Ronald Reagan, elected president in November 1980 on a platform of restoring American prestige and influence, was willing to up the ante. Even though his advisers were skeptical about the military capacities of the mujahideen, Reagan instructed the CIA to do what it could. During his first administration, direct aid remained at fairly modest levels, rising to around $250 million in 1984. Of greater consequence, the United States decided to overlook its disagreements with Zia and throw its weight behind Pakistan. In September 1981, Reagan approved a six-year $3.2 billion military assistance package for Pakistan, with options to sell 40 F-16 fighter jets.

The deal was large enough to keep Pakistan's army happy and thus keep Zia in power. It also made it easier for him to stand up to the Soviet-Indian alliance. Perhaps most important, the renewal of the U.S.-Pakistan alliance made it impossible for the Soviets to bomb or strafe mujahideen bases in Pakistan, which might have relieved pressure on their troops across the border.

The CIA under Bill Casey had no problem finding sturdy Soviet bloc arms and ammunition to outfit the rebels; U.S.-made arms would have advertised the source of the equipment, which the United States was not prepared to do. Former Soviet and now U.S. clients such as Egypt had huge quantities of such weapons in their warehouses, as did Israel as a result of its victorious campaigns against Egypt and Syria. If that was not enough, the agency contracted with China, through the ISI, to manufacture copies; factories in Egypt and the United States were eventually added to the supply chain. At least one huge shipment of rifles reportedly came from Soviet ally India. Funding was arranged in part through Saudi intermediaries, anxious to help the Afghan jihad, and distribution was largely controlled by the ISI, operating from its operations base at Ojhri near Rawalpindi.

Many of the purchased weapons proved to be damaged or obsolete, and arms dealers and corrupt middlemen made off with huge amounts of money. Nevertheless, the rebels never seriously lacked for arms and ammunition.

Reagan was reelected in a landslide in 1984, on a theme of restored confidence ("morning in America"). By now, both Congress and the media had taken note of the Afghan resistance and began pressuring the administration to get involved. In response, the president issued a national security directive calling for a mobilization of "all available means" to help the Afghan resistance. In 1985 alone, the United States sent more than a half-billion dollars in aid to the mujahideen, more than in all previous years combined. The total rose to $670 million in 1987.

The effects of this infusion of cash were apparent on the ground by the winter of 1985–86. Soviet scorched earth tactics and the flight of most of the rural population had deprived the rebels of food and other basic supplies, but thanks to U.S. aid, the problem was easily surmounted. A steady stream of rations, blankets, boots, radios, binoculars, and maps found their way across the border. Shoulder-fired land missiles and large-bore, long-range Chinese rockets put nearly every city and Soviet base within range of the rebels.

Perhaps most important, in the summer of 1986, the United States made the decision to supply the mujahideen with shoulder-fired, heat-seeking Stinger anti-aircraft rockets (and British blowpipe missiles). In 1985, the mujahideen had taken down an Afghan Airlines plane, apparently using a black market SAM-7 Russian anti-aircraft weapon, which demonstrated both the skill of the fighters and the enormous potential of such weapons to change the course of the war. Both the United States and Pakistan had resisted the idea, fearing that the arms might fall into the hands of the Soviets. Worse, they could potentially be diverted to Middle Eastern terrorist groups, who had already blown up, shot down, or hijacked civilian aircraft in the West. Ultimately, the temptation to turn the tide against a weakening Soviet Union could not be resisted.

The Course of the War

In all likelihood, the Soviets never intended to do much fighting. They expected their display of force to cow most of the country and allow the Afghan armed forces to deal with tribal resistance. Ironically, their intervention dramatically weakened Afghan fighting capabilities. The mass desertions that began with the Saur Revolution accelerated after the invasion, while the Parcham regime imposed by the Soviets carried out massive purges in the Khalq-dominated officer corps and replaced trained commanders with political appointees. When it became clear that the Afghan army was not up to the task, the Soviets soon found that their heavily armored forces, trained for set-piece battles in China or the North European Plain, were not ideally suited to fight local militias on difficult terrain.

A Russian T-54 tank destroyed by an RPG-7 antitank grenade launcher in 1987 in Chankani (Photo by Bruce Richardson)

The first major fighting in 1980 was in the east, between Kabul and the Pakistan border. The Soviet 201st Motorized Rifle Division launched offensives in the Konar Valley. Their tanks were useless in uprooting rebel forces in the hills; according to the mujahideen, the Russians took revenge on the civilian population in the valley, killing 1,800 villagers and uncounted animals. In retaliation, an entire battalion of the 201st was massacred in Paktia in June. The Soviets were never able to subdue the Ghilzai Pashtun tribal areas, which were easily reinforced and resupplied from across the border.

To the northeast, in 1980, the Soviets launched the first two of many offensives into the Panjshir Valley, where guerrillas had been harassing the vital Salang Pass supply route and Bagram Air Base. The Soviet offensives were successful but had no lasting results, as the mujahideen simply relocated farther up the hills, only to retake the valley villages as soon as the Soviet forces withdrew.

Throughout the country, Afghan troops were stationed along the most important communications routes in fortified outposts surrounded by minefields extending out to the maximum range of rebel mortars. There, they were safe but not of much use. The major land routes remained under Soviet control throughout the war (though all travel was in convoys), but the rebels often blew up bridges—the resulting pileup of military traffic was a perfect target for ambush. The rebels also became adept at mining the roads, sometimes using explosives from undetonated Soviet shells. In the cities, demonstrations and strikes were common in the first years, along with targeted assassinations, but they petered out long before the end of the war.

The Soviets had helped write the rules of modern guerrilla warfare; now they would have to reorganize and rewrite their battle plans to deal with a populist rural resistance of the type they had often supported in the past. They beefed up their helicopter strike force from 50 in 1980 to 300 the following year, including troop transports and gunships, and raised their fighter force to 130. Mi-24 gunships, equipped with four-barrel machine guns and 64 rockets, each proved devastating to the rebels. Heavy bombers were brought close to the front in Turkmenistan, where they could reach rebel bases high in the mountains. Soviet tanks were upgraded to fire at higher angles (into the mountains), and troops and armored vehicles were equipped with both faster and more accurate weapons.

However, the Soviets never raised their troop strength above 115,000, nearly half of them stationed around Kabul and the southeastern provinces. The war was costing them between $7 and $12 billion per year, plus a massive logistics effort to feed and resupply the troops already in place. In addition to 6,000 dead and 10,000 wounded by 1983, in the primitive conditions of wartime Afghanistan, Soviet forces suffered from the diseases of poor hygiene and poor medical care. Many demoralized troops, who quickly understood they were unwelcome in the country, succumbed to alcoholism or drugs, which were far more readily available in Afghanistan than anywhere in the tightly controlled Soviet Union.

In 1981, the Soviets returned to their targets of the previous year, launching two more ineffective offensives into the Panjshir Valley and wiping out some rebel bases near the road to Jalalabad. Another major offensive around Farah and Herat brought the war to the west of the country.

Chastened by Soviet air power, the rebels were nevertheless able to come back in 1982 with powerful weapons upgrades of their own. RPG-7 rocket-powered grenade launchers could pierce Soviet armor, and tough AK-47 Kalashnikov semi-automatic rifles became almost standard issue. Land and antiaircraft machine guns were widely distributed as well.

In 1982, fresh Soviet troops, many brought in across the new "Friendship Bridge" over the Amu Darya, retraced the well-worn routes their predecessors had blazed. Thousands of civilians were killed in Herat as the Soviets tried to suppress chronic unrest that had claimed the lives of hundreds of government officials. But the biggest offensive was once again into Panjshir, where Massoud had raided the Bagram Air Base.

The methodical attack began in May with a week of bombing, followed by commando landings all along the hillsides. Afghan government troops spearheaded the ground attack. They were allowed into the valley, but the Soviets behind them were blocked by massive landslides set off by mines. The Afghans surrendered or went over to the rebels, who captured several tanks in the bargain. The Soviets eventually worked their way into the valley from two ends, collecting the commandos who had been driven off the hills, and retreated with several hundred dead. They came back in late August, holding on to the low ground just long enough for a methodical campaign of destruction, leveling villages, uprooting fields, and destroying irrigation systems.

After three years of fighting, both sides nursed their wounds during 1983; even Massoud agreed to a cease-fire in the Panjshir. The United States and Pakistan were both tiring of the conflict, which was not producing the clear victory they had hoped for. In the absence of Soviet offensives, the mujahideen often fought one another or descended into banditry. The mighty flow of U.S. and Arab money and arms streaming into Pakistan was providing fat pickings for corrupt officials within the ISI as well. In 1984, Zia again tried to impose operational unity between the mujahideen parties, without much success.

The Karmal government had managed to survive and even implement some of its programs: Many women took advantage of unprecedented employment opportunities; the education system improved. Karmal was assisted by Najibullah's KHAD secret police and by widespread revulsion in some areas against the mujahideen's often brutal tactics and infighting.

The army gradually became more effective as well, partly because the mujahideen by now were routinely executing any government soldiers who fell into their hands—the window for defection had passed. The many KHAD agents were now routinely gathering useful intelligence, too. But despite forced recruiting in the cities, troop strength did not exceed 40,000 until the final years of the struggle, nor was the army able to do without large numbers of Soviet advisers, even after the main Soviet force withdrew.

Afghans who lived in the vast areas under mujahideen influence were now subjected to a ferocious near-genocidal Soviet campaign of depopulation. Villages were destroyed in gunship attacks, herds were annihilated, crops were burned with napalm, and fields were littered with mines to prevent their use. Hundreds of thousands of butterfly mines were dropped, designed to maim rather than kill; some were disguised as toys.

By the middle of 1984, as many as 5 million Afghans had been driven out of the country, mostly to Pakistan, the rest to Iran; another million were to join them in the following few years. More than a million more rural residents were driven to find safety in Kabul, which swelled with destitute refugees; many thousands crowded the other cities as well.

The mass atrocities committed by the Soviets, together with many individual acts of violence by demoralized Soviet troops against Afghan civilians, occurred far from the cameras of the world press. They generated only a fraction of the condemnation that dogged the United States throughout the Vietnam War, but they wore out any remaining sympathy for the Soviets in the Muslim world, where the information eventually did penetrate. The French aid group Médecins sans Frontières (Doctors without Borders), fearful of jeopardizing its presence by criticism of the government, reported only that its hospitals were bombed.

Afghanistan is one of the heaviest mined countries in the world. During the Soviet occupation, land mines were planted indiscriminately over most of the country by all parties in the conflict, but particularly by the Soviet forces. An estimated 10 to 12 people each day were killed by land mines in Afghanistan in 1999. Since then, demining agencies have made great progress. Afghanistan signed the international Mine Ban Treaty in 2002. (Photo by Bruce Richardson)

In March 1985, the United Nations Commission on Human Rights (UNCHR) reported "serious and widespread" abuses. "Foreign troops" had deliberately bombed villages, massacred civilians, and executed captured fighters. The commission reported that the government had jailed 50,000 political opponents. A later report claimed that torture had become routine and that mines disguised as toys had been laid down around the country (Ewans 2002, 227).

The War Drags On

During veteran hard-liner Konstantin Chernenko's brief reign of power in the Soviet Union from February 1984 until his death in March 1985, the Soviets tried one more time to impose a favorable outcome through the massive deployment of force. This included high-altitude carpet bombing, the dispersion of staggering quantities of air-dropped mines, and several major ground offensives.

In April 1984, the "Panjshir 7" offensive (there were to be several more) put 15,000 Soviet troops and 5,000 Afghans into the fray after

Massoud refused to extend the cease-fire of the previous year. Soviet commandos were ferried all along the hills to block escape routes. They faced the best-trained, -equipped, and -led mujahideen force in the country, numbering around 5,000, but felt successful enough after several weeks of fighting to leave the valley garrisoned for the first time. Similar massive offensives made some headway in the old Konar Valley and Paktia Province battle grounds (where Soviet bombers attacked targets on the Pakistani side of the border) and in the region around Herat.

The exact same pattern continued through 1985, as Soviet commanders tried to use the new premier Mikhail Gorbachev's one-year grace period to squeeze out a victory. Early the following year, their efforts were finally crowned with some successes. In the spring of 1986, a joint Soviet-Afghan force captured the major mujahideen base at Zhawar just inside the Pakistan border; they used Pakistani airspace with impunity. Massoud was finally driven out of Panjshir in the summer; he redeployed in Badakhshan to the northeast, which became his base for the next 15 years.

But the delivery to the resistance of significant quantities of anti-aircraft missiles and Chinese ground-to-ground rockets meant that the

In 1987, 270 Soviet aircraft were destroyed with the help of missiles delivered by the United States, Pakistan, and China. (Photo by Bruce Richardson)

mujahideen could continue to damage their opponents no matter how high up into the mountains they were driven. According to ISI chief General Yousaf, the Soviet victory at Zhawar was the last straw that convinced the United States and Pakistan to deliver Stingers. Over the next year, 270 Soviet aircraft were destroyed in the air. Without their low-flying fighters and bombers and their Hind helicopter gunships, there was no way Kabul could ever suppress the resistance. Morale soared among the mujahideen and plunged among the Soviet troops.

Following Gorbachev's decision at the end of 1986 to withdraw the Red Army before very long, the pace of operations slowed. Nevertheless, the Soviet leadership still hoped to bequeath a more favorable security balance to the Najibullah government and launched a major offensive near Khost in Paktia in November and December.

Soviet forces gradually withdrew in 10 months' time beginning in the spring of 1988, fighting rear-guard action when necessary. After mujahideen sacked the northern town of Kunduz during the Soviet retreat, a joint government-Soviet force retook the town and killed many of the rebels. On the whole, the mujahideen permitted an orderly retreat. Kabul was almost cut off from food and fuel in the winter of 1988–89, but a major joint effort, especially from the air, cleared the supply routes by January. Afghan army forces pulled back from many newly exposed positions but were able to regroup closer to the major cities.

After nine years of fighting, the Soviets counted some 15,000 dead and 37,000 wounded, although most observers believed the true numbers were higher. Thousands of mujahideen and government troops also died, but civilian deaths dwarf these figures, probably exceeding 1 million. The 1986 UNCHR report, which detailed some of the atrocities, described "a situation approaching genocide" (Ewans 2002, 235).

The USSR finally put behind it the nine-year quagmire in Afghanistan in February 1989, but for Afghanistan, the nightmare was far from over. The Najibullah regime was able to hold out for another three years. Fighting on a smaller scale continued throughout those years, through the four years of divided rule that followed, and during the five-year Taliban regime. A total of 24 years of harrowing struggle stretched from the Saur Revolution through the fall of the Taliban in 2001.

The Beginning of the End for the PDPA Regime

Pakistan, the United States, the mujahideen, and perhaps the Kabul government itself expected the Soviet withdrawal to be followed by the rapid collapse of the regime. Perhaps for that reason, the opposition showed little interest in accepting Najibullah's offer to negotiate a coalition government; in any case, it did not trust the brutal former KHAD director. Had a coalition government taken office, infighting might have been kept to a minimum.

In February 1989, the Pakistanis hosted a *shura* in Peshawar of all the opposition factions based there. Its stated aim was to create a broad-based government in exile. Despite much talk, the ISI made sure that the new Afghan Interim Government (AIG) was dominated by familiar faces from among the seven Sunni groups recognized by Pakistan all along. The long-despised Hazaras, whose economic and political status had improved both in Communist Kabul and in the autonomous Hazarajat, were left out in the cold. But even the seven Peshawar-based groups were as divided as ever.

In March, the rebel government ordered a joint attack on Jalalabad by some 15,000 fighters from several mujahideen groups. A government based on Afghan territory, it was argued, could attract more local and international support. In any case, Pakistan was eager to see the rebel armies depart from its soil. Jalalabad, everyone assumed, would be a good first takeoff point for an assault on Kabul.

Since the government army had abandoned many indefensible frontier posts after the Soviet withdrawal, the mujahideen expected an easy victory. The city was quickly surrounded and the airfield taken, but to everyone's surprise the Jalalabad garrison held out. The slaughter of 70 captured officers by Khalis's Hezb-i-Islami militia worked to dissuade any defenders from changing sides. In preparation for the attack, the government had moved in 20,000 non-Pashtun troops to the area and built up the city's defenses. Frequent ground sorties from the city kept the ill-coordinated mujahideen off balance until reinforcements could be brought in from Kabul by land and air. Four batteries of Scud-B missiles newly deployed in the capital kept up a frightening barrage of 2,000-pound rockets on rebel positions, while air force jets had easy pickings in the flat, open terrain.

The weakness of the mujahideen forces soon became apparent. Well armed for a resistance force, they lacked the air power or heavy armor that would have enabled them to oust the army from heavily fortified defensive positions. Nor were they able to forge cooperation between units on the battlefield. The Kabul government, on the other hand, had received delivery of new MiG-27 fighters and quickly absorbed the vast armamentarium left behind by the Soviet troops. Army strength was back up to 60,000 men, and the air force could now field more than 200 jet fighters and helicopters. The regime was also feverishly building up a coalition of autonomous local and regional militias, often subsidizing clans and tribes who were the traditional rivals of mujahideen-affiliated tribes.

By the summer, the army crushed the rebel attack on Jalalabad, the most massive in the history of the war, and cleared the road all the way to the Pakistan border. The rebels suffered 1,000 dead and 2,000 other casualties. In the autumn, the army defeated another major attack, this time against Khost in Paktia Province. These two battles shifted the psychological balance in favor of the government.

In the absence of the Soviets, and with a further moderation of the government's radical rhetoric, the rebels could no longer count on a national front against Kabul. It was they who now represented foreign intervention, as well as Pashtun religious extremism. National minorities and whatever was left of the secular middle class had reasons to rally to the government. Those clans and tribes who were now freed of Soviet or government overlords returned to their traditional localist orientation; many were willing to work with Najibullah, who was more than happy to accept local autonomy.

In fact, the president deliberately encouraged progovernment warlords to build up local militias outside the control of the army's Khalq officer corps. One of the most prominent was Uzbek general Abdul Rashid Dostum (born in 1954), who by 1991 ruled his north-central domain with 40,000 ethnically diverse soldiers armed by the government. Dostum had long supported the DRA, leading a 20,000-man militia in fights against the mujahideen. Even some mujahideen leaders settled into the same pattern after the Soviet withdrawal; they were not eager to carry the battle into the cities, where many of their relatives now lived as refugees.

Rebel unity proved short lived. After seven of Massoud's Jamiat commanders and 23 other fighters were murdered in an ambush by Hekmatyar's Hezb-i-Islami followers, the two groups became fierce blood rivals, and Hekmatyar formally quit the AIG. For his part, Massoud ruled his territory through a *shura* and administration based in Taloqan in the north. Those mujahideen still willing to fight reverted to their original hit-and-run guerrilla tactics, peppered with rocket shelling of the cities.

For the next two years, Soviet aid to the Kabul regime continued at a rate of $3–$4 billion per year. This was enough to buy more tanks, artillery, and other weapons than the army could use. It was also sufficient to put a large number of tribal leaders and even mujahideen commanders on the payroll, a time-honored Afghan tool to build support.

The United States, on the other hand, was showing less enthusiasm now that its chief objective had been achieved. The new administration of George H. W. Bush was increasingly alarmed about Islamic militancy in Afghanistan and elsewhere, the growing role of Iran in Afghanistan

OSAMA BIN LADEN

Osama bin Laden was born in 1957 in Saudi Arabia to a Syrian Alawite mother and a Yemeni father who owned a major construction company. He inherited some $80 million after his father's death in 1968, which ballooned into $250 million or more by the time he graduated as a civil engineer from a Saudi university in 1979. He first visited Afghanistan in 1980, recruited by Saudi intelligence, and by 1982, he was using his construction background to build a mujahideen base complex in Pakistan. At around the same time, he joined his university mentor Dr. Abdullah Azzam in organizing the Maktab al-Khidmat (Services Bureau) to encourage and support Arab fighters among the mujahideen. Maktab exploited bin Laden's political and financial connections to help recruit, support, and train non-Afghan Muslims for the battle. As an example of his support, bin Laden paid $300 a month to the families of volunteer fighters. These early activities were endorsed and supported by both the ISI and CIA.

Using his family's heavy construction equipment, bin Laden built a network of well-fortified cave redoubts south of Jalalabad and around Khost as a territorial base. His first camp, called al-Ansar, was abandoned after a Russian attack in April 1987, but the battle was widely reported in the Arab media as a glorious victory, helping to build up bin Laden's image.

In 1989, bin Laden split from Maktab and became one of the founders of al-Qaeda (the base). The new group would channel many of the 35,000 non-Afghan fighters who had participated in the anti-Soviet jihad to other Islamic struggles around the world. After the Soviet withdrawal in 1989, bin Laden returned to Saudi Arabia to devote his efforts to building up al-Qaeda.

After condemning the Saudi government for stationing American troops on its sacred territory, bin Laden was forced to move once again in 1992. He spent the next four years in Sudan, coordinating various anti-U.S. terrorist attacks in the region, until U.S. pressure forced the Sudanese government to expel him in 1995. The following year, the Taliban victory in Afghanistan seemed to offer him the ideal base for building up al-Qaeda.

following the end of its war with Iraq, and the threat that Middle East terrorism might spread to other regions. In 1989, after the death the previous year of President Zia ul-Haq, the CIA was finally able to pressure the new government in Pakistan under Benazir Bhutto into allowing the United States to allocate aid directly to individual mujahideen groups. The United States now targeted its aid to local military coalitions within Afghanistan and cut off Hekmatyar and Sayyaf, leader of the Wahhabi-supported Ittihad. The agency was increasingly concerned about the "Afghans," those Arab terrorists who had been armed, trained, and indoctrinated while fighting with Hekmatyar's or Sayyaf's groups or as part of Saudi Arabian Osama bin Laden's organizations.

Victory for the Mujahideen
Kabul had succeeded in buying time by the army's effective use of Soviet assistance and by Najibullah's patient reconciliation efforts. But internal dissension, the bane of the PDPA regime from its inception, once more arose, this time pitting Najibullah against rival Parchamis as well as his old Khalq enemies.

In December 1989, a number of officers were arrested in Kabul and charged with plotting a coup. When, at their March 1990 trial, the Khalq defense minister, General Shah Nawaz Tanai, was implicated, the latter quickly moved to seize power; he ordered the presidential palace bombed and, according to some reports, ordered the troops defending Kabul's south to stand aside and allow Hekmatyar's forces into the city. These reports speak of a proposed Khalq–Hezb-i-Islami government, joining radical Communists with radical Islamists whose only common link was Ghilzai Pashtun ethnicity. The plan was allegedly supported by Saudi Arabia and the ISI. The coup failed, in part because the United States encouraged the other mujahideen groups to withhold their support. Tanai fled to Pakistan, where Hekmatyar put him in charge of his troops. Later in 1990, Hekmatyar once more tried to take Kabul in a massive armored attack backed by the ISI; Najibullah repelled the attack decisively.

The Tanai incident marked a growing divergence between the United States on the one hand and Pakistan's military and ISI on the other. The gap widened during the Persian Gulf War of 1991, when the latter, together with Hekmatyar and Sayyaf, supported Saddam Hussein, while most other mujahideen and Pakistan's civilian government backed the United States–Saudi Arabian coalition that opposed Iraq's invasion of Kuwait; a small force of traditionalist mujahideen actually fought in the coalition's ranks. In March of the following year, however, the two sides once more joined forces when a coalition of mujahideen captured the government garrison at Khost in Paktia; the coalition immediately fell apart as the rival forces looted the city.

Najibullah continued his moderate tack. In 1990, he renamed the PDPA Hezb-i-Watan (Homeland Party) and tried to market the regime as nationalist and Islamic. In November, he traveled to Geneva to meet with mujahideen representatives.

Following the end of the Gulf War, diplomatic attempts to bring peace to Afghanistan resumed. In May 1991, United Nations Secretary general Javier Pérez de Cuéllar presented a peace plan calling for a cease-fire, an end to arms shipments, and a transitional setup leading to elections. The Kabul regime endorsed the plan, as did Pakistan, Iran, the United States, the Soviet Union, and the traditionalist mujahideen. Once again, however, Hekmatyar and Sayyaf played the role of spoilers (along with some of the Shiite parties), preventing the AIG from accepting the proposal. Nevertheless, in September, the United States and the USSR agreed to cut off all military aid from January 1, 1992. The point became moot when the Soviet Union itself ceased to exist in October, setting free the Central Asian republics and entirely removing Afghanistan from Moscow's priority list.

Muhammad Najibullah, the last Communist president of Afghanistan, was forced to step down in 1992 by the mujahideen. When the Taliban took Kabul in September 1996, Najibullah was executed. This photograph was taken in Dakha in 1996. (Photo by Bruce Richardson)

Early in 1992, Russia stopped sending food and fuel into Kabul. Pakistan also cut off all aid to the mujahideen, but the Islamists could still count on financial aid from the Saudis. In the north, Dostum defected from the regime and joined forces with Massoud; together they captured Mazar-e Sharif in February. At the advice of the Russians, Najibullah agreed on March 18 to resign. In an address to the nation, he called on the various factions "to actively enter the process for political and peaceful settlement of the Afghan question and practical realization of the U.N. peace formula."

On April 10, UN special envoy Benon Sevan announced he had brokered a transitional council of unaffiliated political figures to accept a handover from Najibullah at the end of that month. But it was too late for such an ad-hoc arrangement. The president tried to flee the country on April 15 with Sevan's help but was barred by airport security. He disappeared from public view as he took sanctuary at the UN compound in Kabul. Following Najibullah's abdication, General Yakubi, the last head of the KHAD, committed suicide. Kabul was there for the taking.

Two forces rushed in to fill the vacuum. A cobbled coalition of Massoud, Dostum, Sayyaf, and various lesser allies (including defecting army units) reached the northern suburbs in late April. Before entering the city, Massoud called on the AIG, sitting as the Islamic Jihad Council, to provide a political framework for post-Najibullah Afghanistan. Before the council could act, Hekmatyar and his supporters arrived with a larger force from the south and began infiltrating the city. In three days of fighting, Massoud prevailed, thanks to careful planning and coordination. Hekmatyar and the Shiite Hezb-i-Wahdat remained in control of the southern and western sections of the now-sprawling capital.

By defeating the larger and better-financed Pashtun rebel groups and the Shiites, Massoud and Dostum effectively established a Tajik/Uzbek dominion over the capital, later supported by the Tajik warlord Ismail Khan (born in 1942), who ruled the west from Herat. This situation was unacceptable to many Pashtuns, who saw it as almost a reversal of the natural order after hundreds of years of Pashtun rule.

Faced with the prospect of being shut out of the new regime, the groups based in Pakistan decided to accept a power-sharing accord brokered by Pakistan's new prime minister, Nawaz Sharif. The Islamic Jihad Council signed the Peshawar Agreement on April 24, 1992. The moderate Mujadidi was named a compromise temporary president. On April 28, he and 30 delegates of the council formally accepted Kabul's surrender from officials of the Najibullah government; they went on to proclaim the Islamic Republic of Afghanistan. Rabbani was slated to take over as president after two months for an additional four-month transition period, to be followed by a council that would prepare elections. Massoud was named interim defense minister, Gailani foreign minister, and Sayyaf interior minister. The position of prime minister was held open for Hekmatyar. He refused to join the government on various pretexts, probably unwilling to play second fiddle to the Tajik Rabbani.

In much of the rest of the country, army commanders and governors hurried to turn over local power to mujahideen leaders or local notables. Often, the former enemies cooperated to set up joint councils to manage local affairs. The councils continued to function for several years. Similar arrangements at the national level might have spared the Afghan people another decade of war.

The new government had the formal support of most of the Peshawar resistance parties who had represented the opposition to the world. It won recognition from the United Nations and most of the international community.

The Communist era in Afghanistan was clearly over. What would take its place, however, was no clearer in April 1992 than it had been at any time since the Soviet pullout three years before. Thirteen years of war had torn the country apart; the new government did not possess the power or resources to put it back together again.

9

MUJAHIDEEN RULE
(1992–1996)

The dogged resistance of the mujahideen had worn out the Soviets, toppled the regime they left behind, and eliminated the PDPA as a credible force. Thirteen years of Communist rule and mass emigration had also effectively eliminated the independent political and social life that had existed beneath the surface in Kabul and other cities and emerged during rare periods of political freedom. The Afghan armed forces, deprived of legitimacy and financial support, ceased to exist as a national body.

Thus, by 1992, the mujahideen had a near monopoly of political legitimacy, diplomatic recognition, military strength, and financial support from abroad. They, especially the seven opposition parties designated by Pakistan (and thus the United States) to receive aid, were the obvious successors to the Najibullah regime. Furthermore, a few of them had amassed considerable experience in regional government and were led by skilled negotiators able to maintain coalitions across regional and ethnic lines. Finally, the groups shared at least a few common political principles: They all rejected the reforms of the previous era, such as women's rights, and supported the concept of an Islamic state, though they interpreted such an ideal in different ways.

It soon became clear, however, that the long-feuding mujahideen parties and militias would be unable to unite. Respect for central authority had always been a weak instinct in Afghanistan; now it all but disappeared. Local warlords became laws unto themselves, and the long-suffering Afghan people became subject to random atrocities and injustice. Soviet bombs, mines, napalm, and explosives had already laid waste the countryside; now it was the turn of the cities. Kabul was largely reduced to rubble in the struggle between the different mujahideen forces. Some refugees returned from abroad, especially those living in Iran, but the urban warfare created a huge new wave of internal and external emigration.

With the country and even the capital city divided into a patchwork of de facto sovereignties, economic life remained depressed. The opium trade became the country's main industry, bringing huge profits to criminal gangs and warlords and a desperately needed subsistence income to many peasants. After four years of such misery and hopelessness, the country was ready to accept any power that could end the state of eternal warfare.

A Patchwork Country

The mujahideen commanders who carved up Kabul in April 1992 and set about fashioning a national government were already well known to Afghans and international observers. Hekmatyar, Dostum, and Massoud each commanded the loyalty of tens of thousands of hardened fighters and thousands of political adherents. They each had a territorial power base and could also project their power or influence to other regions.

Up to 70 percent of the buildings in Kabul were destroyed during the majahideen rule, from 1992 to 1996. This photograph of Tajbeb Palace was taken in 1997. (Photo by Bruce Richardson)

Even so, these powerful warlords and their mujahideen political movements were only part of the picture. A host of smaller, localized militias, many of which had been cultivated by Najibullah, also came to play important roles. Their loyalties shifted according to circumstance or were purchased by the highest bidder in money and arms. Collectively, they constituted a serious obstacle in the path of national unity or economic recovery.

For example, Sayyid Mansur Naderi, the powerful leader of the Ismaili Shiites in the eastern Hazarajat, led a militia of at least 13,000 troops in Baghlan Province, with his son Jaffar as commander. The elder Naderi, known as the Sayyid-i-Kayan after his prominent family's

ISMAILIS

Ismailis constitute the second largest grouping of Shiites in the world. They disagree with the Imami Shiites, dominant in Iran and Iraq, as to the legitimate succession in the line of imams. While all Shiites await the return of the last, "hidden" imam, Ismailis recognize new substitute imams upon the death of the previous leader (although several competing lines have emerged over the centuries). The majority of Ismailis recognize Prince Karim Aga Khan IV as their 49th imam. While their external practices are similar to other orthodox Muslims, they are reputed to hold a variety of syncretic beliefs in private, drawing on many of the world's ancient Middle Eastern and Eastern religions.

The Afghan Ismailis, who worship in secret, were considered heretics or even devil worshippers by both Sunnis and mainstream Shiites, probably because they used the peacock to symbolize the hidden imam. The peacock often represents the devil in folk iconography in the Muslim world. The Ismailis constituted a low socioeconomic rung wherever they lived in Afghanistan. Most of them are ethnic Hazaras, with a substantial Tajik contingent in Badakhstan. Like their fellow Hazaras, they were persecuted under the Taliban, and much of their property in the eastern Hazarajat was destroyed.

stronghold in Baghlan Province, had served as vice president of parliament under King Zahir. When jihad was first declared and the Jamiat and Hezb-i-Islami began recruiting fighters in his area, Naderi organized his own community, in part for self-defense.

Ismailis lived in small numbers across northeast Afghanistan, but their heavy concentration just north of the Salang Tunnel, the vital route for Soviet aid, made them valuable to the Communist regime, especially after the withdrawal of the Soviet units who had guarded the route. In 1989, the 24-year-old Jaffar (who had been educated partly in England and the United States) was made governor of Baghlan and general of the 80th Division of the Afghan army, as the Ismaili militia was styled under Najibullah. Jaffar was furnished with Soviet weapons, some of which he distributed to other progovernment forces in the region. He was also appointed to the Revolutionary Council in Kabul.

The Naderis worked closely with the powerful warlord Abdul Rashid Dostum, whose sphere of influence abutted their own to the north. Unlike Dostum, they commanded enough respect beyond their community to be useful as intermediaries when Najibullah became interested in talking with the mujahideen. The Naderis followed Dostum's lead when the latter abandoned the Najibullah government in early 1992 and later when he turned against his one-time ally Massoud. The Naderis ruled southern Baghlan as a virtual fiefdom from a lavish palace complex at Kayan until expelled by the Taliban in 1999. Like most of the warlords, they returned after the fall of the Taliban, but they were unable to regain the level of influence they had enjoyed in the mujahideen era. The elder Naderi was, however, elected to the Wolesi Jirga in the September 2005 parliamentary elections.

The militia of the Achakzai Pashtuns, who lived between Kandahar and Chaman on the Pakistan border, played a similar role as an independent force controlling a strategic route. Ismatullah Muslim, a Soviet-trained major in the Afghan army, had taken this militia into the opposition in 1979. His border tribe's traditional occupations of smuggling, raiding, and collecting "road tolls" flourished in the chaotic conditions of the times. For five years, Muslim was a useful ally to Pakistan's ISI; however, he lost favor with the Pakistanis when he refused to join any of the official mujahideen parties of Peshawar.

In 1984, Muslim went over to the government, and he was rewarded with a seat on the Revolutionary Council. He spent much of his smuggling profits on famously wild parties in his Kabul mansion, where he freely dispensed alcohol. Smelling defeat after the Soviet withdrawal, he tried to defect once more, but he was too late. His militia was routed by forces loyal to the ISI near Spin Boldak in 1991. The absence of a stabilizing Achakzai presence in the southern border zone was to have dire consequences, by clearing the way for the Taliban's first successes in 1994.

Hazarajat and the West

Like the Ismailis, the much larger Hazara community was traditionally oppressed and despised on grounds of religion (Shiism) and, in their case, because of race (Mongol ancestry). Also like the Ismailis, they were able to use the war to improve their relative social and political position.

For 20 years, from the Saur Revolution until they were finally subdued by the Taliban in 1999, the Hazaras in their remote Hindu Kush homeland enjoyed the independence they had lost to Emir Abdur Rahman in the late 19th century. Freed from outside interference, the Hazara squandered their resources in bitter factional fighting until the time of the Soviet withdrawal, when they finally united in the Hezb-i-Wahdat party, under heavy pressure from their Iranian sponsors.

The impoverished Hazara manual and domestic laborers of Kabul, their numbers increased by war refugees, benefited from Communist policies that favored minorities. Sultan Ali Keshtmand, Karmal's ally and the country's prime minister from 1981 to 1988, was a Hazara. Other Kabul Hazaras stepped into commercial niches abandoned by the disappearing traditional middle class. Fully armed by the Democratic Republic of Afghanistan as a local militia against sabotage or raids, the Hazara of Kabul provided a ready-made power base in the capital for the Hezb-i-Wahdat after the fall of Najibullah. The Hezb-i-Wahdat ruled a large sector of Kabul for the entire mujahideen period, usually in alliance with Hekmatyar.

To the west of the Hazaras, another powerful militia leader, Ismail Khan, now moved into the front ranks of warlords, where he remained through years of vicissitudes up until September 2005, when President Hamid Karzai dismissed him as part of his proclaimed antiwarlord policy. Khan, an ethnic Tajik born in 1946, was one of the army officers who led the bloody uprising in Herat in 1979. After his defeat, he took a large force of deserting soldiers from the 17th Division into the mountains of Ghowr Province. There he organized a conventional military force of about 7,500 troops under his direct command, which grew to as many as 25,000 in the mujahideen period.

From this base, Khan coordinated mujahideen activity all across the western provinces, by means of a council of commanders. He set up a rudimentary administration for those areas under rebel control, with committees on finance, health, education, agriculture, and the judiciary.

The steady flight to Iran of the civilian population weakened Khan by the mid-1980s. Nevertheless, he managed to hold out long enough to negotiate the surrender of Herat and the western region after the fall of Najibullah and to emerge as provincial governor and warlord. Herat, historically the most cosmopolitan and perhaps best-educated center in Afghanistan, became a model of relatively efficient rule under Khan and was one of the few areas to enjoy economic growth. Iran provided assistance in exchange for Khan's help in repatriating 1.5 million citizens to the region.

Khan aligned himself with the Jamiat commanders ruling Kabul, thus creating a fairly continuous swath of non-Pashtun controlled territory in the north. However, his refusal to submit his administration to central control and his self-appointment as "Emir of the West" caused tensions with the government, which Pakistan and the Taliban were later able to exploit. The Taliban drove Khan into exile in 1995 and imprisoned him two years later when he tried to return, but he gained power in Herat after the fall of the Taliban in 2001.

The Northern Warlords

During the fight against the Soviets and their Afghan clients, it was probably Ahmad Shah Massoud who had built up the strongest and most competent military force. This force enabled him to dominate Kabul during the entire mujahideen era and to provide the core of resistance to the Taliban thereafter.

Massoud's personal talents and his ability to call on a large strata of educated Tajiks from Kabul had given him pride of place among the mujahideen of the northeast from the early 1980s, attracting support from many ulemas and commanders nominally associated with the traditionalist parties of Mujadidi and Gailani. His base was in the Panjshir Valley and later in Takhar Province to the north. He fielded village-based militias as well as an elite mobile force. Massoud organized many of the local Jamiat commanders throughout the northeast into the Supervisory Council of the North (SCN) under his leadership. They continued to run their local militias but contributed elite troops to the Central Forces, under Massoud's command. Unlike most mujahideen, this force followed standard military discipline; orders were issued in Dari, as they were in Afghan's national army.

Unlike Hekmatyar and some other mujahideen leaders, Massoud encouraged the population to remain on the land. Using the SCN, he succeeded to a degree in extending the successful administrative structure of the Panjshir into the other areas under his indirect control, recruiting village elders and religious figures to serve alongside commanders in local councils. A few thousand trained employees worked for various ministry-like committees to supervise education, health, and culture; their influence reached inside Kabul. In addition to relatively small subsidies from Peshawar, Massoud could count on taxes from the lapis and emerald mines of Badakhshan, contributions, and captured equipment and supplies. He was thus able to supply food and fuel to some of the most desperate peasants. Other Jamiat leaders, including the party's longtime political leader Burhanuddin Rabbani and his Badakhshis, may have resented Massoud's role, but they never threatened his dominance.

Massoud was well positioned to take a commanding role in the post-DRA arrangements. With Dostum on his side, he was clearly the dominant party, especially vis-à-vis his Pashtun opponents, still riven by tribal and factional discord.

Abdul Rashid Dostum began his career as a Communist union leader in the government-owned gas fields of the north, where he organized self-defense units. A supporter of the Saur Revolution (he was 24 when it erupted), he started organizing a wider militia based on Uzbek peasants from Jowzjan Province; these peasants had long been subservient to northern Pashtun landlords under the monarchy, and they cherished their new power. After training in the Soviet Union, Dostum eventually built an army that crossed ethnic lines. He brought it over to the rebel side as the Communist cause disintegrated in early 1992. The one-time Communist now set up a political movement called Jumbesh-i-Melli-i-Islami, or the National Islamic Movement.

Dostum spent two years fighting for Kabul alongside and then against Massoud. After his defeat, he retreated north to focus on building a mini-state in the six provinces surrounding the city Mazar-e Sharif and to cultivate ties with the newly independent Central Asian republics. Called "pasha" by many of his followers, he reportedly dreamed of reviving the Uzbek supremacy of Timur's days. A harsh disciplinarian in rule, he was often accused of atrocities, especially against Pashtuns. Dostum was driven into exile by the Taliban in 1997.

The Battle for the Government—and for Kabul

By May 1992, the largest organized forces in the country were deployed in and around Kabul, whose population had swollen to 2 million as a result of the war. Armed to the teeth with their own and captured government equipment, they were to hold the city hostage for the next four years, in the process driving much of the population back to the countryside or abroad.

The travails of the Kabulis began with the entry of tens of thousands of mujahideen fighters, some of whom treated the inhabitants as conquered enemies and subjected them to large-scale looting, rape, torture, and killings, according to many Afghan and international observers. Street blockades and territorial divisions between the groups were soon laid down along the various informal cease-fire lines.

For the next four years, the mujahideen leaders fought over control of the central government. In practical terms, however, that government had little authority of its own, even in Kabul. Local leaders in various parts of the country may have looked to it for guidance, but its real power extended only into the territories personally ruled by its various ministers. Foreign assistance continued to be dispersed largely to individual leaders and factions, even though the United Nations and most foreign countries recognized the government as the only legitimate authority.

The Peshawar agreement of April 24 had established an Islamic republic and an interim government consisting of a president, an executive council of 51 members, and various interim ministers. But Hekmatyar refused to sign the accord, despite his appointment as prime minister. He demanded a more powerful role in the government for his party and insisted that Dostum's formerly Communist army be expelled from the city—although Hekmatyar himself was still allied to the former Khalq generals Shah Nawaz Tanai and Aslam Watanjar. As a pressure tactic, Hekmatyar launched rocket attacks against city neighborhoods.

Only 22 council members attended its first session, called by interim president Mujadidi, who issued a decree for a general amnesty (excluding Najibullah). Two compromise power-sharing agreements were reached over the next several months in an attempt to placate Hekmatyar, but neither was implemented. This provoked even angrier rocket barrages; by August, some 1,800 civilians had been killed and about 500,000 had fled the city. Hundreds more were killed in fighting in early June between the Shiite Hezb-i-Wahdat and the Saudi-backed anti-Shiite Ittihad-i-Islami of Abdul Rasul Sayyaf; many of the victims were civilians kidnapped across factional lines and never seen again. Later, in 1994, the Shiites also fought with the Harakat-i-Inqilab-i-Islami, with similar results.

Kabul faced a severe food crisis in the winter of 1992–93, as Hezb-i-Islami imposed a blockade of shipments from the south and Pakistan. All in all, in the first year of mujahideen rule, some 30,000 civilians were killed in Kabul and 100,000 wounded, mostly by Hekmatyar's rockets. By 1996, the total of civilian deaths in Kabul had probably reached 50,000.

Later in 1992, a *shura* convened by President Rabbani, packed largely with his supporters and boycotted by his opponents, extended his term for another 18 months, further inflaming Hekmatyar and most Pashtuns. Though a subsequent agreement in Islamabad in March 1993 confirmed Hekmatyar's appointment as prime minister, he once again failed to enter the city to take up the position, whether of his own volition or because he was barred.

In January 1994, Dostum once more switched sides. He, Hekmatyar, Mujadidi, and the Shiite Hezb-i-Wahdat joined forces to try to take the city. Failing in that objective (Dostum was driven back to his northern base in June), Hekmatyar threw all his artillery and rockets at the city and reimposed the blockade. The attacks, as well as the failure to take Kabul, finally discredited Hekmatyar among most of his Pashtun allies and, more important, persuaded Pakistan's ISI to begin searching for a more effective and popular protégé.

Four years of intermittent war had left Kabul largely in ruins, with up to 70 percent of its buildings destroyed. Its remaining population was at the mercy of criminals and undisciplined soldiers and lived on the verge of starvation. No other region suffered quite as much during this era, although the Pashtun south also suffered as a multitude of factions and criminal gangs vied for control with Hekmatyar's Hezb-i-Islami and other mujahideen militias. In some areas, including the city of Kandahar, the situation approached complete anarchy, with all its negative consequences for civilians. The victims included workers for nongovernmental aid organizations, starting with an Icelandic nurse working for the Red Cross in Maidan Shahr who was killed in 1992. Frequent roadblocks and checkpoints disrupted commerce and terrorized citizens.

Fighting between competing warlords in Kabul caused an estimated 50,000 civilian deaths in the city. Chilsitoon Palace, as seen in 1997. (Photo by Bruce Richardson)

In March 1994, a United Nations mission to Afghanistan headed by Tunisian diplomat Mahmud Mestiri began working toward a peace agreement between the major mujahideen groups, supported by a Security Council resolution in August. All such efforts became moot by 1995 in the face of the conquest of southern Afghanistan by the Taliban.

Opium

Historically, opium poppies, reportedly introduced to the country by Genghis Khan, were not a major crop in most parts of Afghanistan, and its drug products were not widely used locally. According to one U.S. report, about 200 tons of raw opium were produced yearly in Afghanistan before the Saur Revolution of 1978. Within a decade, however, that total quadrupled; the country became the world's major opium grower, producing up to 75 percent of the crop and posing major problems for every subsequent regime.

Several factors contributed to this change. The Communist government and their Soviet supporters never managed to extend their authority to most agricultural regions, which either fell into anarchy or were ruled by warlords with few other sources of steady income and no incentive to obey the law. Soviet landmining of agricultural lands and destruction of irrigation systems left many peasants with few alternatives to poppy, a high-value-added crop that can be grown on small patches in mountain valleys and is resistant to drought. Any moral concerns were allayed by the fact that the end product was destined for consumption primarily by non-Muslims in Europe or America.

The conduits for transporting weapons and money to the mujahideen in all parts of the country from their international supporters in Pakistan were soon exploited to move opium in the opposite direction. The drug dealers took advantage of the clandestine nature and worldwide reach of the arms smuggling networks that supplied the rebels and the growing corruption of Pakistani customs and other officials in the presence of large sums of gray-market arms and aid money.

A new northern route for the trade to Europe opened up after 1991, when the Soviet Union, with its tight police controls, broke apart into 15 different states, nearly all of them plagued by organized crime with ties to the new regimes. The Soviet successor states also became important new markets for the drugs.

The Helmand Valley saw the first opium boom. Its mullah warlord Nasim Akhunzada, affiliated with the Harakat party, supervised the spread of poppies from traditional fields in the mountainous north of the valley into southern Helmand. He forced peasants to grow poppy on 50 percent of their holdings. He would purchase the entire crop and sell it to refiners controlled by Hekmatyar's Hezb-i-Islami. The output was smuggled to Pakistan or Iran.

In 1989, Akhunzada accepted a pledge of $2 million from the U.S. ambassador in Pakistan, in exchange for a cutback in production. Perhaps as a result of this deal, in March 1990, Akhunzada was murdered in a mob-style hit in Peshawar, reportedly carried out by Pakistani drug dealers working with Hekmatyar. The killing sparked a war in the Helmand between the mujahideen factions. Eventually production rebounded to former levels. Other centers of opium production and trade grew up around Kandahar and Jalalabad, under the aegis of various local warlords, who thus became more independent of ISI handouts.

Rise of the Taliban

Taliban is a Pashto and Persian word of Arabic origin referring to lower-level students of Islam, usually from poor, rural backgrounds and always males. Such students constituted the core of the Taliban movement that ruled most of Afghanistan in the second half of the 1990s.

The majority of the Taliban's fighters were recruited from madrassas, or religious schools, in the Pashtun areas of Pakistan. These students included thousands of Afghan refugees for whom the madrassas were often the only education available; the free schools provided food and lodging. Thousands of ethnic Pashtun Pakistanis also joined the movement, as well as Arab and other non-Afghan Muslim volunteers. Their ranks were later reinforced by Urdu-speaking Pakistanis from the Punjab and Sindh and by students and others within Afghanistan.

Compared to the relatively cosmopolitan and well-educated Muslim intellectuals who created and ran the Jamiat, the Hezb-i-Islami, and some of the other mujahideen groups, the Taliban mullahs were mostly ignorant of Islamic history, law, and scholarship. The curriculum of the madrassas was based on repetition of the Qur'an and a handful of other texts and inculcated the simple messianic, puritan values of an imagined primitive Islam. The mullahs who ran the schools often confused Pashtun custom with Islamic law, especially in matters of gender roles.

The young, inexperienced rank and file Taliban, many of whom had been raised on foreign handouts in refugee camps, bore little resemblance to veteran mujahideen, who were often family men with land or trades who had grown up steeped in their local social, ethnic, and religious traditions.

The Taliban as a political force traced their origin to the 1980s, when small groups of religious students in several different provinces joined the mujahideen of Yunis Khalis or the traditionalist Harakat-i-Inqilab group or organized their own independent local bands. As early as 1984, Western reporters observed madrassas among the Pashtun of Oruzgan, Zabol, and Kandahar Provinces, where students divided their time between study and fighting. The schools drew students from across local tribal and clan boundaries. Like many Afghans, they were quickly disillusioned by the corruption, violence, and disunity of the mujahideen groups after they seized power in 1992.

The national movement eventually coalesced around a core group under the leadership of Maulvi (master) Mohammed Omar, a local mullah from the southern frontier area. Born in 1959 to landless Ghilzai Pashtun peasants, Omar had become a mullah in 1980 and opened a madrassa as a way to support his family. Sometime after the Soviet withdrawal, he joined the Khalis faction of Hezb-i-Islami, lost an eye fighting against the Najibullah regime, and retired to Pakistan. He returned to Kandahar around 1992 and set up another madrassa. In July 1994, according to Taliban legend, Omar and 30 of his students responded to the pleas of oppressed citizens near Kandahar and rescued two girls who had been kidnapped and raped by a guerrilla leader; he also intervened when two Kandahari warlords fought for the sexual favors of a young Kandahari boy.

Omar proceeded to execute the reprobates and disperse their troops, and his armed followers began to clean out other lawless elements in the area all the way down to the Pakistan border. Some 200 of them then seized Hekmatyar's arms depot at Spin Boldak. The haul was large enough (18,000 AK-47 rifles and tons of ammunition) to outfit a small army.

Whatever truth there is to this account, Pakistan gave the Taliban its first great opportunity in October that year, when it engaged the group to rescue a 30-truck Pakistani convoy loaded with food and medicine. The trucks had been seized on the Kandahar road by a local highwayman named Mansur, whom the Taliban had apparently overlooked in their cleanup campaign.

Pakistan's prime minister, Benazir Bhutto, had sent the convoy with orders to traverse western Afghanistan and blaze a trade route to the newly independent Muslim countries of Central Asia. Bhutto hoped to thus end Pakistan's historic isolation; she also coveted a share in the sought-after rights to Central Asia's rich oil and gas fields. Despairing of the messy situation in Kabul and the east, Bhutto had recently met in Turkmenistan with Dostum and Ismail Khan, who had pledged their cooperation on her western transport and trade plan. Pakistan had also flown foreign investors to Kandahar and Herat, without consulting the government in Kabul.

The Taliban soon disposed of Mansur; reinforced by new recruits, they marched back to Kandahar. They captured the city after a couple of days of light fighting and, reportedly, after paying the local commanders some $1.5 million to change sides. In addition to their rifles, they now came into possession of a sizable number of tanks, artillery pieces, helicopters, and a dozen MiG-21 jets. Hundreds and then thousands of students began streaming to Kandahar as Omar dispatched heavily-armed units to Helmand Province to the west and Zabol to the east.

Among those who welcomed these Taliban gains were the private truckers bringing supplies to western Afghanistan and contraband goods back into Pakistan. The roads became much safer. Besides, a monthly charge from a single Taliban paymaster in Kandahar was a big savings over the repeated tolls levied by a long line of large and petty warlords all along the route. The truckers later donated to Omar's campaigns to capture the northwest; although the ISI was allied with Khan, the Herat warlord's tolls were becoming onerous.

In a three-month lightning campaign, the Taliban took control of 12 southern provinces, placing nearly the entire Pashtun homeland in Afghanistan under a unified, ultraconservative rule that brought law and order to regions that had not known it for 15 years. After capturing Ghazni in a battle with Hekmatyar's mujahideen in January 1995, the Taliban quick marched through the mountains of the east. Most guerrilla groups along their route either surrendered without a fight or voluntarily joined up with the triumphant new army. Swollen with new recruits, the Taliban stunned the country by driving Hekmatyar's Hezb-i-Islami from its base at Charasyab south of Kabul in February, sending its leader into retreat.

Massoud and the Kabulis were grateful to be rid of Hekmatyar. Having no reason as yet to fear the Taliban, which had been active only in the anarchic Pashtun zone, Massoud turned his full strength against the Hazara Hezb-i-Wahdat, the only anti-Massoud force left in the capital. In a desperate measure, Hezb-i-Wahdat commander Abdul Ali Mazari turned to the Taliban, whose anti-Shiite views made it an unlikely ally. Undefeated so far, the Taliban rashly accepted his invitation and sent forces into the city for the first time while Mazari visited Taliban leaders for consultations.

The Hazara rank and file, however, refused to cooperate. Together with the pro-Iranian faction of Sheikh Akbari, most Hazara fighters joined government forces in attacking the Taliban advance party, which suffered many casualties. In retaliation, the Taliban murdered Mazari; this mutual betrayal was a bad omen for the fate of the Hazaras under Taliban rule.

The Taliban now unleashed a massive bombardment of Kabul, which made it a clear threat to the government for the first time. The remaining Hezb-i-Wahdat abandoned Kabul to Massoud, who completed his conquest of the capital region in mid-March 1995 by driving the Taliban well to the south. He thus freed what was left of the city from the threat of rockets and artillery for the first time in years.

The reverses in Kabul did not seem to cool the ardor of Taliban leaders—taking the capital may not yet have been on their agenda in any case. The Taliban pivoted its main force to the west of the country and started pushing north from Helmand. It seemed determined to take Herat from Khan against the strong advice of Pakistan, which had been assiduously cultivating the leader for some time.

The campaign proved that the Taliban as yet lacked the logistical capacity and supplies to win against seasoned troops. Khan was able to deflect the overextended Taliban force of 20,000 troops with the help of 2,000 commandos sent from Kabul by Massoud and with the help of air power, which was still a government monopoly. The Iranians also increased their aid to Khan in the face of the Sunni Pashtun threat and clashed with Taliban forces near the border. By April, the Taliban had been beaten back in the west.

After losing badly to both Massoud and Khan, Mullah Omar issued an emergency jihad call from Kandahar. Thousands of new recruits poured in from the Pakistan madrassas, most of them armed and quickly trained by the ISI. Another 2,000 troops arrived from Khost, where the local mujahideen leader Jalaluddin Haqqani had signed on to the Taliban cause. By the end of 1995, Omar commanded a force of about 25,000 fighters.

Pakistan used the time to beef up training and improve supplies. It mobilized financial resources: Osama bin Laden reportedly gave $3 million to the Taliban at this time, and the Saudi government contributed large numbers of pickup trucks to enhance mobility. The Pakistanis arranged for Dostum to contribute technicians to repair the aircraft that had fallen into Taliban hands. On August 3, 1995, the Taliban succeeded in forcing down a Russian plane that was carrying ammunition to the government in Kabul. Massoud then ordered a general offensive in the west to deal with the growing Taliban threat.

The Taliban, however, had regained its earlier momentum. Thousands of fresh, highly motivated recruits rushed up the road from Kandahar, flanked by two-thick columns of pickup trucks fitted with machine guns. They stunned and scattered Khan's collection of militias. The warlord called a panicky retreat, abandoning the airbase at Shindand on September 3 with its 52 MiG-21s and fleeing toward Iran two days later. The Taliban marched unopposed into Herat, perhaps the most forward-looking city of Afghanistan, with its thousands of educated women and glorious cultural heritage.

Massoud and the entire Rabbani regime now understood the danger. Rioters invaded the Pakistani embassy and beat up the ambassador. With at least half the country in its hands, the Taliban turned back to Kabul in the fall. The city remained impregnable, and the stymied Taliban fell back to the tactics it had condemned when used by Hekmatyar: It laid down a blockade and subjected the city to rocket and artillery barrages all through the winter and spring of 1996, this time punctuated by repeated air attacks. Thousands more civilians were added to the tragic death toll of Kabul. A United Nations airlift brought in emergency food rations over the winter.

The mujahideen now closed ranks. In October 1995, Massoud arranged a cease-fire with Dostum, who had joined the Taliban in its campaigns against Khan. In June 1996, Hekmatyar showed up in Kabul to formally assume the prime minister's post, although by this time he was so discredited that his accession may have hurt the government politically. Even the Hezb-i-Wahdat joined the coalition after Taliban forces began slowly fighting their way through the Hazarajat.

In the meantime, the Taliban was mopping up Hekmatyar's old bases in the east, taking Jalalabad in September 1996, reportedly with the help of a $2 million bribe to its commander. With no enemies in the rear, the Taliban threw all its forces against the Kabul region in a well-planned campaign that included political and financial appeals to neutral and even progovernment forces. As Taliban pincer columns were about to cut off the capital from the north, Massoud abandoned the city on September 26. The following day, the Taliban marched in unopposed. It wasted no time in entering the United Nations compound to seize Najibullah, castrate and kill him, and leave his body hanging at a crossroads for several days for the edification of the public.

The Foreign Role

Nearly all observers assert that the government of Pakistan was instrumental in the rapid rise of the Taliban, possibly even in its creation. The conclusion is based in part on ample evidence but also on the high level of military skill, planning, coordination, communications, and logistic support displayed by the Taliban forces from the very start.

The impressive professionalism of the Taliban, including accurate mortar and artillery aim, was well above that shown by the mujahideen and beyond what can reasonably be attributed to untrained students and inexperienced mullahs, however strongly motivated. The heavy equipment deployed by the Taliban in its rapid advance, including tanks and aircraft, could only be operated and maintained by experienced soldiers, or at least with battlefield advice from seasoned advisers. At the very least, former Khalq army officers and technicians, possibly coordinated from Pakistan by former Afghan defense minister Shah Nawaz Tanai, may have played an important role. The lack of any significant media presence during the Taliban advance makes a final judgment difficult.

Pakistan interior minister Naseerullah Babar, a Pashtun, had been behind Bhutto's Central Asia overture and her hopes for a road and railway link through western Afghanistan. He had organized the famous truck convoy, and his ministry provided much of the Taliban's early support until the ISI was convinced to switch from Hekmatyar. Babar set up an interministerial Afghan Trade Development Cell within the Pakistani government, which provided extensive communications assistance to the Taliban and coordinated other military and infrastructure assistance.

Another major Pakistani supporter was the Jamiat-i-Ulema-i-Islam (JUI) party, which ran many of the Taliban madrassas. The party's firm stand against religious innovation seems to have informed the Taliban ideology. It condemned any role for women outside the home and rejected all secular tribal government or feudal social arrangements in favor of rule by Islamic scholars and judges and a certain degree of egalitarianism.

The JUI had joined the Pakistani government in 1993. After party leader Maulana Fazlur Rehman became chairman of the National Assembly's Foreign Affairs Committee, he was able to arrange funding for the Taliban from Saudi Arabia and the Gulf States, a crucial necessity at least until revenues from traditional sources such as road tolls and drug trafficking could kick in. At several crucial junctures in the fighting, many madrassas were shut down and their students sent into battle across the border.

Apart from the hoped-for benefits of regional trade, Pakistan had no doubt tired of the constant warfare on its borders and had lost faith in the ability of the mujahideen to end the turmoil. The government was also anxious to be unburdened of several million pauperized refugees. A pliant government in Kabul could also be counted on to keep a lid on the old Pashtunistan issue.

In the United States, the administration of Bill Clinton at first viewed the Taliban favorably and sent high-level officials to consult with its leaders. After all, the puritanical mullahs bid fair to suppress the opium trade. Furthermore, it seemed possible that the country would be united and stabilized at last, which might prepare the way for UNOCAL, an American oil company, to pipe crude from Central Asia to Pakistan. In addition, an Afghanistan firmly in the hands of America's traditional Pakistani allies would be a bulwark against Iran, still a U.S. bugbear. All these illusions, and many of Pakistan's exaggerated hopes, were soon enough dispelled.

10

THE TALIBAN ERA
(1996–2001)

With the capture of Kabul in September 1996, the Taliban enjoyed unchallenged control of 70 percent of Afghanistan, and it subdued much of the remaining territory in the next two years. For the first time since the end of Daoud's regime, two decades before, a kind of peace had been achieved, as nearly all internal enemies were won over or too exhausted to resist.

The new regime in Kabul could count on the full cooperation and sponsorship of Pakistan, its powerful neighbor to the south, for the first time since that country was created in 1947. It also enjoyed the enthusiastic support of the huge rural Pashtun population, and at least grudging acceptance from most other sectors, who hoped that the endless factional war was over.

The very factors that had enabled the Taliban's swift march to victory, however, limited its success. Fired by religious zeal and Pashtun nationalism, the Taliban was unable to maintain alliances with non-Pashtun forces or win genuine support from Shiites or more secular urban dwellers; nor could the repressive religious state win international recognition beyond a small circle of Muslim countries. In the end, it was the close personal and political alliance between Taliban chief Mullah Mohammed Omar and the Islamist terrorist Osama bin Laden that brought the six-year Taliban era to a very rapid end in November 2001.

Nearing the Goal

Whatever other goals motivated Mullah Omar and the Taliban, the military conquest of the remainder of the country was always at the head of the agenda. The regime could never be secure in its power as long as tough warlords like Massoud and Dostum retained their regional bases so close to Kabul. Nor was the regime likely to win international recognition as long as the remnants of the Islamic republic still held sway in parts of the country.

The Taliban was never able to repeat the victorious lightning campaigns of 1994–95, despite continued help from Pakistan, Saudi Arabia, and the growing contingent of foreign Muslim fighters. Nevertheless, it persisted in gnawing away the holdout provinces piecemeal, year by year, reinforced by repeated drafts from the Pakistan madrassas, until by mid-2001, the Taliban ruled more than 90 percent of the country.

In the spring of 1997, it pushed north of Kabul to retake Bagram, which Massoud had won before winter fell, and pushed through the Salang Tunnel with the help of a defecting Massoud commander. The Taliban also moved northeast from Herat to threaten Dostum's Uzbek stronghold and its valuable gas fields. The back-and-forth struggle for the north-central region became one of the bloodiest episodes in the long Afghan tragedy.

The Taliban captured Dostum's capital of Mazar-e Sharif in May, with the defection of another commander, Abdul Malik. Mazar-e Sharif was a fairly modern, cosmopolitan city in which every one of the non-Pashtun ethnic groups of the country was heavily represented, and it had remained prosperous thanks to trade ties with Uzbekistan. The Taliban immediately squandered what welcome the regime might have had by imposing puritanical codes on a population used to a quite different flavor of Islam, driving women from the streets and shutting down Balkh University.

More seriously, the Taliban tried to disarm the Uzbek and Hazara militias, provoking a general revolt at the same time that Malik, frustrated at the Taliban's refusal to give him or his troops a share of power, reversed his loyalties once more. Some 3,000 Taliban were caught in the vise; their bodies were later found piled in mass graves, many apparently killed while in captivity. Other Taliban were slaughtered when the supposed defector closed off the Salang Tunnel, cutting off any escape.

With Hazaras in effective control of Mazar-e Sharif, the Taliban imposed a food blockade on the Hazarajat that came close to causing mass starvation. The Taliban was outraged at the relatively prominent role that Hazara women had assumed during the era of autonomy, in social services, education, nongovernmental organizations (NGOs), and even the Central Council of the Hezb-i-Wahdat.

By now it was clear that a Taliban victory would mean social and ethnic repression combined with economic stagnation and international isolation. In June, Massoud called an emergency meeting of all the remaining non-Taliban forces in the country, essentially representing the non-Pashtun ethnic groups, including Malik and Khalili, the Hezb-i-Wahdat chief. They founded the United Front for the Liberation of Afghanistan, soon known as the Northern Alliance, with Massoud as military commander and Rabbani as titular head. The alliance was later to be the core of the United States–led coalition that toppled the Taliban in 2001. Unfortunately, the alliance did not preclude fierce fighting between the various forces, and even within them.

The following year, 1998, saw the Taliban move north once again, this time more successfully. They captured Taloqan, with its key airfield, and retook Mazar-e Sharif, wreaking a horrifying vengeance. In two days of killings, some 6,000 Hazara civilians were massacred wherever they could be found, on the streets or in homes. Columns of civilians fleeing the city were bombed from the air. When the slaughter subsided, the new governor proclaimed that all Shiites had to leave for Iran, convert, or die. For good measure, 11 Iranian diplomats found in the city were killed, reportedly on orders from Omar himself.

Fierce fighting continued in 1999 and 2000 in the Hazarajat and the north, with little mercy shown to prisoners, military or civilian. Many towns changed hands repeatedly, but the overall trend was in favor of the Taliban. Apart from pockets of local resistance, only the extreme northeast, including Panjshir and Badakhshan, remained free by 2001. In that year, the suffering of the Afghan people was now compounded by the effects of three years of drought, driving still more refugees from the country and placing those in the battle zones in danger of starvation.

Minimalist Rule

Mullah Omar and his circle of like-minded advisers had no experience in government and little interest in acquiring it. Most of the institutional structure of the state, never well developed in Afghanistan and profoundly weakened through war and disunity, now collapsed entirely.

In March 1996, a *shura* of 1,200 ulemas and mullahs convened in Kandahar and bestowed on Omar the title of *emir al-muminin* (commander of the faithful), as he wrapped himself with the cloak of Muhammad, the country's most sacred relic. The Taliban thus ignored the specifically Afghan institution of *loya jirga*, harking back instead to the early days of Islam when similar shuras would choose the caliph.

Omar, a reclusive man devoid of charisma or oratorical powers, remained the ultimate authority for all religious and civil matters anywhere in the country for the next five years. It was understood that the only law would be the Islamic sharia, bolstered by the Pashtunwali, the traditional tribal code of the Pashtuns. After Kabul was taken in September, a 10-man Supreme Shura was established in Kandahar, composed entirely of Omar's old companions; on many occasions, however, a variety of other military or civil officers participated in deliberations.

Two subsidiary *shuras* reported directly to Omar—a military *shura* and a Kabul *shura* (which included no native Kabulis). The latter functioned as the civil government of the country, with each of its 14 members having quasi-ministerial responsibilities. These ministers tended to be more pragmatic than the mullahs, but their decisions were often overruled. They were never properly funded in any case. All disbursements came from Kandahar, where the national treasury, so everyone believed, was stored in tin chests under Omar's bed. In October 1997, the name of the country was formally changed to the Islamic Emirate of Afghanistan, and Omar was named head of state.

The army and air force operated without formal hierarchies or budgets and were run on an ad-hoc basis. Local commanders were given lump sums to equip and feed their recruits. The only salaried soldiers were the former Khalq army technicians, specialists, pilots, and others whose services were crucial to the Taliban's offensive operations.

The Taliban conducted a widespread purge of already understaffed government and municipal departments, which the mullahs viewed as nests of corruption or heresy. Non-Pashtuns were replaced in important posts all across the country by inexperienced Pashtuns, usually Kandaharis, who could speak neither Dari nor the language of their constituents; they were frequently shifted around to keep them from building local power bases. When most government services ceased to function as a result, the authorities appeared unconcerned. Resources were dedicated mostly to military needs or to provide the minimum infrastructure needed to support the military, the opium trade, smuggling, and the transshipment of goods.

Nearly all women were dismissed from employment outside their homes. Since women were the mainstay of the education system and a key component of health care, such services were decimated. Without the presence of a host of United Nations agencies and NGOs, the humanitarian crisis might have overwhelmed the country. That did not prevent the Kandaharis from putting obstacles in their path, especially concerning the many women, local and foreign, who worked for the agencies. Many groups suspended or ceased their Afghanistan operations under the Taliban, or were expelled from the country.

To give the Taliban its due, those under its control benefited from a greatly enhanced sense of security, whose value cannot be exaggerated for a people who have endured decades of war and banditry. Many refugees were able to return to Taliban-controlled areas, and foreign aid was more easily distributed there, especially by the World Food Program, which in June 2001 was feeding 3 million people each day within the country.

Furthermore, many Afghans were relatively well equipped to survive in the absence of government services beyond the local level, thanks to a culture of cooperative tribal and clan rule. Though the Taliban was in principle against rule by hereditary tribal chiefs, it often tolerated such arrangements, especially in Pashtun areas. Eventually, UN agencies and NGOs began targeting self-governing local communities for development assistance.

The Taliban presided over a limited amount of economic growth as well, in a context of complete laissez-faire. Agriculture revived in some regions, and cross-border trade flourished, much of it in the form of goods flown in from the United Arab Emirates (where many Afghans worked) or trucked in from Central Asia and then smuggled into Pakistan. A huge volume of illicit trade also took place under cover of the 1950 Afghan Transit Trade Agreement, under which goods were shipped from the port of Karachi, ostensibly for Afghan use, but then reloaded and shipped into duty-free bazaars in the Tribal Agencies on the Pakistan side of the border. Pakistan lost several hundred million dollars a year in customs duty as a result of this activity, which soared as the Taliban restored security to the country's road network. Kandahar, which was now effectively the country's capital city, became a thriving center of trade.

In the last year of Taliban rule, however, a new crisis loomed. Three years of drought had sharply reduced crop yields. According to estimates by foreign aid workers, several million Afghans were facing starvation in the coming winter. Theoretically, the existing food assistance programs could be expanded to meet the need, but the regime remained suspicious of and hostile toward the foreign aid community, and its policies had alienated most of the countries best able to help.

Repression

Outside Afghanistan, the Taliban is remembered largely for its extreme, idiosyncratic application of Islamic laws as interpreted by Mullah Omar and the Kandahari *shura*. At least to the residents of Kabul and the north, who made up more than half the population, such laws often seemed cruel, oppressive, irrational, and completely disruptive of normal life.

Several factors contributed to the Taliban's extreme views. In part, they simply reflected the puritanical orientation of the Afghan and Pakistani madrassas, made more extreme under Saudi Wahhabi influence in the 1980s and 1990s. In part, they reflected the social background of the Kandahari rulers, all of them rural clerics little used to female company.

In part, however, the Taliban was merely expressing the century-old resentment felt by many members of Afghan tribal society against the centralizing and modernizing programs of the Kabul elites, who sometimes imposed their reforms with insensitivity, arrogance, and even cruelty, particularly during the Communist era. Modern values, especially with regard to gender roles, were also associated with hated foreign imperialists, whether British or Russian. Worse, many Afghans may have associated such values with the feckless and sexually liberated hippies and other adventurers who flocked through the country in the 1960s and 1970s, providing many rural Afghans with their first contacts with Europeans or Americans.

Whatever the source of these values, they were consistently applied. The sole ministry known for efficiency and vigor was the Department for the Propagation of Virtue and Suppression of Vice, which deployed a religious police force to enforce the law with the help of severe corporal punishment.

Some exceptions were made, as when some rural communities wanted to keep girls' schools open. The Taliban was also able to maintain an alliance with Hazara Shiite clerics under the leadership of Sheikh Akbari, despite the Taliban's anti-Shiite views and their persecution of Hazaras outside the Hazarajat. Mullah Omar was also willing at times to overrule Pashtun custom when it clearly violated Muslim law, as in a 1998 decree that restored certain property rights to women and their right to reject a proposed husband.

The Taliban became notorious for its assault on the archaeological and artistic legacy of Afghanistan's rich pre-Islamic civilizations. On orders from Omar in February 2001, the regime destroyed the famous third- and fifth-century C.E. stone Buddhas at Bamiyan. The Taliban called the Buddhas pagan relics that might seduce Muslims into idolatry, although the monumental torsos had been tolerated by a thoroughly Muslim Afghanistan for a thousand years (their faces and arms were long ago mutilated anyway) and had been admired locally as a sign of

TALIBAN LAW

 mong the onerous laws imposed by the Taliban were the following:

- a ban on playing or listening to music
- a ban on dancing
- a ban on television
- a dress code for men
- a requirement that women be covered from head to toe in public; a ban on white socks, perceived as an insult to the white Taliban banner; a ban on makeup and nail polish
- a limited list of Muslim names that could legally be given to newborn children
- separation of the sexes on public transport
- the institution of stoning, amputation, and public execution as punishments
- a general ban on photographs of people or animals
- special identifying garments for the vanishingly few Hindus and Jews still in the country
- a minimum beard length for men
- a ban on flying kites
- a ban on keeping caged birds
- a ban on soccer
- prohibition of women leaving their home without a male family member
- prohibition of male doctors treating women, or vice-versa
- a ban on the traditional Nawruz spring festival, considered of pagan origin
- a ban on most education for girls (even in private homes)
- a near total ban on women working outside the home

ancient greatness. Thus the emir's decision can be seen as an aberrant exception to the more tolerant attitudes of Islam in Afghanistan.

Shortly after this incident, Taliban officials spent several days at the Kabul Museum systematically destroying 3,000 non-Muslim artifacts. Other items were reportedly taken and removed from Kabul by the retreating Taliban later that year. In any case, most of the 100,000 treasures of the museum, carefully collected over decades, had already been looted after the Soviet withdrawal in 1989 and sold out of the country, but at least they survive and may at some date be repatriated.

This family returned to Bamiyan after living for many years as refugees in Iran. Unable to afford housing, they reside in a cave close to where two monumental statues of Buddha once stood. The statues were destroyed by the Taliban in February 2001. (Photo by Shaista Wahab)

The Taliban had ignored the museum for the first four years of rule in Kabul; in fact, the regime's draconian law-and-order policies had put an end to looting there. Thus, the shocking vandalism in 2001, carried out over vigorous objections by virtually the entire world (including the Taliban's religious mentor and key supporter Sami ul-Haq of the JUI in Pakistan), was taken as evidence of the increasing sway in the country of Osama bin Laden.

Global Jihad

The Taliban leaders were not in principle averse to good relations on their own terms with the United States, the United Nations, or any other foreign power. However, their commitment to the pan-Islamic cause outweighed any other foreign policy goal, guaranteeing their isolation and eventual defeat.

The Taliban understood the need for good relations with the new Central Asian republics. They were a source of lucrative trade revenues for the Taliban regime on the one hand and a potential lifeline for their enemies in the Northern Alliance on the other.

In May 1999, the Taliban allowed Tahir Yuldashev, leader of the violent Islamic Movement of Uzbekistan (IMU), to set up a base in the north, where he trained antigovernment Islamic fighters from Uzbekistan, Tajikistan, Kyrgyzstan, and the autonomous region of Xinjiang in China, and facilitated their instruction by Saudi Wahhabi extremists. The Taliban (and bin Laden) provided Yuldashev and other Central Asian rebels with arms and training, which helped destabilize the entire region. Afghanistan also became a source of military, financial, and political support for the most extreme and aggressive Chechen rebels, including Shamil Basayev and Abdul Rahman Khattab, also known as Emir Khattab.

Through these actions, the Taliban, already the natural enemies of Shiite Iran, managed to antagonize most of the rest of their neighbors and earn the enmity of Russia and China. They apparently thought the price was worth paying, as it turned the country into a source of inspiration and support for thousands of young recruits to Islamic revolutionary groups from around the world.

Iran and Russia were determined to do all they could to keep alive the anti-Taliban resistance and to forestall international recognition of the regime, but Omar had good reason to doubt that either country would intervene directly. However, by drawing ever closer to bin Laden, Omar risked provoking the United States, the one power that possessed the military strength and the ideological inclination to take the battle to the territory of Afghanistan.

Bin Laden had been expelled from Sudan in May 1996 following pressure from the United States, after he was implicated in attacks that killed 42 American soldiers in Somalia and Saudi Arabia. Sudan apparently offered to deliver bin Laden to the United States, but the Clinton administration deferred (Ijaz 2001). Bin Laden found refuge in Afghanistan, where he set up al-Qaeda headquarters in the base complex he had built near Khost in the 1980s.

The "sheikh," as he was called, sealed his alliance with Emir Omar by taking the latter's daughter as his fourth wife. The deal gave bin Laden a secure base for training fighters and terrorists, plus the propaganda value of association with the apparently victorious and virtuous Taliban. In the five years after 1996, al-Qaeda trained some 11,000 recruits in Afghanistan, up to 3,000 of them aspiring terrorists and suicide bombers. At the time of the U.S. intervention late in 2001, some 6,500 foreign al-Qaeda fighters were stationed at dozens of bases around the country, the majority in Kabul and the east.

In exchange, bin Laden was able to offer Omar money, training, occasional military support from his fighters, and special favors, such as the assassination of Ahmad Massoud in September 2001 by two suicide bombers. He also provided Omar access to his network of supporters around the world.

By 1998, however, bin Laden was beginning to become a serious liability for the Taliban. In August, al-Qaeda operatives blew up the U.S. embassies in Kenya and Tanzania, killing hundreds of people, including 12 Americans. President Clinton responded two weeks later by firing dozens of cruise missiles at bin Laden's bases near Khost. The long-distance missile attack did hit some of the targets; however, it also paradoxically handed bin Laden a major propaganda coup, by enhancing his legendary invincibility.

More to the point for the Taliban, the Saudis withdrew their diplomats from Kabul after the government refused to extradite bin Laden, who by now was a sworn enemy of the Saudi regime; they probably cut off direct financial aid at this time as well. When the Taliban rejected a UN Security Council extradition demand in November 1999, the United Nations imposed serious economic sanctions and an arms embargo against the Taliban (but not against their opponents); President Clinton had issued an executive order imposing such sanctions in August. Nevertheless, a further al-Qaeda suicide attack in October 2000, this time against the destroyer USS *Cole* in Yemenite waters, failed to provoke a military response, perhaps allowing Omar to preserve a false sense of security.

Opium, Oil, and International Isolation

One of the Taliban's few saving graces for the United States and others in the mid-1990s was that it vociferously opposed the opium trade as a violation of Islamic principle and promised to suppress it. Once in power, however, leaders disregarded their promise, as opium production soared under the first four years of Taliban rule.

According to figures issued by the United Nations Drug Control Program, the country's farmers produced more than 2,000 tons of dried opium in 1995. Within two years, the yield shot up to 2,800 tons, most of it produced in Helmand and Nangarhar Provinces, both Taliban strongholds. Climate conditions held the crop down in 1998, but by 1999, Afghanistan collected a bumper crop of 4,600 tons—20 times the amount produced before the Saur Revolution of 1978.

Laboratories in both Afghanistan and Pashtun areas of Pakistan refined the raw opium to morphine and heroin. Their output supplied 90 percent of the European market and much of the American market via multiple trade routes through Pakistan and Russia. A good deal of the product was siphoned off by the growing illegal drug cultures in Pakistan, Iran, and Central Europe.

Most of the estimated $80 billion in profits went, as always, to criminal middlemen and corrupt officials all along the distribution route, but hundreds of thousands of impoverished Afghan farmers were able to live from their modest share of the take of perhaps 1 percent of the final consumer price. The Taliban is believed to have earned up to $300 million a year in taxes and payoffs from farmers, truckers, and others.

In 1999, Mullah Omar called for a cut of one-third in poppy production; in fact, the United Nations estimated that the crop fell to 3,300 tons. In July 2000, Omar ordered a complete ban on the crop. He either felt moral qualms or wanted to prop up the value of the Taliban's own inventory, said to have reached 2,800 tons. Once again, the regime demonstrated its complete control, as almost no poppies were grown in the provinces it controlled.

The Taliban believed they could derive additional much-needed revenue from the transport of Central Asian petrochemicals. The breakup of the Soviet Union and the introduction of quasi-capitalist systems in the successor republics opened up a potential oil bonanza for Western countries and companies. The Soviets had preferentially exploited oil and gas resources in Siberia or the Caucasus, leaving proven and promising fields in Central Asia relatively unexploited.

Turkmenistan, a relatively stable country, is blessed with rich gas fields near its borders with Iran and Afghanistan; it is also a terminus for existing gas pipelines and proposed oil pipelines from fields farther north. Both Pakistan and India could make good use of these resources, if they could be piped across Afghanistan; gas brought to Pakistan could also be moved through existing infrastructure for export via Arabian Sea ports. The United States has consistently favored this route, as opposed to alternatives that pass through Iran or Russia, and successive Pakistani governments have shown keen interest as well.

When the Taliban seized Kandahar in 1994, two contenders for development and pipeline rights had already been discussing possible pipeline deals with the Turkmen government—Bridas Production, an Argentine firm (which began investing in exploration and extraction as early as 1991), and UNOCAL, an American-based consortium in alliance with the Saudi firm Delta. Both parties engaged the Taliban in negotiations, set up offices in Afghanistan, and reached tentative agreements. As early as 1996, UNOCAL agreed in principle to subsidize Afghan warlords along the proposed pipeline route. The following July, the company signed an agreement with Pakistan and Turkmenistan that set a target date in 1998 to start work on a $2 billion pipeline from the Daulatabad field to Sui in Pakistan. Taliban delegates visited Ashkabad in October 1997 and traveled to the United States in November, where UNOCAL executives shepherded them through the State Department and other key addresses.

The long-sought project became yet another casualty of the impasse over bin Laden. After the cruise missile attacks in August 1998, UNOCAL suspended the project and pulled American personnel out of the country. In December, following protests from stockholders and women's groups in the United States, UNOCAL abandoned the project. In May 2002, the governments of Turkmenistan, Afghanistan, and Pakistan signed a memorandum in Islamabad officially reviving the gas pipeline project, this time with a proposed terminus at the port of Gwadar on the Arabian Sea. The three countries invited tenders from foreign companies; UNOCAL denied any further interest.

Only three countries ever recognized the Taliban: Pakistan, Saudi Arabia, and the United Arab Emirates. By 1998, the Saudi government had soured on its former protégés and withdrew from the country. Pakistan, for its part, was tired of running interference for its Afghan client and disappointed in the collapse of its pipeline hopes. Worse yet, the cumulative effects of two decades of involvement with Afghanistan were taking a negative toll on the country. Islamic militance and violence were spreading, fueled in part by the madrassas that had given birth to the Taliban; vast quantities of weapons of all sorts could be found in civilian hands; and the bureaucracy was increasingly corrupted by opium, the arms trade, and smuggling. The country was also suffering from years of economic stagnation compounded by international sanctions imposed in reaction to its nuclear weapons testing.

In October 1999, General Pervez Musharraf deposed the elected government of Pakistan and set up a military dictatorship. Dependent for survival on the army and the ISI, Musharraf could not have jettisoned his country's long-standing Afghan policy overnight, even if he had so desired. Nevertheless, his government was not closely identified with the Taliban and its supporters, and he was publicly committed to a new start for his country. When an outraged United States decided to act against the Taliban after September 11, 2001, it found a willing pragmatic ally in Musharraf.

September 11, 2001

The modest dwelling near Kandahar where Mullah Omar held court stood as far as could be from New York City, in a cultural and economic if not quite geographic sense. That city was surely not in the emir's thoughts on September 11, 2001, as al-Qaeda operatives implemented their most spectacular plan, the successful attacks on the World Trade Center in New York and on the Pentagon in Washington, D.C., and the unsuccessful attacks on Congress and the White House.

Intelligence agencies around the world immediately recognized the signature of al-Qaeda; the United States quickly documented that suspicion, to the satisfaction of nearly all the world's governments and security agencies. Most of those in the Muslim world, including Mullah Omar, who doubted bin Laden's role, were disabused of their doubts by his own acknowledgment in candid videotapes released afterward.

In Washington, the reaction of the administration of George W. Bush, who had taken office less than eight months before, could not be predicted. Even well-informed al-Qaeda leaders, let alone the insular Kandaharis surrounding Omar, could hardly have expected to be engaging U.S. forces on the ground a few weeks later.

Under President Clinton, the country had seemed reluctant to put American troops in harm's way. His administration preferred to project U.S. power via high-altitude bombing (in Kosovo and Iraq) or long-distance missiles (in Afghanistan and Sudan, in response to the African embassy attacks). During the recent election campaign, Bush had seemed to go even further, opposing the use of American forces in "nation-building" implying that he would not have gone into Somalia, for example, in the first place. Bush was convincingly portrayed by his opponents as uninformed and uninterested in foreign policy.

However, the death of nearly 3,000 civilians on American soil—a numerical loss even greater than that sustained at Pearl Harbor in 1941—and the attack on the citadels of government in the nation's capital drew a swift and fierce response, and not just to al-Qaeda. The United States demanded that the Taliban government extradite bin Laden and threatened to "make no distinction between the terrorists who committed these acts and those who harbor them," as Bush told the nation the night of September 11.

Mullah Omar refused to accede to this demand, overruling the advice of even ISI chief Faiz Gilani. The attack had transformed bin Laden into a hero for thousands of Muslims around the world, especially among the Taliban's Islamist constituency. Unfortunately for the Taliban, it had also focused the fears of many of the world's major countries.

Governments around the world who faced or had reason to fear Islamist violence, including those of Russia, China, India, the Central Asian republics, France, Britain, Germany, most Arab countries, Israel,

OSAMA BIN LADEN, ON THE PAPER TIGER

In a May 1998 interview with ABC reporter John Miller, conducted in Afghanistan, Osama bin Laden, the al-Qaeda leader, explained his confidence in ultimate victory against the United States: "The Soviet Union entered Afghanistan in the last week of 1979, and with Allah's help their flag was folded a few years later and thrown in the trash, and there was nothing left to call the Soviet Union." According to bin Laden, this experience "cleared from Muslim minds the myth of superpowers."

If the Russians could be defeated, he reasoned, the Americans should be much easier to overcome. "After leaving Afghanistan, the Muslim fighters headed for Somalia and prepared for a long battle, thinking that the Americans were like the Russians," bin Laden said. "The youth were surprised at the low morale of the American soldiers and realized more than before that the American soldier was a paper tiger and after a few blows ran in defeat ... dragging their corpses and their shameful defeat" (Miller 1999).

the Philippines, and even Pakistan, either supported a U.S. military response or were unwilling to oppose it. For 170 years, Afghanistan had faced competing powers on its north and south; in the weeks following September 11, U.S. and British forces set up forward bases on both sides, in Pakistan, Tajikistan, and Uzbekistan, the latter two in close proximity to the strongholds of the Northern Alliance.

Almost immediately, the Bush administration decided that its "war on terror" required that Afghanistan cease to be a sanctuary for al-Qaeda and other violent Islamist groups. As the Taliban regime was not willing to cooperate (and might not have had the power to do so), it had to be overthrown.

The U.S. forces that quickly converged on the region began the campaign by arranging air drops of food packages around the country in response to the reports of famine and the fear that war would complicate famine relief. Taliban charges that the food was poisoned, as well as U.S. fears that the Taliban might try to poison the food, put a quick end to this program.

On October 7, the real campaign began, less than a month after the World Trade Center and Pentagon attacks. It combined massive bombing of Taliban and al-Qaeda formations and resources; the introduction of U.S. Special Forces units around the country to guide the air campaign, coordinate among opposition forces, and buy off tribal or militia leaders (in time-honored Afghan fashion); and massive financial and military assistance to the Northern Alliance, including dozens of tanks supplied by Russia and money, arms, ammunition, and uniforms supplied by a host of coalition partners.

A month of bombing, the first phase of the attack, began to alienate the public both within the country and abroad, but the allies were using the time to line up support in Pashtun zones behind opposition figures like Populzai Pashtun chief Hamid Karzai and mujahideen commander Abdul Haq, whom the Taliban meanwhile captured and executed. Such leaders were to be incorporated into a multiethnic provisional government. Plans for an orderly transfer of power, however, could not keep pace with Northern Alliance advances once the old mujahideen forces broke out of their fixed positions. On November 9, they took Mazar-e Sharif; on the 12th, Ismail Khan returned to Herat, and on the 13th, the alliance walked into Kabul to widespread civilian cheers, as Taliban forces melted south. The Jalalabad warlords turned coat on November 15.

In response to looting and acts of retaliation, the United Nations, on November 13, provided for a multinational force to patrol Kabul. A force of 3,000 troops recruited from the armies of 18 NATO countries began deploying in December. Some 15,000 government forces and foreign volunteers holed up in Kunduz agreed to surrender on November 21. Hundreds, or as some claim several thousand of them, were killed despite promises of safety. Some 20,000 ethnic Pashtuns also fled the northern areas.

On December 6, a day after anti-Taliban Afghan delegates approved the Bonn Agreement setting up an interim government, Mullah Omar surrendered his remaining troops in Kandahar to local chiefs, effectively ending the Taliban's five years of rule. Coalition forces turned their focus on al-Qaeda. In short order, its facilities in Afghanistan were destroyed and nearly all its forces (now deprived of any local allies) were captured, killed, or driven from the country. However, top leaders such as Omar and bin Laden and hundreds of followers managed to escape over the Pakistan border into more welcoming territory in the Tribal Agencies.

11

THE LEGACY OF THE CIVIL WAR

Few of the faction leaders and technical experts who made up the interim government of Afghanistan under the 2001 Bonn Agreement had wide government experience. But even the most seasoned ministers of the largest countries in the world would have been daunted by the challenges of restoring and maintaining some semblance of a functioning state in Afghanistan after 23 years of war.

At the most basic level, the country's people were either missing or in the wrong place. Vast numbers had been killed or died of privation. One out of three Afghans was living in refugee camps in Pakistan and Iran. Many others were living in camps within the country far from their homes, or holing up wherever they could in the ruins of Kabul and other cities. Worse yet, the entire population, in- or outside the country, had to deal with the debilitating emotional scars left by decades of violence, insecurity, hatred, and human rights abuses. Added to all this, the female half of the population had to overcome the legacy of severe repression that had been imposed by religious rulers.

Refugees

More than 6 million men, women, and children had fled from war and persecution in Afghanistan to take refuge in neighboring countries in the years following the Saur Revolution of 1978. More than another million had been forced to escape to the cities or to other parts of the country.

Together, these refugees accounted for more than one-third of the country's population, and constituted the largest single refugee group in the world in the 1980s and 1990s. Although the humanitarian crisis began to abate after the fall of the Taliban and the implementation of the Bonn Agreement in 2001, it may take years to resettle all the refugees and repair the social, economic, and educational damage Afghans have suffered.

The first wave of refugees fled the country in the period immediately following the PDPA takeover in April 1978, when the government of the Democratic Republic of Afghanistan staged mass arrests of real or potential enemies of the revolution. Those rounded up were interrogated under torture, and many were executed.

Fearing a similar fate, anyone with a history of government service or political activity, or anyone lucky enough to be released from prison, escaped as soon as he or she could. Among the first groups to leave were a large number of intellectuals and other educated people from Kabul and the other major cities. Many joined the exile circles that had formed in Peshawar during the Daoud regime; thousands of others found refuge in Europe and North America. Most businesspeople and professionals soon realized they lacked a future as the government's communist character became clear, and they, too, began making plans to leave the country.

Factional battles within the PDPA continued throughout the Communist era, based on ideology and ethnicity; losers in the power struggle often fled the country, sometimes finding refuge in the Communist countries of Eastern Europe. By the end of 1978, monarchists, Islamists, and liberals were joined in exile by members of the Parcham faction of the PDPA; many of these leaders returned following the Soviet invasion.

Within a few months of the Communist takeover, major rebellions broke out in Konar, Badakhshan, Herat, and other areas, followed by brutal reprisals. Thousands escaped the fighting toward the nearest border, generally Pakistan or Iran. Others soon ran away after the government decreed and began to impose revolutionary measures that undermined the traditional rural economy and society. Still others left in compliance with religious strictures requiring Muslims to leave a country where Islam has been overturned.

Refugee numbers swelled to epic proportions during the Soviet occupation years (1979–89). Some regions were nearly depopulated as entire clans and tribes fled across the Pakistan border to fill makeshift camps all across the Pashtun regions of that country. Human rights abuses drove many away, as did the unremitting 10-year war between the Soviet army and its government allies on the one hand and the mujahideen and tribal militias on the other; the Soviet scorched earth policy left large rural areas uninhabitable. Intermittent fighting among the various opposition groups made matters worse.

After the Soviet withdrawal, civil war continued between the mujahideen and the Najibullah government, and even urban areas that had been secure now came under attack, driving still more people to join the millions already scratching out a bare existence in Pakistan and Iran. In 1992, the Communist government was replaced with the interim government of the mujahideen, led at first by Sebghatullah Mujadidi and then by Burhanuddin Rabbani; however, this long-awaited change merely created new waves of refugees.

The new refugees included many employees of the old Najibullah government who feared that the new Islamic government would punish them for their cooperation with the Communists. At the same time, many refugees who had enthusiastically returned to Afghanistan soon found themselves trapped in bitter fighting between the mujahideen factions and reluctantly returned to the safety of refugee camps in Pakistan and Iran.

Between 1992 and 1996, an estimated 50,000 civilians were killed in Kabul, largely due to shelling by Gulbuddin Hekmatyar's Hezb-i-Islami. Thousands of others were victimized by ethnic cleansing as the cumulative effect of years of civil war poisoned interethnic relations. The old patchwork distribution of ethnic and tribal groups across the country

Many refugees who returned home after the fall of the Taliban cannot afford the high price of housing in Kabul and live in ruined buildings and tents. This photo was taken in 2003. (Photo by Shaista Wahab)

229

had left many isolated pockets of ethnic groups exposed to retaliation and expulsion.

Once the Taliban took control of most of the country in 1996, most of the key mujahideen militias fell apart or were defeated, and most of their leaders fled the country along with many of their followers. Only Ahmad Shah Massoud continued to resist the Taliban from inside Afghanistan, from his bases in the Panjshir and Badakhshan.

The Taliban came to power, and was kept there, with the help of thousands of foreign fighters, who supported the new regime as an Islamic cause rather than as the Afghan government. Unfortunately, the resulting oppression helped drive thousands more native citizens from the country, including an estimated 50,000 just between October and December 1996.

During their five years in power, the Taliban compiled a brutal record of repression and violation of human rights and imposed oppressive laws, especially against women, in the name of their ill-informed, idio-syncratic interpretation of Islam. Those who escaped the worst punishments could be subjected to public whipping—women and children included. Fear and humiliation became the lot of those considered hostile to the Taliban, which included most city dwellers, Shiites, and non-Pashtuns in general.

Refugee Existence

For most refugees, the desperate decision to leave their homes did eventually win them respite from the ravages of war, but it was also the

---

MAJOR WORLD'S REFUGEE GROUPS IN 2000

Afghanistan	3,580,400
Burundi	568,000
Iraq	512,800
Sudan	490,400
Bosnia-Herzegovina	478,300

Source: G. Matoso, United Nations High Commissioner for Refugees, "Refugees by Number 2001 Edition," (booklet) (found at www.safecom.org.au/opendoc.pdf)

---

first step in a long, difficult life of privation and insecurity. Typically, refugees had to trek for days across rugged terrain, often mountainous and barren. Most of them hired guides who were familiar with the escape routes and had safe contacts along the way. Refugees hid during the day and moved in the dark of night to avoid confronting DRA and Soviet forces. Any escapees caught by government troops without travel documents or authorizations were subject to punishment and could even face imprisonment or execution.

The journey was particularly difficult for children and the elderly. However, as the government did not have much control over the border areas, most families managed to reach the safety of refugee camps intact—but with almost no resources. Their homes and livestock had been destroyed, and they had escaped with what little they could carry on their backs.

The majority of the refugees, mostly farmers or unskilled laborers, settled down in refugee camps located close to Afghanistan borders. Many passed more than two decades of their lives in the harsh conditions of the camps. Proud, hard-working Afghans, deprived of their traditional livelihoods, became dependent on handouts from a large variety of international agencies.

More than 150 camps were eventually set up in Pakistan, where most of the refugees lived. The government required refugees to register with one of the political parties in order to be eligible for aid. A much smaller number of Afghans with the requisite financial resources or skills were able to move to Pakistani cities, where they set up businesses or found jobs; their children were among the few with access to education.

The camps lacked decent housing, clean water, or health care facilities. Maternal and infant mortality rates, always high in Afghanistan, were even higher among the refugees. Depression and mental health problems were commonplace; more than a few who were unable to endure years of insecurity committed suicide.

The majority of refugees were ethnic Pashtuns, most of whom fled to Pakistan, where the Pashtun population was roughly as large as that in Afghanistan. Other major ethnic groups that reached Pakistan included Tajiks, Turkmens, and Hazaras; the latter joined a community that had set down roots there under British rule in the late 19th century, when Abdur Rahman first subdued their home territory in the Hindu Kush.

Most of the refugees who fled to Iran were Shiites and Dari speakers from Hazarajat and Herat. These refugees shared a common language with the Iranians; they found themselves culturally more akin to Iranians than to Pakistanis, or even at times to Afghan Pashtuns. A smaller number of Afghans migrated to other countries. In the United States, many settled in the Bay Area of California and in the New York metropolitan area. After living much or all of their lives outside Afghanistan, most Afghan refugee children adopted the culture of their host countries.

Human Rights Abuses

No country has a perfect record on human rights, nor is there even a universal consensus on many rights issues. Afghanistan before 1978 was no model state by international standards; in fact, the regime of President Muhammad Daoud, established in a palace coup, was undemocratic in operation, intolerant of dissent, and unconcerned about the fine points of police procedure. Furthermore, such concepts as gender equality and the freedom of the individual from family and clan control—almost universally accepted at least in principle—were still controversial in Afghanistan as late as the 1970s.

Nevertheless, it was a stable, relatively peaceful country, where most people could expect to live out their lives without the threat of persecution or excessive violence. Slow progress had been made during the 20th century, especially in the cities, toward greater rights for women, progress for repressed ethnic minorities, academic freedom, and other items on the typical human rights agenda.

The Communist Saur Revolution of April 1978 changed the status quo. From the very start, the "democratic republic" subjected thousands of innocents to torture and execution without trial. Many Afghans fled the country, leaving behind property and livelihoods in order to save themselves and their families. A large number of Afghans disappeared into the security system, often between the walls of the notorious Pul-e Charkhi prison in Kabul and similar prisons in the provinces. Fear of the government kept most family members of the disappeared from inquiring about their fate. Some who did inquire were also questioned, tried, and punished as enemies of the "revolution." Even today, decades later, many families have still not discovered their loved ones' fates.

As in all 20th-century Communist states, a vast network of secret police and informers kept tabs on citizens. People feared to speak against the government in their own homes. Children were frequently grilled by teachers or government agents about their parents' opinions. Leaving the country was considered a criminal act; millions managed to flee, but those who were caught were often punished or murdered on the spot. The media and the educational system were considered arms of the state, and absolutely no political activity was tolerated independent of the PDPA itself.

As Soviet forces grew increasingly desperate in the early 1980s, their battle tactics approached genocide. Hundreds of thousands of village dwellers in districts considered sympathetic to the rebels were killed in systematic combined assaults by bombers, helicopter gunships, artillery, and close-range shooting.

Resisting the Soviet occupation, each of the mujahideen parties and militias drew support from a limited ethnic or religious constituency. Their leaders contended for power over the movement in a shifting game of alliance and enmity. On the ground, this often resulted in the arrest, torture, and killing of rival party members and fighters; each group maintained its own brutal prisons.

When the Najibullah regime fell in 1992, mujahideen forces entered Kabul and the other major cities, which had been ruled by the Communists since 1978. Reprisals against those associated with the government were commonplace. The mujahideen, who were nearly all political Islamists, imposed new restrictions especially against women, based on conservative Islamic law.

Fighting between ethnic groups escalated during the civil war. Hazaras, Tajiks, Uzbeks, and Pashtuns each at times found themselves targeted by one or more of the other groups. Tajiks and Pashtuns committed ethnic crimes that were termed *the dance of the dead*. They severed the head of their victim while standing and the headless fell to the ground and wobbled. When control of a piece of territory changed hands, in a neighborhood in Kabul or a rural district, all the residents of the area were subject to retribution. Armed militias often entered the homes of defenseless civilians, killing and frequently raping women. Some women were taken from their homes and married to commanders, and young girls were sold into prostitution. Girls who refused to leave their homes were sometimes killed in front of their families.

Following the Soviet example, mujahideen forces targeted civilian districts with punishing rocket and mortar attacks. In particular, Hekmatyar's Hezb-i-Islami was widely known for its attacks against other rebel forces and against civilians in Kabul.

When the Taliban came to power in 1996, the regime imposed a strict interpretation of Muslim sharia law on the entire country, including regions with quite different historic traditions. The decrees were enforced, often arbitrarily, by the police, who worked for the Department for the Propagation of Virtue and Prevention of Vice.

Women became the prime targets of the Taliban's discriminatory laws. They were not allowed to work or study outside their homes or even venture outside to shop unless covered from head to toe and accompanied by a male relative. Many women committed suicide to end their suffering.

The Taliban also persecuted ethnic and religious minorities. Mass killings of Shiite Hazaras became almost commonplace: For example, when in January 2001 Taliban forces retook the town of Yakaolong in Bamiyan Province from the forces of the Hazara Hezb-i-Wahdat, they arrested some 300 men during house-to-house searches and killed them publicly by firing squad in the town center. Taliban forces also blocked the delivery of humanitarian relief to the Hazara in Bamiyan.

In May 2001, the Taliban announced that Hindus would have to wear distinctive badges to distinguish them from Muslims. Many Hindu families fled the country.

Women's Rights

For more than a century, various Afghan rulers have periodically tried to introduce reforms favorable to women's rights. Typically, the changes provoked serious political and social reactions and thus at times proved counterproductive.

Emir Abdul Rahman Khan put an end to the practice of forcing a widow to marry a relative of her deceased husband. This practice had not been widely observed in any case. In the early 20th century, King Amanullah tried to implement a set of reforms to promote women's rights. He encouraged women to remove their veils by having his wife and other female members of the royal family appear in public in Western dress during official ceremonies. Amanullah established girls' schools and even sent talented young women abroad for further studies and to acquire special skills. His efforts provoked anger among mullahs and tribal leaders and led to his overthrow.

Starting in the 1960s, educated women began to hold prominent positions in the Afghan government. A few were also elected as members of parliament and were appointed as cabinet ministers. The number of female students at universities and institutes of higher education was on the rise. The coeducational systems at these institutions provided equal opportunity for women to learn side by side with their male counterparts, and there were no restrictions on how they should dress prior to 1992. With the support of the government, women were once more sent to foreign countries for further studies.

234

THE CHADRI

The *chadri*—also known as a full, or Afghan, *burqa*—is a head-to-toe garment that women were forced to wear under the Taliban. It is made of heavy pleated material and, when worn, looks like a sack.

In a *chadri,* women see the world through a 2-by-4-inch mesh opening. Women with poor eyesight were unable to wear their glasses under the *chadri;* others, in poor health, were unable to breathe. Both groups were effectively made prisoners of their homes.

Many Pashtun women had been wearing the garment for centuries, but it was not used in all regions of the country. The Taliban made it compulsory everywhere and punished those women who dared to ignore the law.

Many women still wear the chadri, *some out of fear of the mujahideen, the Taliban, and al-Qaeda, who may return to power one day. (Kabul, 2003)* (Photo by Shaista Wahab)

As prime minister, Daoud was an active advocate of women's rights. He abolished the mandatory wearing of the *chadri.* During the celebration of Afghanistan's Independence Day in August 1959, women from the royal family appeared in public with their faces exposed. With the encouragement of the government, a number of young educated women also removed their *chadri.* Many religious leaders responded with anger. Extremists harassed women who did not cover their faces; some even threw acid on exposed legs. Daoud punished the perpetrators and actively suppressed the opposition.

Although women in Kabul and some other cities were beginning to enjoy a less circumscribed life, the status of women in rural and tribal areas remained largely unchanged. By law, men exercised unlimited control over women; women were required to obey their husbands and in-laws. Forced marriages remained commonplace, and young girls were often given in marriage to much older men.

From the time it was established in 1965, the PDPA advocated equal rights for women. Anahita Ratebzad, a leading party member, was the chief promoter of women's rights; she conducted meetings with women to discuss their rights and obligations. Government statistics show that in the period of PDPA rule, the involvement of women increased in social, political, and economic affairs. In Kabul and northern cities, many women wore European clothes and appeared in public unveiled. In 1979, the Communist government issued decrees outlawing both child marriage and forced marriage. Tribal chiefs opposed the laws, and the government was unable to enforce them.

The Islamic government proclaimed by the mujahideen when they entered Kabul in 1992 began imposing restrictions on women. Women were required to cover their heads in public; worse still, they became tempting targets for those avenging ethnic and political attacks.

Between 1992 and 1996, women in Kabul were especially vulnerable as the city was divided among the warlords. Many were kidnapped, raped, tortured, and forced into marriage by the rival factions. Thousands of war widows, often the sole breadwinners of their families, were terrified to leave their homes.

After the Taliban took Kabul in 1996, women lost whatever rights they still retained. A day after entering Kabul, the Taliban's Radio Sharia announced that by order of Mullah Mohammed Omar, women were not permitted to leave their homes. By that one decree, women students were thrown out of school and female government workers lost their jobs. Women were eventually allowed to leave their homes but only if accompanied by a male relative. Those who had lost their close male relatives could not go out, even if they needed medical care. Shopkeepers were forbidden to sell to women customers and were punished if they did.

In short order, women became the chief target of the religious police. They were publicly humiliated and whipped for not complying with the dress codes or other Taliban regulations.

The *chadri* became compulsory for all women in public. Education for girls after the age of eight was prohibited. Women were not allowed to wear white socks or shoes, considered an insult to the white Taliban flag. Women, even war widows with no other means of support, were barred from working outside their homes; the only exception was for women health care workers, who could treat women patients, who could not be seen by male physicians.

In September 1997, the Taliban separated men and women hospitals; of the 22 hospitals in Kabul, only one was allowed to serve women until pressure from the International Red Cross convinced the Taliban to open a few more hospitals to women. Many women suffering from acute mental and physical ailments were never able to obtain medical attention, bequeathing a legacy of untreated problems for the post-Taliban era.

12

OVERCOMING THE LEGACY

The Taliban government seemed to melt away in late 2001, leaving behind almost no clear imprint on Afghanistan's political or military life. The country reverted to its pre-1995 status quo, with mujahideen commanders dividing up Kabul and the non-Pashtun areas of the north, while a larger number of tribal chiefs and local strongmen contended for power in the Pashtun regions of the east and south. Unfortunately, the Taliban years did leave a bitter legacy to social life: a higher level of interethnic mistrust, the final destruction of the educational system, and a reversal of decades of slow progress on the status of women. In addition, opium production had become the cornerstone of the economy.

Balanced against these negative factors were two positives. The people were exhausted by war and anxious to rebuild, and the international community, shocked into action by the events of September 11, 2001, placed a high priority on a peaceful resolution of the quarter-century Afghan crisis.

Political Reconstruction

A gradual if uneven process of political stabilization took hold in the first five years after the fall of the Taliban. Through a messy but mostly peaceful process, a Kabul-based provisional government won recognition from most power centers, although its authority outside Kabul remained tenuous. The first-ever election of an Afghan head of state took place in September 2004, as interim president Hamid Karzai was elected to a full five-year term. Parliamentary and provincial elections took place one year later. On December 19, 2005, the 351 newly-elected male and female members of the upper and lower houses of the National Assembly held a ceremonial opening session. The Wolesi Jirga (House of the People), the lower house, was tasked to draw local district boundaries, which would allow district council elections to proceed in 2006.

The political reconstruction process began on November 28, 2001, when 28 representatives from the Northern Alliance, the Peshawar parties, monarchist circles around King Zahir, and other exiles gathered in Bonn to decide Afghanistan's political future. The meeting was led by United Nation's special envoy Lakhdar Brahimi, who had already spent four years fruitlessly trying to broker an Afghan peace. Many of the details had been hammered out in earlier meetings and in a November 13 New York meeting of the "group of six plus two," consisting of the country's six neighbors, the United States, and Russia.

Longtime Jamiat-i-Islami leader Burhanuddin Rabbani, still the country's nominal president, resisted giving up the post, but in a crucial first step toward ethnic reconciliation, his fellow Tajik leaders threw their support behind Hamid Karzai. Karzai was tribal leader of the Populzai, the large Pashtun tribe that gave the country its first kings in the 18th century. Karzai had parted company with the Taliban early in its rule and helped line up Pashtun support against the regime at the time of the U.S. intervention. On December 5, the Bonn Agreement was signed, providing for a six-month interim government. Karzai was sworn in as chairman on December 22, assisted by five vice chairmen and 29 ministers, many of them Tajiks.

On June 2, 2002, a *loya jirga* was duly convened in Kabul, with 1,450 delegates chosen from all 362 administrative districts. Women held a guaranteed 160 seats; 25 more were allocated for nomads and 100 for refugees living in Iran and Pakistan. The *jirga* voted Karzai interim president for a two-year term over nominal opposition once his two main contenders for head of state, King Zahir (ceremonially dubbed "Father of the Nation" instead) and Rabbani, withdrew. In one stroke, the country effectively repudiated both the 250-year-old monarchy and the movement of political Islam begun by Rabbani and his colleagues nearly 40 years before. Karzai's new cabinet, endorsed by the *jirga,* was ethnically balanced. The president proceeded to name a 35-member constitutional commission, including six women, which presented a document for consideration by another *loya jirga* convened in December 2003, whose more than 500 delegates approved the constitution on January 4, 2004, formally proclaiming Afghanistan an Islamic republic that guaranteed freedom of religion and provided no government role for mullahs or ulemas.

The constitution provided for a strong elected president, who appoints ministers and supreme court justices on approval of the

National Assembly. The president also appoints one-third of the members of the assembly's upper house, the Meshrano Jirga (House of Elder); half of these appointed members must be women. Province and district councils choose the remaining two-thirds of the chamber. The lower house, or Wolesi Jirga, is elected by popular vote. In accord with Afghan traditions of localism, the constitution provides for elected village, city, district, and provincial councils. Constitutional amendments are the province of a *loya jirga* consisting of the National Assembly plus provincial and district council chairs; no amendment can undermine the role of Islam, although the definition of that role was left unclear.

In perhaps the interim government's first major achievement, presidential elections were held peacefully on October 9, 2004, at 25,000 polling sites in Afghanistan and among refugees in Pakistan and Iran. Despite widespread charges of multiple voting and local claims of intimidation, most local and international observers judged that the process of registration and voting (conducted with UN help) was fairly implemented throughout the country and among the refugees. A beefed-up U.S. and NATO troop presence was designed to keep violent disruption by the Taliban and warlords to a minimum, though a small number of election workers was killed.

In 2004, Hamai Karzai became the first democratically elected president in the history of the country. (Photo by Tim Fitzgerald)

Karzai won with 55 percent of the 8 million votes cast, a turnout of about 75 percent of those registered. None of the three other major candidates—the familiar mujahideen commanders Abdul Rashid Dostum, an Uzbek general; the Shiite leader Muhammad Mohaqiq; and Yunus Qanuni, a Tajik and a leading figure in the old Northern Alliance—managed to break out of his ethnic bases.

Masooda Jalal, the only woman candidate and Karzai's only challenger at the 2002 *loya jirga*, captured only 1 percent of the vote, but she and two women vice presidential candidates helped pressure the major candidates to support women's rights publicly. Karzai appointed her minister of women's affairs in his first cabinet, alongside two other women ministers.

The new cabinet, announced on December 24, 2004, excluded most of the familiar warlords such as the previous defense minister Mohammed Fahim, successor to Ahmad Massoud; it instead included several well-regarded technocrats in the economic and rehabilitation ministries. Karzai did appoint Ismail Khan as energy minister, in compensation for removing him as governor from his fiefdom in Herat, where he had restored order and prosperity with characteristically brutal and high-handed tactics. In March 2005, Karzai named Dostum to a top army post in which his responsibilities remained unclear.

Both appointments were attempts at coopting the old commanders. Karzai compiled a mixed record, sometimes cycling warlords and/or drug lords through various local or national positions; a more thorough purge may not be possible until the successful conclusion of programs to expand the national army and disarm the militias. In February 2005, Karzai succeeded in replacing six troublesome provincial governors.

Parliamentary elections were held in September 2005. More than 5,000 candidates competed for the 249 seats in the Wolesi Jirga. Voting was by candidate rather than party, to reduce the influence of the old mujahideen groups—although a majority of those elected are tied to those groups. A possible unintended effect was to reduce turnout; only about half of the more than 12 million registered voters (who included about a half-million *kuchi* nomads) cast ballots. Turnout was low in Kabul and in many Pashtun areas, especially where insurgent activity was reported. Provincial council elections were held at the same time. In the following weeks, the 102-seat Meshrano Jirga was gradually filled through votes in the provincial councils and presidential appointments.

By 2006, a majority of the 20,000 planned village councils had been elected; half of them have had their development plans approved. The U.S. Agency for International Development (AID) has committed to fund these plans at the rate of $200 per local family. The plans provide for schools, roads, irrigation, and drinking water systems; they are expected to include human rights codes.

Foreign Intervention

When the United States (and Great Britain, its ally, led by Prime Minister Tony Blair) launched a military intervention in Afghanistan in late 2001, the U.S. military and foreign policy elite was anxious to avoid repeating the mistakes of the 1980s. In their single-minded goal of driving out the Soviet army, the administrations of Ronald Reagan and George H.W. Bush had allowed Pakistan to control the distribution of money and arms to anti-Soviet forces. After the withdrawal of the Soviets in 1989, the United States effectively washed its hands of the problem, turning its focus instead to Iraq. More consistent attention might have forestalled the country's slide into the grip of Osama bin Laden, in the prevailing view.

The administration of George W. Bush, by contrast, made the decision to keep substantial forces in the country until a government was in place, strong enough to resist the Taliban and al-Qaeda. It quickly won backing from Britain and the NATO alliance and an unusual level of support and cooperation from the United Nations. Most Afghan political forces accommodated to the reality of a foreign military presence; the first U.S. ambassador, who was said to consult with Karzai on a daily basis, was nicknamed "the Viceroy." Since a 2002 assassination attempt, Karzai has been protected by U.S. Special Forces. A low level of violent resistance by residual Taliban units increased somewhat in 2005 and 2006, and foreign troops inevitably became embroiled at times in tribal feuds and opium-related violence. By late 2006, the American combat death toll stood at around 200.

Most U.S. casualties were incurred during occasional active sorties against Taliban strongholds, although roadside bombs took their toll as well. American troops had not, as of 2006, become routine targets for reprisal, as had the Soviets before them. Nevertheless, charges of U.S. mistreatment of prisoners, especially those kept at the Guantánamo Naval Base in Cuba, periodically stirred up protests in Kabul and other cities. At least 15 anti-U.S. protesters were killed in clashes with the police in May 2005 after prisoners charged that U.S. guards at Guantánamo had disrespected the Qur'an in their presence. Riots also took place in Kabul in May 2006 after a runaway U.S. army truck caused a crash, killing three Afghans.

Only about 4,000 U.S. troops were on the ground at the start of 2002, including air support units, engineers, and interrogators; by August, the number had doubled. Total troop strength rose as the military began tackling a wider variety of responsibilities in various parts of the country (in addition to the ongoing anti-Taliban campaign). It topped off at over 20,000 in the run-up to the 2004 presidential elections and remained close to that level through 2006.

On November 13, 2001, the day the Northern Alliance entered Kabul, the United Nations called for an International Security Assistance

Force (ISAF) to control looting and retaliation in the capital region. Some 3,000 troops from 18 members of NATO began deploying in Kabul in December; their six-month mandate was later repeatedly extended. NATO itself formally took command of the ISAF (which also included units from Australia and New Zealand) in August 2003, the first-ever alliance mission outside the Euro-Atlantic area. In October of that year, the United Nations authorized the force to operate outside Kabul. Non-U.S. NATO troop strength reached some 17,000 by July. Some of the smaller NATO members contributed specialized personnel such as motorized or helicopter companies, medics, and air traffic controllers.

Foreign troops have played a key role in extending Kabul's control over the country, especially in the context of Provincial Reconstruction Teams (PRT). Each provincial team includes some 80–200 foreign troops working with civilian experts from Afghan ministries, government agencies from NATO members and other European countries, and the UN mission. By early 2006, 23 PRTs were in place, providing security and helping with infrastructure and other "nation building" projects. They have intervened to stop local fighting and have helped in

After the fall of the Taliban, in November 2001, the International Security Assistance Force (ISAF) provided security in Kabul, as Afghanistan lacked a regular army. (Photo by Shaista Wahab)

243

UN disarmament programs. Many nongovernmental organizations (NGOs) in Kabul have criticized the concept; they charge that the PRTs often benefit local warlords and generate resentment against foreigners that make their own work more difficult. NATO took over the U.S. military role in southern and southeastern Afghanistan in the summer of 2006 and across the entire country in October 2006.

The United Nations, in addition to providing legitimacy to U.S. and NATO intervention, has been active in several key fields in post-Taliban Afghanistan. Apart from relief and development work by such familiar agencies as the United Nations International Children's Emergency Fund (UNICEF) and the World Health Organization (WHO), a United Nations Assistance Mission in Afghanistan (UNAMA) was authorized by a March 2003 Security Council resolution to help prepare elections and coordinate other aid; it employs a staff of 500, 75 percent of them local citizens.

One of the international body's most promising programs has been its Disarmament, Demobilization, and Reintegration (DDR) program. By the end of 2005, the DDR (funded largely by Japan) claimed to have disarmed around 63,000 militia members, mostly former soldiers of the Northern Alliance, who exchanged their weapons for job training, cash, and other assistance. By no means have all militia commanders cooperated. A follow-up program was launched in 2005 to deal with some 125,000 members of up to 2,000 smaller, less formal militias.

The DDR had also cantoned (disarmed and stored) more than 12,000 tanks, missiles, anti-aircraft guns, and armed personnel carriers by early 2006. It began the effort with an estimate that only 4,000 such weapons existed, but given that the country has received lavish foreign arms assistance from all around the world for decades, an accurate estimate is probably not possible.

A host of NGOs have a long history in Afghanistan. More than 2,000 organizations, large and small, remain, struggling in impossible conditions against remaining Taliban, local warlords, and criminal gangs. Scores of staffers have been killed since the fall of the Taliban. After five of its doctors were killed in Badghis Province in June 2004, the celebrated Médecins Sans Frontières pulled out of the country, after having worked there for 24 years.

At the December 2001 Bonn conference, the Afghans identified a need for $22–$45 billion in reconstruction assistance, perforce from the outside world. The next month, representatives of more than 60 donor countries met in Tokyo to assess a report compiled by the UN Development Program, the World Bank, and the Asian Development Bank that called for a 10-year $15 billion plan that focused on de-mining, education, health care, and infrastructure. Of this, a total of $4.5 billion was pledged for the first five years by states and NGOs. A further conference was held at Berlin in April 2004 at which some 50 countries and 11 NGOs pledged $8.2 billion for the next three years. The same participants gathered for a follow-up conference in London early in 2006.

Security Gains

Security is in the eye of the beholder, as different observers continue to provide starkly divergent assessments. While major NGOs avoid large areas of the country (10 of 35 aid workers were killed in 2005), the government and its U.S. military allies point to many signs of improvement.

The Taliban, at least, may have suffered badly from its inability to derail the 2004 and 2005 elections or impact the huge turnout with threats of violence. The few thousand Taliban fighters still active in 2006 were no longer a serious military threat to the existence of the government. An increase in Taliban attacks in the spring of 2006 led to heavy counterattacks, including airstrikes, that reportedly killed hundreds of rebel fighters. Nevertheless, some 1,600 government troops and civilians died during 2005. Insurgents retained the capacity to complicate reconstruction projects by random attacks against workers, local police, or local coeducational schools. Yet, they were widely reported to be short of funds and equipment. Any hope Islamist insurgents had for a revival rested with the madrassas and mosques on the Pakistan side of the border, especially in the Quetta area, where local Pashtuns and refugees, militants alike, continue to stoke the flame of jihad in sermons and lectures. Taliban and al-Qaeda forces continued to enjoy the hospitality of Pashtun tribes in western Pakistan as late as 2006.

Intrawarlord fighting became far more sporadic than in the past. In late 2004, Dostum's Uzbeks and Tajiks under warlord and Balkh governor Atta Muhammad fought pitched battles in the north with heavy equipment. In 2005, they both disarmed the majority of their fighters in order to run in the elections for parliament.

A promised amnesty program at the national level finally materialized in May 2005, despite opposition from non-Pashtun groups. Many provincial officials, in cooperation with enthusiastic U.S. army officers, had been offering their own amnesty and rehabilitation programs with some success. Some former Taliban officers have been integrated into local police forces.

Afghanistan has never enjoyed civil peace without a strong central army. Rebuilding such an army from scratch takes years. By 2006 the

Afghan army claimed to have fielded 35,000 trained troops and to be training another 4,000; 28 of 31 battalions were deemed combat ready and many of them had already participated in fighting. Unofficially, recruiters seek to maintain ethnic balance throughout the military. Many potential recruits, it was reported in mid-2005, had to be rejected due to undernourishment or vitamin deficiencies, a reflection on the poor state of health care; illiteracy is not a bar, as even many officers are reportedly unable to read. The United States, with much NATO assistance, has assumed the dominant role once played in the 1960s and 1970s by the Soviets in training and equipping the Afghan armed forces. The National Military Academy was formally opened in March 2005, with 30 professors and 112 cadets; the school was established in "partnership" with the U.S. Military Academy at West Point.

The integrated multiethnic army has had a few successes suppressing battles between rival militias but relies in many regions on cooperation with local militias, as do the Americans. By the end of 2005, a 3,000-man army brigade was stationed at each of the four regional commands outside the capital.

As of early 2006 nearly 60,000 national highway and border police had been hired and stationed around the country. Many former mujahideen and even Taliban fighters could be found in their ranks. The government has endorsed training the police in human rights, with some NGO participation, but the level of compliance is reported to be spotty. The police in some areas have proved less successful than the Taliban had been at suppressing such crimes as ransom kidnapping and drug-trade violence. In March 2005, Human Rights Watch, a U.S.-based advocacy group, charged that former warlords now ensconced as provincial governors and top police officials "have been implicated in widespread rape of women and children, murder, illegal detention, forced displacement, human trafficking and forced marriage." (http://hrw.org/english/docs/2005/03/10/afghan10299.txt.htm)

Even once all opposition and private militias are disbanded, land mines will continue to present a safety problem for years to come. Some 5–7 million of them were left over from the wars. The United Nations Mine Action Center for Afghanistan (UNMACA) spent some $64 million in 2002 to deploy 200 clearance teams that removed 40,000 mines, marked off many uncleared areas, and destroyed 900,000 items of ordnance. Many ordnance caches continued to be uncovered with the help of local citizens in 2006. In 2004, about 100 people, often children, were killed or maimed by land mines every month. By 2005, some 8,000 de-miners were working for 15 organizations toward a goal of effective clearance of all dangerous zones in populated areas by 2015. By early 2006, the UNMACA claimed a total of 2.8 million explosive devices (mines and ordnance) had been removed from 320 square kilometers (124 square miles) of land.

Economic Recovery

Billions of dollars of military and economic assistance and billions more in opium money have helped spark an economic revival, at least compared with the depressed level of the war years. The return of the majority of refugees and the somewhat improved security situation leads most observers to expect continued improvement, though sustainability is still a distant goal.

The country's gross domestic product has finally rebounded to pre–Saur Revolution levels. From a figure of $3.7 billion in 1977, it fell continuously to around $2.7 billion in 2000 but reached around $4 billion in 2004 and more than $5 billion in 2005. (Opium exports bring in an additional $2.7 billion a year.) Postwar growth rates hit 29 percent in 2002 and 18 percent in 2003 but fell to 7.5 percent in 2004, partly as a result of a continuing drought, which finally ended in the winter of 2004–05. In September 2002, a new currency was issued in a successful attempt to promote financial stability; one new afghani replaced 1,000 old ones; by early 2006, it had lost only some 15% of its value, trading at 49 to the U.S. dollar.

Major infrastructure projects, if completed successfully, should encourage internal and external trade and link the country closer together. The rebuilt Kabul-Kandahar segment of the key Highway 1 (financed mostly by the U.S. AID) was completed in late 2004, and work on the Kandahar-Herat segment continued; many local highway and bridge projects were advancing as well. The U.S. military announced plans in March 2005 for a $28 million vehicle and pedestrian bridge to Tajikistan, scheduled for completion in early 2007. Other international road or rail links with Uzbekistan, Turkmenistan, and Iran (which could link the Arabian Sea directly to Central Asia or even China for the first time) have been the subjects of numerous state visits and press releases, though none of them had passed the planning stage by mid-2006.

As in many other poor countries, wireless technology has brought an explosion of telephone usage. Only 33,000 landlines served the country in 2002, plus some 15,000 mobile units; by the end of 2005, the two major mobile companies in Afghanistan had about 1.3 million enrolled customers, after investing some $240 million. The country was awarded the ".af" Internet domain name in 2003, and Internet clubs began to appear in the cities.

The long-proposed pipeline between the gas fields of Turkmenistan to consumers in Pakistan was still languishing in 2006 for lack of serious private interest, largely due to the security situation. However, on a March 2005 visit to Pakistan, Karzai and several ministers signed cooperation pacts with their Pakistani allies in the U.S.-sponsored "war on terror"; the agreement provides for regular political consultations, as well as measures to promote trade, transport, and tourism.

Whereas in 2001 electricity production had been limited to portable generators, by 2005, partial services had been restored in much of Kabul and other cities, though only about half the limited prewar generating capacity was in operation. Border areas have been supplied from the grids of the country's neighbors.

Even in the best of times, only 12 percent of the country is suitable for agriculture, but the neglect and destruction of the wars brought increased desertification in the south and deforestation in the east. Several years of drought have complicated efforts to revive agriculture,

A farmer plows his land in preparation for the winter crop. (Bamiyan, 2002) (Photo by Shaista Wahab)

but snows and rains improved food production in 2005. The continued distribution of seed and fertilizer, the de-mining program, and the reconstruction of damaged irrigation systems are bound to help raise output at least to prewar levels—as long as security can be assured—as will the reconstruction or reclamation of the country's 22 prewar agricultural research stations.

Many stands of wild and rare fruits and nuts were cut down during the war, and the precious national seed collection in Kabul was destroyed. Fruits and nuts, many of them native to Afghanistan, once accounted for half of all exports. Fortunately, some native seed varieties were preserved abroad and have been shipped back for propagation or hybridization.

After 2001, opium production once more soared, from just 185 tons in 2001 (when production was depressed by a Taliban ban) to 2,700 tons the following year and to a near-record 4,200 tons in 2004, constituting a staggering 87 percent of world production. A British-run program to suppress the crop had failed to make much of a dent, but in 2006, the UN Office on Drugs and Crime reported that output had declined by about one-fifth in the previous year. In March 2005, the Pentagon reported that U.S. forces would dramatically increase their role in support of eradication efforts.

Drug money is believed to finance most insurgent and criminal violence. However, a successful eradication program against opium, which has brought in an estimated 60 percent of export income, could have a depressing effect on the economy, both in the producing regions and in the cities where much of the money is spent.

Repatriation and Rehabilitation

Early in 2002, the UNHCR began a voluntary repatriation program in cooperation with refugee host countries and the Afghan government. After five years, more than 4 million people had returned. The continued poverty and insecurity in the country may keep away indefinitely many of the 2.5 million refugees still in Pakistan and 900,000 in Iran.

The UNHCR actively encourages refugees to return. It verifies their identities and provides them with a minimal amount of aid to get started. When the program began, the aid package consisted of $20 in cash per person, with a maximum of $100 per family; 150 kilograms (330 pounds) of wheat; two plastic sheets; two water buckets; one kerosene lantern; five bars of soap per family; and some sanitary materials. As more Afghans became willing to return, the aid package was reduced.

The majority of the refugees have moved to Kabul, rather than their home provinces, for reasons of security and in hopes of finding jobs. Many cannot afford the high price of housing in Kabul, however, and live in tents provided by aid agencies or in ruined buildings. The UNHCR officially supports the reintegration of returnees to their places of origin. It claims to have rebuilt more than 140,000 homes all across the country by 2006, in cooperation with other agencies, and to have dug some 8,000 wells or water points in areas with many returning refugees. It has also helped mediate disputes between returning refugees and those who stayed behind or moved into the returnees' regions in the intervening years.

Human Rights

After the fall of the Taliban, innocent Pashtun families living in predominantly non-Pashtun areas were made to pay for the crimes of the Taliban. Hazara, Uzbek, and Tajik militias raided Pashtun homes, looting, beating, raping, and murdering the inhabitants.

Such attacks were reported in Balkh, Dawlatabad, the Shur Darya region in Faryab Province, Mazar-e-Sharif, and Herat. In a period of three months, early in 2002, Human Rights Watch reported more than 150 violent attacks against Pashtuns in northern Afghanistan. Those seeking revenge often demanded payments of $1,700 to $2,500 from Pashtuns to spare their lives, a sum beyond the means of most families. Several thousand Taliban and foreign prisoners were apparently killed in the north after surrendering to Northern Alliance commanders.

Many of the warlords guilty of such crimes managed to secure positions in the post-Taliban national government or in local governments after the Taliban were driven from power. Although President Karzai has managed to marginalize a few of the more prominent leaders, others continue to use their positions to persecute opponents and would-be reformers. The continued presence of Taliban units in southern provinces and skirmishes between warlords and tribes have impacted the rights scene as well.

The Afghan independent Human Rights Commission (AIHRC) recorded some 2,700 significant human rights complaints in 2005. The commission reported that poor security had fueled "child trafficking, land grabbing, torture by police and extra-judicial killings."

On the other hand, a vigorous independent press has emerged in Kabul, with more than 200 newspapers and magazines by 2004, although most have limited circulation. The provinces have seen far less activity. By 2005, about 30 independent radio stations had been set up around the country with the assistance of foreign aid agencies, and several more operated in Kabul. Press freedoms have not been a major issue, although television (which has a limited audience) came under pressure from prominent Muslim authorities in 2005 for broadcasting "un-Islamic" material such as dance programs. Self-censorship is reportedly widespread, and issues such as violence and women's rights are covered delicately if at all.

Opposition political activity is consistently tolerated as well, probably for the first time in Afghan history. Yunus Qanuni, who lost a presidential bid to Karzai in 2004, announced in March 2005 that 11 opposition parties had formed a new coalition to contend in parliamentary elections scheduled to take place in the fall. Although the opposition bloc failed to win a majority of seats, Qanuni was elected speaker when parliament took office in December.

Education

No sector suffered as much from the deprivations of the Communists and the Taliban as education. In fact, the entire physical and human system must be rebuilt almost from scratch. After the Saur Revolution, university professors, schoolteachers, education bureaucrats, and students alike were subjected to interrogation, torture, and imprisonment; many fled the country permanently for the West. The one-third of the Afghan population who languished for decades in refugee camps lost almost all access to modern education, depriving an entire generation of basic literacy. Furthermore, under the Taliban, almost all girls were driven from school. As for physical facilities, the Asian Development Bank estimated that 80 percent of school buildings were destroyed in the wars.

The reopening of school in March 2002 was a huge morale boost for the country. In 2005, some 5 million children attended elementary or high school, about 35 percent of them girls. Unfortunately, an estimated 60 percent of girls under 11 years old are still not in school. About 50 "secret" girls' schools were still in operation in Kabul in 2005, to accommodate girls whose families oppose government schools or fear to let their daughters venture far to attend. Attendance, for boys as well as girls, varied greatly by province; the northern provinces tended to surpass other areas in numbers.

251

The U.S. AID began an accelerated learning program in 2003 for those who had missed out on their education during the war years. As of mid-2005, 170,000 students were enrolled in 17 provinces, 56 percent of them females. About 40 percent of the 6,800 teachers in this program were women.

UNICEF reached agreements in 2005 with the Ministry of Religious Affairs to use mosques and government-supported clergy to encourage families to enroll their girls in schools. The agency also committed funds to set up informal local schools for 500,000 additional girls and train an additional 25,000 teachers.

A variety of foreign aid projects have focused on reviving higher education, in Kabul and in regional centers. The United Arab Emirates agreed in 2004 to set up a medical school in Kabul. The United States has allocated funds for an American University in the capital, as well as a kindergarten–grade 12 American school.

Archaeology has also shown signs of a revival. In March 2005, Afghanistan's National Institute of Archaeology signed an agreement with Ryukoko University, a Buddhist school in Kyoto, Japan, to excavate ancient Buddhist remains in Keligan, about 70 miles west of the monumental Buddhas that the Taliban destroyed at Bamiyan. The same month, it was announced that a 20,000-item collection of Bactrian objects, unearthed in 1978 and believed to have been destroyed by the Taliban, had been found and recataloged and was being taken on a world tour by the U.S. National Geographic Society.

Health

Afghanistan has always lagged in health indicators, but the wars wiped out what little there was of modern health care, especially outside Kabul. The vast majority of trained doctors fled the country long ago. As a result, tuberculosis and leishmaniasis are endemic, and malaria has begun to spread as well. Recent psychological studies have found that two-thirds of the population suffers depression, anxiety, or post-traumatic stress syndrome.

Some progress has been made, especially with childhood vaccination. In March 2005, 35,000 health workers gave oral polio vaccines to some 5.3 million children while distributing vitamin A supplements to boost immunity; reported cases of polio had already fallen to just four in 2004. More than half the country's children have been immunized against whooping cough and measles. In March 2004, some 5 million children were medicated against intestinal worms. By 2005, several hundred health care centers had been renovated or built; 3,300 new community health care workers, 4,860 clinic staff, and a few hundred midwives had been trained.

Women's Rights

After years of war and negligence, the status of women in Afghanistan requires considerable attention from the new government. Progress in the face of traditional values of male domination will be difficult, especially since prominent traditionalists continue to hold powerful positions in the new state, especially in the provinces.

The new government has taken several positive steps toward protecting women's rights. A large number of women delegates were elected to the constitutional *loya jirga* that was held in Kabul in December 2003. The new constitution formally guarantees equal rights for women. It also sets aside 25 seats in parliament for women, which were duly filled during the elections in late 2005.

Women are becoming more aware of their rights. In 2002, for the first time in the history of Afghanistan, a woman ran for the office of president during the *loya jirga*. Masooda Jalal ran again in the presidential

About 25 percent of the delegates to the constitutional loya jirga, *held in Kabul in December 2003, were women.* (Photo by Shaista Wahab)

election in late 2004, garnering 90,000 votes. This constituted only 1 percent of the total votes, but her campaign, and that of two female vice presidential candidates, focused attention on women's issues.

In 2005, Jalal was named minister for women's affairs, taking her seat alongside two other female ministers. Her leadership qualities encouraged many other educated Afghan women to become politically and socially active and to defend their rights. A couple of months later, President Karzai appointed Habiba Surabi as governor of Bamiyan Province, the first female governor in the country's history.

In another potentially hopeful sign, women have been playing a more public role in the media. They regularly anchor radio and television news broadcasts, even in conservative provinces. Nevertheless, female journalists face far more obstacles than do their male colleagues, such as their circumscribed ability to travel around the country or even in the cities at night.

Despite the vocal opposition of many powerful mullahs, tribal leaders, and warlords, women's rights are supported by many Afghan men. As far back as 2001, the NGO Physicians for Human Rights found that

MILESTONES IN WOMEN'S RIGHTS IN AFGHANISTAN

1920s—Women gain the right to vote

1920s—King Amanullah opens first girls' school in Kabul and encourages women to remove their veils

1946—Women's Welfare Society established

1959—Mandatory wearing of *chadri* abolished

1964—Four women appointed to the advisory committee for drafting the new constitution

1977—Women constitute more than 15 percent of parliament members

Early 1990s—70 percent of schoolteachers, 50 percent of government employees, and 40 percent of medical doctors in Kabul are women

2004—Constitution grants women equal rights; woman runs for president

2004—Three women named to new cabinet, including minister of women's affairs

2005—Woman named governor of Bamiyan Province

90 percent of the more than 1,000 Afghan men and women they interviewed strongly backed a woman's right to an education and to work outside her home.

The status of women has dramatically improved over the very low bar set by the Taliban. Observers claim that one in five women in Kabul go about unveiled; in the non-Pashtun ethnic areas, many women have returned to their traditionally less repressive costumes. Even in Jalalabad, many have reclaimed the right to appear in public without an accompanying male relative.

Some women have also begun to benefit from microcredit programs, helping to lead a revival of small business. Some 35,000 women are employed by the government, a handful in key posts. Driving instructors have seen a rise in women students as well.

The Future

The legacy of the recent past weighs heavily on Afghanistan. Every possible divide—ethnic, gender, religious, class, and political—has been exacerbated; every family suffers from its burden of tragedy.

Nevertheless, there are reasons for optimism. The foundations for civil society are being laid, and at least some physical reconstruction is

Today, the city of Kabul is again crowded with people and street vendors. (2003) (Photo by Shaista Wahab)

visible in most parts of the country. One can hope that the very process of getting back what was lost may produce a momentum to help bring the country closer to prosperity and peace than ever before.

The most important question, however, remains unanswered: What ultimate impact will the 23-year war have on Afghan national identity? Will the common experience of suffering and exile and the common struggle to rebuild finally help cement the different regions and ethnicities into one nation, a century after the death of the unifying emir Abdur Rahman Khan?

The external signs are positive, in the multiethnic government and military and in the modern education curriculum now being taught to several million youngsters in thousands of schools. Pessimists can point to the long legacy of localism, exacerbated by the anarchy of war, and to the dangers posed by chronic instability in neighboring Pakistan and Central Asia. Optimists can, as always, hope.

APPENDIX 1

BASIC FACTS

Official Name
Islamic Republic of Afghanistan

Government
The constitution of January 2004 established a presidential system. The people elect the president, who is both head of state and head of government. Presidential candidates run for a five-year term on a ticket with two vice presidents. The president can be reelected only once. The president nominates cabinet ministers and the nine justices of the Stera Mahkama (Supreme Court), who all must be approved by the Wolesi Jirga (House of the People), the lower house of the National Assembly (parliament). The justices serve 10-year terms.

The Wolesi Jirga is itself elected by popular vote, on a district basis. The Wolesi Jirga can impeach ministers. The president also appoints one-third of the members of the Meshrano Jirga (House of Elders), the upper house of the National Assembly; half of the president's appointees must be women. Province and district councils choose the remaining two-thirds. The constitution also provides for elected village, city, district, and provincial councils.

Political Divisions
Provinces
Afghanistan is made up of 34 provinces, or *welayats,* with populations ranging from barely more than 100,000 (Nurestan) to 3.3 million (Kabul).

Capital
Kabul

Geography

Area

Afghanistan covers an area of about 250,000 square miles (647,000 sq. km), slightly smaller than Texas and slightly larger than Ukraine. It is a landlocked country.

Boundaries

The current boundaries are mostly the result of the 19th-century imperial rivalry between Britain and Russia. Only minor adjustments have been made since then.

The northern boundary between Afghanistan and the former Soviet Union was negotiated between the two countries after Afghanistan gained its independence in 1919. The Soviet government had originally agreed to return the Durrani lands that czarist Russia had seized from Afghanistan but reneged on its promise once its control of Central Asia was secure. In 1946, the two countries signed an agreement drawing the border down the middle of the Amu Darya. After the Soviet Union fell apart in 1991, the new republics of Tajikistan, Uzbekistan, and Turkmenistan simply inherited the old borders, which have not been challenged.

Afghan leaders still formally dispute the Pakistan border. The Durrani kingdom had originally stretched as far as the Indus River, encompassing the historic homeland of the Pashtun people, the dominant ethnic group in Afghanistan. Pakistan, upon its creation in 1947, inherited Great Britain's claim of sovereignty up to the Durand Line, drawn by British India in 1896. Afghanistan always viewed the line as merely a de facto expression of the then-current British Indian sphere of influence.

Topography

Rugged mountains occupy the northeast and center of the country; the Hindu Kush range occupies its geographic heart, dividing it into northern and southern regions. Average elevation in this region is 9,000 feet (2,743 m); the highest peak is Nowshak at 24,557 feet (7,484 m) above sea level. Other mountains are in the northwest (Parapamisus Range) and along the eastern border (Safed Koh); the extreme northeast of the country, in Badakhshan and the Pamir salient, has average elevations of around 13,000 feet (3,962 m).

In the south and southwest of the country are semideserts and plains, while narrow fertile plains stretch across the northern border. Most of the country is made up of high, rocky terrain and is not suitable for agriculture, which can be practiced on only about 12 percent of the land area. Until the 1970s, forests covered about 3 percent of the country, mostly at high altitudes in the eastern and central zones; war and illegal logging by the "timber mafia" have reduced tree cover to only 1 percent. As a result, the country presents an almost unrelieved rocky aspect from the air during most of the year.

Winter snow cover is the source of Afghanistan's many rivers; consequently, water level varies greatly across the year. Afghan geographer Hamidullah Amin divides the rivers into three systems: those that move toward Central Asia, those that feed the Indus, and those that water the Sistan region of Iran and Afghanistan. The major rivers are the Amu Darya, which rises in the Pamir Mountains near China, and, with its tributaries, constitutes the largely fertile border with Tajikistan and Uzbekistan; the Hari Rud, which begins in the Koh-i-Baba Range, runs through fertile lands south of Herat, and then serves as the northern part of the border with Iran before disappearing into the Kara Kum Desert; the Helmand, which begins in the eastern Hindu Kush and flows southwest some 800 miles before it reaches the marshlands near the Iranian border, supplying much irrigation water along the way; and the Kabul River, which starts in the mountains of Paghman west of Kabul and flows east into Pakistan, where it joins the Indus.

Climate

Afghanistan has an arid to semiarid climate. Temperatures vary greatly across the year, soaring to 120 degrees Fahrenheit (49 degrees Celsius) in the summer and then dropping in winter to as low as –12 degrees Fahrenheit (–12 degrees Celsius). Generally speaking, the country has hot, dry summers and cold winters with heavy snow at higher altitudes. Average precipitation is less than 10 inches (245 mm) per year. Kabul lies at approximately 6,000 feet (1,829 m) above sea level and enjoys comparatively mild temperatures.

Demographics

Population

31,056,997 (CIA estimate, 2006)
In the decades of war following 1979, around 6 million Afghans, one-third the 1979 population, left the country to live in refugee camps in Pakistan and Iran, and another few million became displaced within the country. About 1 million more Afghans were killed in the fighting. As of 2006, some 4 million refugees had returned to Afghanistan, and hundreds of thousands of internal refugees had moved back to their home

regions. However, many returnees were living in camps or ruined buildings within the country. The internal and external migrations have made it difficult to prepare an accurate census of the population, as does the continued presence of a seasonal nomad population. Many other refugees have preferred to remain permanent in their countries of refuge.

Growth Rate
2.67 percent (CIA estimate, 2006)

Infant Mortality
160 deaths per 1,000 births (CIA estimate, 2006)

Life Expectancy
43 years (CIA estimate, 2006)

Major Cities
Kabul is the largest city, with an estimated population of more than 3 million people; no other city approaches its size. Other important cities are Kandahar, Herat, Mazar-e Sharif, Jalalabad, Ghazni, Balkh, Bamiyan, Kunduz, and Farah; they all were founded in the distant past and have illustrious histories.

Languages
Pashto and Dari (Persian) are the two official languages of Afghanistan; together they are spoken by the large majority of the population. Other major languages include Uzbeki and Turkmeni, both Turkic languages, and Baluchi and Pashai, both Indo-European languages, as are Dari and Pashto. The constitution of January 2004 declared that any language spoken by the majority of the people in an area can be used as an official language there.

Religions
Almost the entire population adheres to Islam, about 80 percent of them Sunni and the rest Shiite. Most of the small Hindu, Sikh, and Jewish populations, together making up 1 percent of the whole, fled during the long years of warfare, and very few have since returned.

Economy

Gross Domestic Product (purchasing power equivalent)
$21.5 billion (estimate, 2005)

Currency
A new afghani was introduced in 2002; it is pegged at around 50 to the U.S. dollar, although the market rate varied widely from the official rate. Afghanistan was one of the poorest countries in the world even

before the Saur Revolution of 1978 plunged it into 25 years of war. Since the fall of the Taliban in November 2001, the economy has steadily improved with the help of foreign aid, but reconstruction is expected to take many years.

Agriculture

Major agricultural products are wheat, rice, barley, cotton, dairy goods, *qaraqul* (karakul) skins, other animal hides, maize, and vegetables. Afghanistan is also famous for its variety of fruits and nuts including grapes, apples, mulberries, pomegranates, melons, pine nuts, almonds, and pistachios. In recent years, opium has been the largest cash crop and the country's largest export, despite government and foreign eradication programs.

Natural Resources

Afghanistan has rich mineral resources, as yet underexploited, including natural gas, petroleum, coal, copper, salt, chrome, talc, lead, zinc, iron ore, and precious and semiprecious stones.

Industry

Textiles (including rugs), soap, ghee, furniture, shoes, fertilizer, and cement.

Commerce

Major trade partners are Russia, India, Pakistan, Germany, the United States, Japan, the United Kingdom, and the Czech Republic. Natural gas, nuts, carpets, *qaraqul* skins, and dried and fresh fruits are the major export commodities.

Appendix 2

CHRONOLOGY

Early History

3000–2000 B.C.E.	Beginning of urban civilization
2000–1000	Settlement of Indo-Iranian peoples; Afghanistan becomes a crossroad of Asia
550–331	Achaemenid Empire rules Afghanistan
331–150	Greek and Greco-Bactrian rule in northern Afghanistan and spread of Hellenistic art and culture; Mauryan Empire rules southern Afghanistan
125 B.C.E.–224 C.E.	Kushan Empire rules much of Afghanistan
224–651	Sassanian Empire rules much of Afghanistan

Rise of Islam

c. 650	Arab raiders enter Afghanistan
c. 700–961	Muslim dynasties rule Afghanistan: the Abbasids (Arab), Saffarids (Persian), and Samanids (Persian)
961–1151	Ghaznavid dynasty (Afghan Turkish) forms the first Afghan empire in 988
1151–1215	Ghurid dynasty (Afghan Turkish)
1215–21	Khorazmian dynasty (Turkish)
1221–82	Mongols under Genghis Khan invade Afghanistan, destroying many cities; western Afghanistan allotted to the Il-Khanate of Iran and Iraq, ruled under the Tajik Kart dynasty, which gains independence in 1232; remainder of Afghanistan becomes part of the Jagatai Khanate
1364–1506	Timur (Tamerlane) conquers Afghanistan and establishes the Timurid dynasty; Afghanistan experiences its golden age (Timurid Renaissance)
1451	Ghilzai Pashtuns from southeast Afghanistan found the Lodi dynasty in Delhi

1504–30	Babur founds the Mughal dynasty and conquers most of Afghanistan and northern India
1506–1747	Mughal Empire rules Kabul and Pashtunistan; Uzbeks of Samarkand rule Balkh; Persian Safavid dynasty rules western Afghanistan
1736	Nadir Shah becomes king of Persia

The Birth of Modern Afghanistan

1747–72	Ahmad Shah Abdali takes power after the assassination of Nadir Shah; establishes the Sadozai Durrani dynasty and founds modern Afghanistan
1772–1818	Rule of Ahmad's son Timur
1793–1818	Power struggles dominate the country's life during the remaining years under Sadozai Durrani rule
1819–26	Civil war between the Sadozai and Barakzai clans
1826–39	Dost Muhammad gains control of Kabul and consolidates his powers over the following years
1839–42	First Anglo-Afghan War
1863–68	Death of Dost Muhammad; his son Sher Ali gains power
1872	Russians and British establish the northern border of Afghanistan
1878–80	Second Anglo-Afghan War
1880–1901	Reign of Abdur Rahman Khan
1888	Western border with Persia finalized
1893	Establishment of Durand Line between Afghanistan and British India

Twentieth-Century Monarchy

1901–19	Reign of Habibullah Khan
1903	The country's first secondary school opens
1904	Persian border demarcated on the ground
1914–18	Afghanistan remains neutral during World War I
1919	Habibullah Khan is assassinated; his son Amanullah Khan takes power; Third Anglo-Afghan War leads to independence; Afghanistan signs Treaty of Friendship with Soviet Union
1923	King Amanullah proclaims Afghanistan's first constitution
1926	Nonaggression treaty signed between Soviet Union and Afghanistan

1927	First uniform currency, the afghani, introduced
1929	Civil war; Habibullah (Bacha-i-Saqao) rules for nine months
1929–33	Reign of King Muhammad Nadir Shah
1931	Nadir Shah proclaims new constitution based on 1923 document; Hanafi school of Sunni Islam gains official legal status; Bank-i-Melli (Afghan National Bank) founded
1933–73	Reign of King Muhammad Zahir
1934	Afghanistan joins the League of Nations; establishes diplomatic relations with the United States
1938	Da Afghanistan Bank founded
1940	Afghanistan declares neutrality in World War II
1946	Afghanistan joins the United Nations; Shah Mahmoud replaces Muhammad Hashim Khan as prime minister and introduces a series of liberal reforms; opposition newspapers, political groups, and student organizations form and demand additional reforms; brief liberal era ends in 1951–52
1947	New nation of Pakistan closes its borders with Afghanistan
1953–63	Muhammad Daoud Khan replaces Shah Mamoud as prime minister; under Daoud educational system, women's rights, and economy improve; border dispute with Pakistan escalates
1954–55	Series of trade, development, and military agreements signed with Soviet Union; United States increases assistance
1963	Prime Minister Daoud resigns and is replaced by Muhammad Yousuf
1964	New constitution establishes a constitutional monarchy with a bicameral legislature
1965	Following student protests, Yousuf is replaced as prime minister by Muhammad Hashim Maiwandwal, leader of the Progressive Democratic Party; Nur Muhammad Taraki founds the People's Democratic Party of Afghanistan (PDPA); Gholam Muhammad Nyazi establishes the Jamiat-i-Islami (Society of Islam); women vote for the first time in national elections

1967	Nur Ahmed Etemadi becomes prime minister when Maiwandwal takes seriously ill
1969–72	About 100,000 die due to widespread famine
1972	Musa Shafiq named prime minister

A Coup and a Revolution

1973–78	Daoud establishes a republic in a palace coup; King Zahir goes into exile
1977	Daoud promulgates new constitution, establishing a one-party state
1978	Saur Revolution: President Daoud is killed in coup by Communists, who establish Democratic Republic of Afghanistan; Nur Muhammad Taraki becomes head of state; Secret police agency AGSA (Da Afghanistan de Gato de Satalo Adara) founded; New Treaty of Friendship and Cooperation is signed with Soviet Union

Soviet Afghanistan

1979	President Taraki is assassinated by Hafizullah Amin; Soviet Union invades Afghanistan; President Hafizullah Amin is killed; Babrak Karmal is appointed president
1980s	Increasing resistance against the Soviet occupation
1985	Islamic Union of Afghan Mujahideen (IUAM) forms to fight Soviets; Mikhail Gorbachev comes to power in Soviet Union
1986	Gorbachev withdraws about 8,000 troops from Afghanistan
	Karmal steps down as president and is replaced by Muhammad Najibullah
1988	Soviet Union and Afghanistan sign the Geneva Accords
1989	Soviet Union withdraws its forces from Afghanistan; Afghan Interim Government is created by Afghan exiles in Pakistan; Osama bin Laden founds al-Qaeda; Mujahideen lay siege to Jalalabad for seven months but fail to take the city
1992	Mujahideen take Kabul; President Najibullah steps down; Islamic Republic of Afghanistan is

established with an interim mujahideen government led by Burhanuddin Rabbani

Mujahideen Rule

1992–94   Afghanistan is ruled by a patchwork of competing local warlords, including Sayyid Mansur Naderi in Baghlan Province, Ismail Khan in the western provinces, Ahmad Shah Massoud in the northeastern provinces, and Abdul Rashid Dostum in the north; Gulbuddin Hekmatyar fights in the regions north of Kabul as well as in the Pashtun south

1992–96   Fighting between competing warlords in Kabul causes an estimated 50,000 civilian deaths in the city; up to 70 percent of Kabul's buildings are destroyed

1994   With assistance from Pakistan, the Taliban movement establishes control over southern Pashtun lands of Afghanistan

1995   Ahmad Shad Massoud wins control of Kabul in March

The Taliban Era

1996   Taliban takes Kabul and assassinates former president Najibullah

1998   United States attacks al-Qaeda training camps inside Afghanistan; United Nations withdraws its staff from Kandahar

1999   United States and United Nations impose trade sanctions on Afghanistan

2000   Al-Qaeda attack against the U.S. destroyer *Cole* in Yemenite waters

2001   Taliban destroys two monumental statues of Buddha in the Bamiyan Valley in March; Massoud is killed by al-Qaeda agents in September; almost 3,000 people are killed in al-Qaeda attacks against the World Trade Center in New York City and the Pentagon in Washington, D.C.; United States bombs Afghanistan in October to destroy terrorist camps created by Osama bin Laden; Taliban are removed from power in November; at a conference held in Bonn, Hamid Karzai is named as chairman of the interim government in Afghanistan for six months, beginning in December

The Post-Taliban Era

2002 Muhammad Zahir Shah returns from his nearly 30-year exile in Italy

2003 In June, Karzai holds a *loya jirga* of 1,450 delegates from the 362 administrative districts to elect the interim government president for the next two years; delegates reelect Karzai; in December, a constitutional *loya jirga* is held in Kabul to review the draft constitution

2004 On January 4, the *loya jirga* ratifies the new constitution and declares Afghanistan an Islamic republic; constitution establishes a presidential form of government, with important powers reserved for the National Assembly; in an attempt to rein in warlords, Karzai removes Ismail Khan from the governorship of Heart in September; violent protests follow; in October, Karzai is elected president in country's first democratic presidential elections

2005 In May, details emerge of alleged prisoner abuse by U.S. forces at Bagram Military Base in Afghanistan; in September, country's first parliamentary and provincial elections in more than 30 years take place; new parliament holds its first session in December

2006 More than 4 million refugees return from Pakistan and Iran; Taliban units increase local attacks in south and east; Kabul hit by suicide bombs; NATO takes over U.S. military role in October

Appendix 3

Bibliography

Adamec, Ludwig W. *Historical Dictionary of Afghanistan: Third Edition.* Lanham, Md.: Scarecrow Press, 2003.

Afghan Independent Human Rights Commission. Annual Report, 2005. Available online. URL: www.aihrc.org.af/anl_rpt=2005.pdf.

Afghan Network iNteractive. "Khushal Khan Khattak." Available online: URL: http://www.afghan-network.net/biographies/khattack.html. Accessed September 1, 2006.

Afghan Tourist Organization. *Afghanistan Tourist Information.* Kabul: Afghan Tourist Organization, 1977.

Afghanan Dot Net. "Afghanistan History: Mongols (1220–1332)." 2005. Available online. URL: http://www.afghanan.net/afghanistan/mongols/htm. Accessed May 1, 2006.

Ahmed-Ghosh. "A History of Women in Afghanistan." *Journal of International Women's Studies* 4, no. 3 (May 2003).

Ali, Mohammad. *A Cultural History of Afghanistan.* Kabul, Afghanistan: Printed by Malik Muhammad Saeed at the Punjab Educational Press, Lahore, Pakistan, 1964.

Allchin, F. R., and N. Hammond. *The Archaeology of Afghanistan from Earliest Times to the Timurid Period.* London, New York: Academic Press, 1978.

Amin, Hamidullah, and Gordon B. Schilz. *A Geography of Afghanistan.* Omaha, Neb.: Center for Afghanistan Studies, 1976.

Amstutz, J. Bruce. *Afghanistan: The First Five Years of Soviet Occupation.* Washington, D.C.: National Defense University, 1986.

Atta, Yama, and Haidari, Hashmat. "An Afghan Intellect: Mahmoud Tarzi." afghanmagazine.com. September 1997. Available online. URL: http://www.afghanmagazine.com/articles/tarzi.html. Accessed May 2, 2006.

Benawa A. R. "Selections from Early and Contemprary Pashto Literature." *Pasto Quarterly* 5, no. 1 (Autumn 1981): 1–2.

Boaz, John. *Afghanistan.* San Diego, Calif.: Greenhaven, 2004.

Bollyn, Christopher. "Mineral-Rich Afghanistan a Valuable Corporate Property." Available online. URL: http://www.americanfreepress.net/NWO/Mineral-Rich_Afghanistan_a_Val/mineral-rich_afghanistan_a_val.html. Accessed May 10, 2006.

Brezhnev, Leonid. *On events in Afghanistan.* Moscow: Novosti Press, 1980, pp. 1–23. Available online. URL: http://agitprop.org.au/lefthistory/19800113_lb_on_events_in_afghanistan_php. Accessed May 5, 2006.

Brzezinski, Zbigniew. "U.S. Memos on Afghanistan: From Brzezinski to President Carter." Episode 20: Soldiers of God. CNN Interactive. Available online: URL: http://edition.cnn.com/SPECIALS/cold.war/episodes/20/documents/brez.carter/. Accessed May 10, 2006.

Central Intelligence Agency. "Afghanistan." *The World Fact Book.* Available online. URL: http://www.cia.gov/cia/publications/factbook/geos/af.html/. Accessed May 10, 2006.

Danishjuyan-i Musalman Payraw Khatt-i Iman. *GDR Ambassador Reports That Soviets Hope to Replace Prime Minister Amin with a Broader Based Government, July 18, 1979.* Tehran, Iran: Danishjuyan Musalman Payraw Khatt-i Iman, 1979.

Diamonds Gemstones Jewelry. "Koh-i Noor Diamonds." Available online. URL: http://www.diamondsgemstonesjewelry.com/diamond-famous/koh-i-noor-diamond.aspx. Accessed May 10, 2006.

Dupree, Louis. *Afghanistan.* 2d ed. Princeton, N.J.: Princeton University Press, 1980.

———. *The 1969 Student Demonstration in Kabul.* Hanover, N.H.: American Universities Field Staff, 1979.

Dupree, Nancy Hatch. A *Historical Guide to Afghanistan.* Kabul: Afghan Air Authority, Afghan Tourist Organization, 1973.

Embassy of Afghanistan in Washington, D.C. Available online. URL: http://www.embassyofafghanistan.org. Accessed May 10, 2006.

Ewans, Martin. *Afghanistan: A Short History of Its People and Politics.* New York: HarperCollins, 2002.

Forbes, Archibald. *The Afghan Wars, 1839–42 and 1878–80.* London: Seeley and Co., 1892.

Gasper, Phil. "Afghanistan, the CIA, bin Laden, and the Taliban." The Third World Traveler. November–December, 2001. Available online. URL: http://www.thirdworldtraveler.com/Afghanistan/Afghanistan_CIA_Taliban.html. Accessed May 10, 2006.

Gregorian, Vartan. *The Emergence of Modern Afghanistan: Politics of Reform and Modernization, 1880–1946.* Stanford, Calif.: Stanford University Press, 1969.

Guha, Analendu. "The Economy of Afghanistan during Amanullah's Reign, 1919–1929." *International Studies.* 9, no. 2 (October 1967): 161–182.

Hammond, Thomas T. *Red Flag over Afghanistan: The Communist Coup, the Soviet Invasion, and the Consequences.* Boulder, Colo.: Westview Press, 1984.

Herold, Marc W. "War and Modernity: Hard Times for Afghanistan's Kuchi Nomads." Cursor. Available online. URL: http://www.cursor. org/stories/kuchi.html. Accessed May 10, 2006.

Ijaz, Mansqor. "Clinton Let Bin Laden Slip Away and Metastasize." *Los Angeles Times.* December 5, 2001. B. 13.

Johnson, Chris. *Afghanistan.* 2d ed. Oxford U.K.: Oxfam, 2004.

The Kabul Times Annual. 1st ed. Kabul, 1967.

Khalilzad, Zalmay. *Prospects for the Afghan Interim Government.* Santa Monica, Calif.: RAND, 1991.

Knobloch, Edgar. *Beyond the Oxus.* London: Benn Limited, 1972.

MacKay, Ernest John Henry. *The Indus Civilization.* London: Lovat Dickson and Thompson, 1935.

Macmunn, George Fletcher. *Afghanistan: From Darius to Amanullah.* Quetta, Pakistan: Gosha-e-Adab, 1977.

Madani, Hamed. *Afghanistan.* San Diego, Calif.: Greenhaven Press, 2004.

Miller, John. "Greetings, America. My Name Is Osama Bin Laden." Frontline. 1999. Available online. URL: http://www.pbsorg/ wgbh/pages/frontline/shows/binladen/who/miller.html. Accessed May 8, 2006.

National Security Archives, U.S. *Afghanistan, the Making of U.S. Policy, 1973–1990.* Washington, DC: National Security Archives, 1990.

Newell, Richard S. *The Politics of Afghanistan.* Ithaca, N.Y.: Cornell University Press, 1972.

Palka, E. J. *Geographic Perspectives: Afghanistan.* Gilford, Conn.: McGraw-Hill/Dushkin, 2004.

"Radio-TV Address of President Najibullah." *Afghanistan Forum* 20, no. 3 (May 1992): page 33.

Rasanayagam, Angelo. *Afghanistan: A Modern History.* New York: I. B. Taurus, 2003.

Republic of Afghanistan. *Social, Economic and Development Plan.* Translated and edited by United Nations Development Programs. Kabul: United Nations Development Program, 1975.

Roberts, Jeffery. *The Origins of Conflict in Afghanistan.* Westport, Conn.: Praeger, 2003.

Rodenburg, Willem F. *The Trade in Wild Animal Furs in Afghanistan.* Kabul: United Nations Development Programs, 1977.

Sastri, Kedar Nath. *New Light on the Indus Civilization.* Delhi, India: Atma Ram and Sons, 1965.

Schreiber, Gerhard, Bernd Stegemam, and Detlef Vogel. *Germany and the Second World War, Volume III.* Translated by Dean S. McMurray, Ewald Osers, and Louise Wilmot. New York: Oxford University Press, 1995.

Stevens, Ira M. *Agricultural Production, Industrial Production and Marketing: Helmand Valley Afghanistan.* Kabul: 1963.

Synovitz, Ron. "Afghanistan: Experts Say Soviet Military Withdrawal Holds Lessons for Future (Part 1)." Radio Free Europe. February 13, 2004. Available Online. http://www.rferl.org/featuresarticleprint/2004/02/d251c79b-277d-42a8-a8b3-fb0324a72342.html. Accessed May 10, 2006.

Tanner, Stephen. *Afghanistan: A Military History from Alexander the Great to the Fall of the Taliban.* Cambridge, Mass.: Do Capo Press, 2002.

Turton, David, and Peter Marsden. *Taking Refugees for a Ride? The Politics of Refugee Return to Afghanistan.* Afghanistan Research and Evaluation Unit, 2002.

Wahab, Shaista. 1993. *United States–Afghanistan Diplomatic Relations: September–December 1979: Hafizullah Amin's Struggle for Survival.* Master's thesis. University of Nebraska at Omaha.

Walker, P. F. *Afghanistan: A Short Account of Afghanistan, Its History, and our Dealings with it.* London: Griffith and Farran, 1881.

Wikipedia: The Free Encyclopedia. "Brezhnev Doctrine." Available online. URL: http/en.wikipedia.org/wiki/Brezhnev_Doctrine. Updated April 22, 2006.

Appendix 4

Suggested Reading

A Brief History of Afghanistan is intended to provide general information on the country. The following suggested reading is provided for in-depth research on specific aspects of the topic.

Introduction: The Challenge of Afghanistan

Ali, Mohammad. *A Cultural History of Afghanistan.* Kabul: Printed by Malik Muhammad Saeed at the Punjab Educational Press, Lahore, Pakistan, 1964.

Bacon, Elizabeth Emaline. 1951. *The Hazara Mongols of Afghanistan: A Study in social organization.* Ph.D. diss., University of California.

Barfield, Thomas Jefferson. *The Central Asian Arabs of Afghanistan: Pastoral Nomadism in Transition.* Austin: University of Texas Press, 1981.

Bellew, Henry Walter. *The Races of Afghanistan.* Delhi, India: Shree Publishing, 1982.

Dupree, Ann, Louis Dupree, and A. Motamedi. *A Guide to the Kabul Museum, the National Museum of Afghanistan.* 2d ed. Kabul: Afghan Tourist Organization, 1968.

Dupree, Louis. *Afghanistan.* 2d ed. Princeton, N.J.: Princeton University Press, 1980.

Singh, Ganda. *Ahmad Shah Durrani, Father of Modern Afghanistan.* Bombay: Asia Publishing House, 1959.

Tabibi, Abd al-Hakim. *Afghanistan, a Nation in Love with Freedom.* Cedar Rapids, Iowa: Igram Press, 1985.

Land and People

Abdullah, Shareq. *Mineral Resources of Afghanistan.* 2d ed. Kabul: Republic of Afghanistan, Ministry of Mines and Industries, Afghan Geological and Mines Survey 1977.

Ali, Mohammad. *Aryana: or, Ancient Afghanistan.* Kabul: Historical Society of Afghanistan, 1957.

Anderson, Clay J. *A Banking and Credit System for the Economic Development of Afghanistan.* Washington, DC: Robert R. Nathan Associates, 1967.

Bali, Anila. 1985. *The Russo-Afghan Boundary Demarcation 1884–95: Britain and the Russian Threat to the Security of India.* Ph.D. diss., University of Ulster.

Barakat, Sultan. *Reconstructing War-Torn Societies: Afghanistan.* Houndmills, U.K.; New York: Palgrave Macmillan, 2004.

Bechhoefer, William B. *Serai Lahori: Traditional Housing in the Old City of Kabul.* College Park: University of Maryland School of Architecture, 1975.

Central Intelligence Agency. *Afghanistan-Pakistan Border.* Washington, DC: Central Intelligence Agency, 1988.

Chakravartty, Sumit. *Dateline Kabul: An Eye-Witness Report on Afghanistan Today.* New Delhi, India: Eastern Book Centre, 1983.

Curzon, George Nathaniel. *The Pamirs and the Source of the Oxus.* London: Royal Geographical Society, 1896.

Department of Forestry, Afghanistan. *Final Report of the Department of Forestry.* Kabul: Department of Forestry, 1954.

Dupree, Louis. *Afghanistan, 1977: Does Trade Plus Aid Guarantee Development?* Hanover, N.H.: American Universities Field Staff, 1977.

Dupree, Nancy Hatch. *Kabul City.* New York: Afghanistan Council of the Asia Society, 1975.

Dupree, Nancy Hatch, Louis Dupree, and A. Motamedi. *The National Museum of Afghanistan: An Illustrated Guide.* Kabul: Afghan Air Authority, 1974.

Economic and Social Commission for Asia and the Pacific. *Atlas of Mineral Resources of the ESCAP Region.* Vol II: *Geology and Mineral Resources of Afghanistan.* New York: United Nations, 1995.

Foreign Office, Great Britain. *Exchange of Notes between His Majesty's Government in the United Kingdom and the Government of India and the Government of Afghanistan in Regard to the Boundary between India and Afghanistan in the Neighborhood of Arnawai and Dokalim.* London: H.M. Stationery Office, 1934.

Fry, Maxwell J. *The Afghan Economy: Money, Finance, and the Critical Constraints to Economic Development.* Leiden, Netherlands: Brill, 1974.

Ganss, Ortwin. *On the Geology of SE Afghanistan.* Kabul: Afghan Geological and Mineral Survey, 1970.

Gerard, M. G. *Report on the Proceedings of the Pamir Boundary Commission.* Calcutta, India: Office of the Superintendent of Government Printing, 1897.

Ghani, Ashraf. 1982. *Production and Domination: Afghanistan, 1747–1901*. Ph.D. diss., Columbia University.

Grace, Jo. *One Hundred Households in Kabul: A Study of Winter Vulnerability, Coping Strategies, and the Impact of Cash-for-Work Programmes on the Lives of the "Vulnerable."* Kabul: Afghanistan Research and Evaluation Unit, 2003.

Gulzad, Zalmay. *External Influences and the Development of the Afghan State in the Nineteenth Century.* New York: P. Lang, 1994.

Gulzad, Zalmay Ahmad. 1991. *The History of the Delimitation of the Durand Line and the Development of the Afghan State (1838–1898).* Ph.D. diss., University of Wisconsin–Madison.

Hendrikson, Kurt H. *Afghanistan's Foreign Trade, 1336–1348 and Its Prospective Development During the Fourth Five Year Plan, 1351–1355.* Kabul: German Economic Advisory Group, 1972.

Holdich, Sir Thomas Hungerford. *The Indian Borderland, 1880–1900.* Delhi, India: Gian Publishing, 1987.

Kamrany, Nake M. 1960. *The First Five Year Plan of Afghanistan (1956–61): An Economic Evaluation.* Ph.D. diss., University of Southern California.

Khan, Azmat Hayat. *The Durand Line: Its Geo-Strategic Importance.* Peshawar, Pakistan: Area Study Centre (Russia & Central Asia), University of Peshawar, 2000.

Lamb, Alastair. *Asian Frontiers: Studies in a Continuing Problem.* New York: Praeger, 1968.

Malleson, George Bruce. *The Russo-Afghan Question and the Invasion of India.* London: G. Routledge and Sons, 1885.

McMahon, A. H. *Letters on the Baluch-Afghan Boundary Commission of 1896 Under Captain A. H. McMahon.* Calcutta, India: Printed at the Baptist Mission Press, 1909.

Mellors, Robert John 1995. *Two Studies in Central Asian Seismology: A Teleseismic Study of the Pamir: Hindu Kush Seismic Zone and Analysis of Data from the Kyrgyzstan Broadband Seismic Network.* Ph.D. diss., Indiana University.

Michel, Aloys Arthur. *The Kabul, Kunduz, and Helmand Valleys and the National Economy of Afghanistan: A Study of Regional Resources and the Comparative Advantages of Development.* Washington, DC: National Academy of Sciences, 1959.

Ministry of Planning, Afghanistan. *Draft Fourth Five Year Plan: National Development Plan for Afghanistan, 1351–1355 (1972/73–1976/77).* Kabul: Ministry of Planning, 1973.

———. *Revised Third Five Year Plan Presented to the Jirga.* Kabul: Ministry of Planning, 1968.

———. *Second Five Year Plan, 1341–45 (March 1962–March 1967).* Kabul: Ministry of Planning, 1963.

———. *Seven Years Economic and Social Development Plan of the Republic of Afghanistan.* Kabul: Ministry of Planning, 1976.

Paul, Arthur. *Constraints on Afghanistan's Economic Development and Prospects for Future Progress.* New York: Afghanistan Council, Asia Society, 1973.

Public Administration Service. *A Final Report on the Land Inventory Project of Afghanistan: January 1972.* Chicago: Public Administration Service, 1972.

Robert R. Nathan Associates and Louis Berger International, Inc. *Final Report: Mineral Resources in Afghanistan.* Arlington, Va.: Nathan Associates, Inc., and Louis Berger International, Inc., February 1992.

Samizay, M. Rafi. *Urban Growth and Residential Prototypes in Kabul, Afghanistan.* Cambridge: School of Architecture and Planning, Massachusetts Institute of Technology, 1974.

Schofield, Victoria. *North-West Frontier and Afghanistan.* New Delhi, India: D.K. Agencies (P), 1984.

Schutte, Stefan. *Urban Vulnerability in Afghanistan: Case Studies from Three Cities.* Kabul. Afghanistan Research and Evaluation Unit, 2004.

Trosper, Joseph F. *The Status of Insurance in Afghanistan.* Bloomington: Indiana University, 1972.

World Bank, Country Programs Department. *Afghanistan, the Journey to Economic Development.* 2 vols. Washington: World Bank, 1978.

Yate, Arthur Campbell. *England and Russia Face to Face in Asia: Travels with the Afghan Boundary Commission.* Edinburgh; London: W. Blackwood and Sons, 1887.

Yate, Charles Edward. *Northern Afghanistan; or, Letters from the Afghan Boundary Commission.* Edinburgh; London: W. Blackwood and sons, 1888.

Zekrya, Mir-Ahmed B. 1976. *Planning and Development in Afghanistan: A Case of Maximum Foreign Aid and Minimum Growth.* Ph.D. diss., Johns Hopkins University.

Early History (Prehistory–651)

Bombaci, Alessio. *The Kufic Inscription in Persian Verses in the Court of the Royal Palace of Mas'ud III at Ghazni.* Rome: Is. M. E. O., 1966.

Bradshaw, Gillian. *Horses of Heaven.* 1st ed. New York: Doubleday, 1991.

Holt, Frank Lee. *Alexander the Great and Bactria: The Formation of a Greek Frontier in Central Asia.* Leiden, Netherlands; New York: E.J. Brill, 1988.

———— 1984. *Beyond Plato's Pond: The Greeks and Barbarians in Bactria.* Ph.D. diss., University of Virginia.

————. *Discovering the Lost History of Ancient Afghanistan (Hellenistic Bactria).* Chicago: The Ancient World, 1984.

————. *Thundering Zeus: The Making of Hellenistic Bactria.* Berkeley: University of California Press, 1999.

International Conference on History, Archeology, and Culture of Central Asia in the Kushan Period. *Kushan Studies in U.S.S.R.: Papers Presented by the Soviet Scholars at the Unesco Conference on History, Archaeology, and Culture of Central Asia in the Kushan Period.* Calcutta, India: Indian Studies, Past and Present, 1970.

Ligabue, Giancarlo, and Sandro Salvatori, eds. *Bactria: An Ancient Civilization from the Sands of Afghanistan.* Venice, Italy: Erizzo, 1988.

Morris, Rekha. 1983. *Prolegomena to a Study of Gandhara Art.* Ph.D. diss., University of Chicago.

Narain, A. K. *The Indo-Greeks.* Oxford: Clarendon Press, 1962.

Narain, R. B. *Buddhist Remains in Afghanistan.* 1st ed. Varanasi, India: Kala Prakashan, 1991.

Prinsep, Henry Thoby, ed. *Historical Results from Bactrian Coins and Other Discoveries in Afghanistan: Based on the Note Books and the Coin-Cabinet of James.* 1844. Reprint, Chicago: Ares Publishers, 1974.

Rawlinson, Hugh George. *Bactria from the Earliest Times to the Extinction of Bactrio-Greek Rule in the Punjab.* Bombay, India: "Times of India" Office, 1909.

Rosenfield, John M. *The Dynastic Arts of the Kushans.* Berkeley: University of California Press, 1967.

Sarianidi, Viktor Ivanovich. *The Golden Hoard of Bactria: From the Tillya-tepe Excavations in Northern Afghanistan.* Translated by Arthur Shkarovsky-Raffe. Photography by Leonid Bogdanov and Vladimir Terebenin. New York: H.N. Abrams; Leningrad: Aurora Art Publishers, 1985.

Schlumberger, Daniel. *The Excavations at Surkh Kotal and the Problem of Hellenism in Bactria and India.* London: Oxford University Press 1962.

Schmidt, Carolyn Woodford. 1990. *Bodhisattva Headdresses and Hair Styles in the Buddhist Art of Gandhara and Related Regions of Swat and Afghanistan.* Ph.D. diss., Ohio State University.

Sidky, H. *The Greek Kingdom of Bactria: From Alexander to Eucratides the Great.* Lanham, Md.: University Press of America, 2000.

Sims-Williams, Nicholas. *New Light on Ancient Afghanistan: The Decipherment of Bactrian; an Inaugural Lecture Delivered on February 1996.* London: School of Oriental and African Studies, University of London, 1997.

Srivastava, V. C. *The Pre-Historic Afghanistan: A Source Book.* 1st ed. Allahabad, India: Ideological Publications, 1982.

Tarn, William Woodthorpe. *The Greeks in Bactria & India.* 3d ed. Chicago: Ares, 1985.

Varma, Kalidindi Mohana. *Technique of Gandharan and Indo-Afghan Stucco Images.* Santiniketan, India: Proddu, 1987.

Vogelsang, W. J. *The Rise and Organisation of the Achaemenid Empire: The Eastern Iranian Evidence.* Leiden, Netherlands; New York: Brill, 1992.

Wenzel, Marian. *Echoes of Alexander the Great: Silk Route Portraits from Gandhara: A Private Collection.* London: Eklisa Anstalt, 2000.

Wilson, Horace Hayman, and Charles Masson. *Ariana Antiqua: A Descriptive Account of the Antiquities and Coins of Afghanistan.* Delhi, India: Oriental Publishers, 1971.

Wood, Michael. *In the Footsteps of Alexander the Great: A Journey from Greece to Asia.* Berkeley: University of California Press, 1997.

From the Rise of Islam to the Afghan State (651–1747)

Bahari, Ebadollah. *Bihzad, Master of Persian Painting.* London; New York: I.B. Tauris Publishers, 1996.

Bosworth, Clifford Edmund. *Early Sources for the History of the First Four Ghaznevid Sultans (977–1041).* London: Islamic Quarterly, 1961.

———. *The Ghaznavids: Their Empire in Afghanistan and Eastern Iran, 994–1040.* 2d ed. Beirut, Lebanon: Librairie du Liban, 1973.

———. *The Later Ghaznavids: Splendour and Decay: The Dynasty in Afghanistan and Northern India, 1040–1186.* New York: Columbia University Press, 1977.

———. *The Medieval History of Iran, Afghanistan, and Central Asia.* London: Variorum Reprints, 1977.

Bruijn, J. T. P. *Of Piety and Poetry: The Interaction of Religion and Literature in the Life and Works of Hakim Sanai of Ghazna.* Leiden, Netherlands: Brill, 1983.

Firishtah, Muhammad Qasim Hindu Shah Mahomed Kasim Astarabadi, and Sir George Olof Roos-Keppel. *Translation of the Tarikh-i-Sultan*

Mahmud-i-Ghaznavi: or, the History of Sultan Mahmud of Ghazni. Allahabad, India: Printed at the Pioneer Press, 1901.

Galdieri, Eugenio. *A Few Conservation Problems Concerning Several Islamic Monuments in Ghazni (Afghanistan): Technical Report and Notes on a Plan of Action.* Translated by Jan McGilvray. Rome: Istituto italiano per il Medio ed Estremo Oriente, Centro Restauri, 1978.

Hashmi, Yusuf Abbas. *Successors of Mahmud of Ghazna: in Political, Cultural, and Administrative Perspective.* 1st ed. Karachi, Pakistan: South Asian Printers and Publishers, 1988.

Herrmann, John A., and Cecil Robert Borg. *Retracing Genghis Khan.* Boston; New York: Lothrop, Lee and Shepard, 1937.

Nazim, Muhammad. *The Life and Times of Sultan Mahmud of Ghazna.* 2d ed. New Delhi, India: Munshiram Manoharlal, 1971.

Nicolle, David. *The Mongol Warlords: Genghis Khan, Kublai Khan, Hulegu, Tamerlane.* Poole, U.K.: Firebird, 1990.

Potter, Lawrence Goddard. 1992. *The Kart Dynasty of Herat: Religion and Politics in Medieval Iran.* Ph.D. diss., Columbia University.

Ramstedt, Gustaf John. *Seven Journeys Eastward, 1898–1912: Among the Cheremis, Kalmyks, Mongols, and in Turkestan, and to Afghanistan.* Translated and edited by John R. Krueger. Bloomington, Ind.: Mongolia Society, 1978.

Samizay, Rafi. *Islamic Architecture in Herat: A Study towards Conservation.* Kabul: Research Section of International Project for Herat Monuments, Ministry of Information and Culture, Democratic Republic of Afghanistan, 1981.

Schurmann, Franz. *The Mongols of Afghanistan: An Ethnography of the Moghols and Related Peoples of Afghanistan.* 's-Gravenhage: Mouton, 1962.

Shephard Parpagliolo, Maria Teresa. *Kabul: The Bagh-i Babur; A Project and a Research into the Possibilities of a Complete Reconstruction.* Rome: IsMEO, 1972.

'Utbi, Abu al-Nasr 'Abd al-Jabbar, James Reynolds, and al-Jarbadakani Nasib ibn Zafar. *The Kitab-i-Yamini: Historical Memoirs of the Amir Sabaktagin, and the Sultan Mahmud of Ghazna, Early Conquerors of Hindustan, and Founders of the Ghaznavide Dynasty.* Translated by Rev. James Reynolds. London: Oriental Translation Fund of Great Britain and Ireland, 1858.

Weatherford, J. McIver. *Genghis Khan and the Making of the Modern World.* 1st ed. New York: Crown, 2004.

The Birth of Modern Afghanistan (1747–1901)

Abdul Rahman Khan. *The Life of Abdur Rahman, Amir of Afghanistan.* Edited by Sultan Mahomed Khan. Karachi, Pakistan: Oxford University Press, 1980.

Army of India, Intelligence Branch. *Frontier and Overseas Expeditions from India. Compiled in the Intelligence Branch, Division of the Chief of the Staff Army Head Quarters.* 6 vols. Simla, India: Government. Monotype Press, 1907–11.

Christian Literature Society for India. *Afghanistan and Its Late Amir: With Some Account of Baluchistan.* London: Christian Literature Society for India, 1902.

Colquhoun, Archibald Ross. *Russia against India: the Struggle for Asia.* London; New York: Harper, 1900.

E., J. M. *The Story of the Frontier Province.* Peshawar, Pakistan: Government Press, 1922.

Gardner, Alexander Haughton Campbell. *Soldier and Traveler: Memoirs of Alexander Gardner, Colonel of Artillery in the Service of Maharaja Ranjit Singh.* Edited by Hugh Pearse. Edinburgh: W. Blackwood, 1898.

Gillham-Thomsett, Richard. *Kohat, Kuram, and Khost; or, Experiences and Adventures in the Late Afghan War.* London: Remington and Company, 1884.

Gray, John Alfred. *At the Court of the Amir of Afghanistan.* London; New York: Kegan Paul, 2002.

Gregson, J. Gelson. *Through the Khyber Pass to Sherpore Camp, Cabul: An Account of Temperance Work among our Soldiers in the Cabul Field Force.* London: Elliot Stock, 1883.

Hanna, Henry Bathurst. *Can Russia Invade India?* Westminster, U.K.: A. Constable, 1895.

Harlan, Josiah. *Central Asia: Personal Narrative of General Josiah Harlan, 1823–1841.* Edited by Frank E. Ross. London: Luzac, 1939.

Haughton, John Colpoys. *Char-ee-kar and Service There with the 4th Goorkha Regiment (Shah Shooja's Force), in 1841: An Episode of the First Afghan War.* 2d ed. London: Provost, 1879.

Kakar, M. Hasan. *Afghanistan: A Study in International Political Developments, 1880–1896.* Lahore: Punjab Educational Press, 1971.

Larminie, E. M. *Report on the Fortress of Ghazni.* Chatham, U.K.: Royal Engineer Institute, 1882.

Macintyre, Ben. *The Man Who Would Be King: The First American in Afghanistan.* 1st ed. New York: Farrar, Straus and Giroux, 2004.

MacMunn, George Fletcher. *Afghanistan: From Darius to Amanullah*. London: G. Bell and Sons, 1929.

Martin, Frank A. *Under the Absolute Amir.* London: Harper and Brothers, 1907.

Morrish, C. *Afghanistan in the Melting Pot*. Lahore, Pakistan: The "Civil and Military Gazette" Press, 1930.

Noelle-Karimi, Christine. *State and Tribe in Nineteenth-Century Afghanistan: The Reign of Amir Dost Muhammad Khan (1826–1863)*. Richmond, U.K.: Curzon Press, 1997.

Northbrook, Thomas George Baring. *The Afghan Question: Speech of the Earl of Northbrook, in the Guildhall, Winchester, on the 11th of November* 1878. London: National Press Agency, 1878.

O'Ballance, Edgar. *Afghan Wars*. London: Brassey's, 2002.

Roberts, Jeffery J. *The Origins of Conflict in Afghanistan*. Westport, Conn.: Praeger, 2003.

Thornton, Archibald Paton. *Afghanistan in Anglo-Russian Diplomacy, 1869–1873*. London: Cambridge University Press, 1955.

Verrier, Anthony. *Francis Younghusband and the Great Game*. London: Jonathan Cape (Random Century Group), 1991.

Wheeler, Stephen. *The Ameer Abdur Rahman*. New York: Frederick Warne and Company, 1895.

Yapp, Malcolm. *The Revolutions of 1841–2 in Afghanistan*. London: School of Oriental and African Studies, 1964.

Twentieth-Century Monarchy (1901–1973)

Dixit, Jyotindra Nath. *An Afghan Diary: Zahir Shah to Taliban*. New Delhi, India: Konark Publishers, 2000.

Dupree, Louis. *The Decade of Daoud Ends: Implications of Afghanistan's Change of Government*. New York: American Universities Field Staff, 1963.

———. *An Informal Talk with Prime Minister Daud*. New York: American Universities Field Staff, 1959.

———. *An Informal Talk with King Mohammad Zahir of Afghanistan*. New York: American Universities Field Staff, 1963.

———. *An Informal Talk with Prime Minister Daud*. New York: American Universities Field Staff, 1959.

———. *The Mountains Go to Mohammad Zahir: Observations on Afghanistan's Reactions to Visits from Nixon, Bulganin-Khrushchev, Eisenhower and Khrushchev*. New York: American Universities Field Staff, 1960.

Katrak, Sorab K. H. *Through Amanullah's Afghanistan, a Book of Travel*. Karachi, Pakistan: Printed by D. N. Patel, 1929.

Miraki, Mohammed Daud 2000. *Factors of Underdevelopment in Afghanistan, 1919–2000*. Ph.D. diss., University of Illinois at Chicago.

Mokhtarzada, Shahla 1996. *The Social Origins of the Neopatrimonial State in Afghanistan*. Ph.D. diss., University of California, Davis.

Nassimi, Azim M. 1997. *An Ethnography of Political Leaders in Afghanistan*. Ph.D. diss., Ball State University.

Nawid, Senzil K. 1987. *Aman-Allah and the Afghan Ulama: Reaction to Reforms, 1919–29*. Ph.D. diss., University of Arizona.

Overby, Paul. *Amanullah: The Hard Case of Reform in Afghanistan*. New York: Afghanistan Forum, 1992.

Poullada, Leon B. *Reform and Rebellion in Afghanistan, 1919–1929: King Amanullah's Failure to Modernize a Tribal Society*. Ithaca, N.Y.: Cornell University Press, 1973.

Rasanayagam, Angelo. *Afghanistan, a Modern History: Monarchy, Despotism or Democracy? The Problems of Governance in the Muslim Tradition*. London: I.B. Tauris, 2003.

Shah, Ikbal Ali Sirdar. *The Tragedy of Amanullah*. London: Alexander-Ouseley, 1933.

Stewart, Rhea Talley. *Fire in Afghanistan, 1914–1929: Faith, Hope, and the British Empire*. Garden City, N.Y.: Doubleday, 1973.

Wild, Roland. *Amanullah, Ex-King of Afghanistan*. London: Hurst and Blackett, 1932.

A Coup and a Revolution (1973–1978)

Amiryar, Quadir A. 1989. *Soviet Influence, Penetration, Domination and Invasion of Afghanistan*. Ph.D. diss., George Washington University.

Amnesty International. *Democratic Republic of Afghanistan: Background Briefing on Amnesty International's Concerns*. New York: Amnesty International USA, 1983.

Arnold, Anthony. *Afghanistan's Two-Party Communism: Parcham and Khalq*. Stanford, Calif.: Hoover Institution Press, Stanford University, 1983.

Democratic Republic of Afghanistan. *On the Saur Revolution*. Kabul: People's Democratic Party of Afghanistan, 1978.

Dupree, Louis. *Red Flag Over the Hindu Kush*. Hanover, N.H.: AUFS, 1980.

Groves, Ralph. *The Cold War in Afghanistan: Soviet Ascendancy in Afghan Aid During the 1973–1978 Regnancy of Mohammad Daoud in*

Post–World War II Soviet-American Competitive Context. New York: Afghanistan Forum, 1992.

Hammond, Thomas Taylor. *Red Flag over Afghanistan: The Communist Coup, the Soviet Invasion, and the Consequences.* Boulder, Colo.: Westview Press, 1984.

Miraki, Mohammad Daoud. *Factors of Underdevelopment in Afghanistan, 1919–2000.* Ph.D. diss., University of Illinois at Chicago.

Tarahk-i, Nur Muhammad. *Message from Our Great Leader Noor Mohammad Taraki on the Occasion of the Opening of the Afghan Academy of Sciences, Hoot 1357.* Kabul: DRA, Ministry of Information and Culture, Afghanistan Publicity Bureau, 1979.

Soviet Afghanistan (1979–1989)

Alexiev, Alex. *The United States and the War in Afghanistan.* Santa Monica, Calif.: Rand, 1988.

Arnold, Anthony. *Afghanistan, the Soviet Invasion in Perspective.* Stanford, Calif.: Hoover Institution Press, 1981.

Avakov, Vladimir. *Afghanistan, on the Road to Peace.* Moscow: Novosti Press Agency Publishing House, 1988.

Borer, Douglas A. *Superpowers Defeated: Vietnam and Afghanistan Compared.* London; Portland, Oreg.: F. Cass, 1999.

Bradsher, Henry St. Amant. *Afghan Communism and Soviet Intervention.* Oxford: Oxford University Press, 1999.

———. *Afghanistan and the Soviet Union.* Durham, N.C.: Duke University Press, 1983.

Brigot, Andre, and Olivier Roy. *The War in Afghanistan: An Account and Analysis of the Country, Its People, Soviet Intervention and the Resistance.* Translated by Mary and Tom Bottomore. Brighton, U.K.: Wheatsheaf, 1988.

Chakravartty, Sumit. *Dateline Kabul: An Eye-Witness Report on Afghanistan Today.* New Delhi, India: Eastern Book Centre, 1983.

Cronin, Richard P. *Afghanistan, Soviet Invasion and U.S. Response.* Washington, DC: Library of Congress, Congressional Research Service, Major Issues System, 1982.

Emadi, Hafizullah. *State, Revolution, and Superpowers in Afghanistan.* New York: Praeger, 1990.

Fazel, Fazel Rahman. *Shadow Over Afghanistan.* San Mateo, Calif.: Western Book/Journal Press, 1989.

Fullerton, John. *The Soviet Occupation of Afghanistan.* Hong Kong: Far Eastern Economic Review, 1984.

Galeotti, Mark. *Afghanistan, the Soviet Union's Last War.* London, Portland, Oreg.: Frank Cass, 1995.

Gall, Sandy. *Afghanistan: Agony of a Nation.* London: Bodley Head, 1988.

―――. *Behind Russian Lines: An Afghan Journal.* New York: St. Martin's Press, 1984.

Giustozzi, Antonio. *War, Politics and Society in Afghanistan, 1978–1992.* Washington, DC: Georgetown University Press, 2000.

Goodwin, Jan. *Caught in the Crossfire.* 1st ed. New York: E.P. Dutton, 1987.

Grasselli, Gabriella. *British and American Responses to the Soviet Invasion of Afghanistan.* Aldershot, U.K.; Brookfield, Vt.: Dartmouth Publishing, 1996.

Grau, Lester W., ed. *The Bear Went Over the Mountain: Soviet Combat Tactics in Afghanistan.* London; Portland, Oreg.: Frank Cass, 1998.

Huldt, Bo, and Erland Jansson. *The Tragedy of Afghanistan: The Social, Cultural, and Political Impact of the Soviet Invasion.* London; New York: Croom Helm, 1988.

Hussain, Syed Shabbir, Abdul Hamid Alvi and Absar Hussain Rizvi. *Afghanistan Under Soviet Occupation: A Study of Russia's Expansion Drama Whose Latest Aggression Has Pushed Mankind to the Threshold of a New Catastrophe.* 1st ed. Islamabad, Pakistan: World Affairs Publications, 1980.

Hyman, Anthony. *Afghanistan under Soviet Domination, 1964–91.* Houndmills, U.K.: Macmillan Academic and Professional, 1991.

Kakar, M. Hasan. *Afghanistan: the Soviet Invasion and the Afghan Response, 1979–1982.* Berkeley: University of California Press, 1995.

Kaul, Rajnish. *Democratic Afghanistan, Forever.* 1st ed. New Delhi, India: Pulse Publishers, 1987.

Kirkpatrick, Jeane J. *Call for Soviet Withdrawal from Afghanistan: November 24, 1982.* Washington, DC: Department of State, Bureau of Public Affairs, Office of Public Communication, Editorial Division, 1982.

Klass, Rosanne. *Afghanistan, the Great Game Revisited.* New York: Freedom House; Lanham, Md.: Distributed by National Book Network, 1990.

Laber, Jeri, and Barnett R. Rubin. *A Nation Is Dying: Afghanistan under the Soviets.* Evanston, Ill.: Northwestern University Press, 1988.

MacEachin, Douglas J. *Predicting the Soviet Invasion of Afghanistan: The Intelligence Community's Record.* Washington, DC: Center for the Study of Intelligence, Central Intelligence Agency, 2002.

Magnus, Ralph H., and Eden Naby. *Afghanistan: Mullah, Marx, and Mujahid.* Rev. and updated ed. Boulder, Colo.: Westview Press, 2002.

Maley, William. *The Afghanistan Wars.* Houndmills, U.K. New York: Palgrave, 2002.

Nair, S. V. *Afghanistan: Perspectives for Reconciliation & Peace.* New Delhi, India: Panchsheel Publishers, 1988.

Odom, William E. *The Strategic Significance of Afghanistan's Struggle for Freedom.* Coral Gables, Fla.: Institute for Soviet and East European Studies, Graduate School of International Studies, University of Miami, 1988.

Richardson, Bruce G. *Afghanistan: Ending the Reign of Soviet Terror.* 1st ed. Bend, Oreg.: Maverick Publications, 1996.

Roy, Arundhati. *The Soviet Intervention in Afghanistan: Causes, Consequences, and India's Response.* New Delhi, India: Associated Publications House, 1987.

Ryan, Nigel. *A Hitch or Two in Afghanistan: A Journey behind Russian Lines.* London: Weidenfeld and Nicolson, 1983.

Saikal, Amin, and William Maley, eds. *The Soviet Withdrawal from Afghanistan.* Cambridge: Cambridge University Press, 1989.

Saikal, Fazel Haq, and William Maley. *Afghanistan: Socialism in One Graveyard.* Canberra: Department of Politics, Australian Defense Force Academy, 1989.

Sarin, Oleg Leonidovich, and Lev Semenovich Dvoretskii. *The Afghan Syndrome: The Soviet Union's Vietnam.* Novato, Calif.: Presidio, 1993.

Sena, Canakya. *Afghanistan: Politics, Economics, and Society.* Boulder, Colo.: L. Rienner Publishers, 1986.

Swing, John Temple. *Afghanistan after the Accords: A Report from Kabul / John Temple Swing.* New York: Council on Foreign Relations, 1988.

Urban, Mark. *War in Afghanistan.* New York: St. Martin's Press, 1990.

Van Dyk, Jere. *In Afghanistan: An American Odyssey.* New York: Coward, McCann & Geoghegan, 1983.

Yousaf, Mohammad, and Mark Adkin. *The Bear Trap: Afghanistan's Untold Story.* London: Leo Cooper, 1992.

Afghanistan in Rebellion (1978–1992)

Ali, Tariq. *The Clash of Fundamentalisms: Crusades, Jihads and Modernity.* London; New York: Verso, 2002.

Farr, Grant M., and John G. Merriam, eds. *Afghan Resistance: The Politics of Survival.* Boulder, Colo.: Westview Press, 1987.

Fuller, Graham E. *Islamic Fundamentalism in Afghanistan: Its Character and Prospects.* Santa Monica, Calif.: Rand Corp, 1991.

Hyman, Anthony. *Afghan Resistance: Danger from Disunity.* London: Institute for the Study of Conflict, 1984.

Karp, Craig. *Afghan Resistance and Soviet Occupation: A 5-Year Summary.* Washington, DC: Department of State, Bureau of Public Affairs, 1984.

Kline, David. *Afghanistan: David Kline's Reports from Behind Rebel Lines on the Resistance to Moscow's Aggression.* 1st ed. Chicago: Call Publications, 1980.

Lessing, Doris May. *The Wind Blows Away Our Words and Other Documents Relating to the Afghan Resistance.* New York: Vintage Books, 1987.

Tabibi, Abdul Hakim. *The Legal Status of the Afghan Resistance Movement.* Cedar Rapids, Iowa: Igram Press, 1986.

Weinbaum, Marvin G. *Pakistan and Afghanistan: Resistance and Reconstruction.* Boulder, Colo.: Westview Press; Lahore: Pak Book, 1994.

Mujahideen Rule (1992–1996)

Ansary, Mir Tamim. *Afghanistan: Fighting for Freedom.* New York: Dillon Press, 1991.

Davidson, Anders, and Peter Hjukstrom, eds. *Afghanistan, Aid and the Taliban: Challenges and Possibilities on the Eve of the 21st century.* Stockholm: Swedish Committee for Afghanistan, 1999.

Dixit, Jyotindra Nath. *An Afghan Diary: Zahir Shah to Taliban.* New Delhi, India: Konark Publishers, 2000.

Dorn, Allen E. *Countering the Revolution: The Mujahideen Counterrevolution.* New York: Afghanistan Forum, 1989.

Gall, Sandy. *Afghanistan: Travels with the Mujahideen.* Sevenoaks, U.K.: New English Library, 1989.

The Geneva Accords: Agreements on the Settlement of the Situation Relating to Afghanistan. New York: United Nations, 1988.

Goodson, Larry P. *Afghanistan's Endless War: State Failure, Regional Politics, and the Rise of the Taliban.* Seattle: University of Washington Press, 2001.

House Committee on Foreign Affairs, Subcommittee on Asian and Pacific Affairs, United States Congress. *Recent Developments in U.S. Policy Toward Afghanistan: Hearing Before the Subcommittee on Asian and Pacific Affairs of the Committee on Foreign Affairs, House of Representatives, One Hundred Second Congress, First Session, June 20, 1991.* Washington, DC: Government Printing Office, 1993.

Jalali, Ali Ahmad, and Lester W. Grau. *Afghan Guerrilla Warfare: In the Words of the Mujahideen Fighters.* St. Paul, Minn.: MBI Publishing, 2001.

Jalalzai, Musa Khan. *The Pipeline War in Afghanistan.* Lahore, Pakistan: Mobile Institute of International Affairs, 2000.

————. *Sectarianism and Ethnic Violence in Afghanistan.* Lahore, Pakistan: Vanguard, 1996.

Khalilzad, Zalmay. *Prospects for the Afghan Interim Government.* Santa Monica, Calif.: RAND, 1991.

Maley, William, ed. *Fundamentalism Reborn? Afghanistan and the Taliban.* New York: New York University Press, 1998.

Menon, Rajan. *Afghanistan after the Geneva Accords: A Report by the International Center for Development Policy on Its April, 1988 Fact-Finding Mission to the USSR and Afghanistan.* Washington, DC: International Center for Development Policy, 1988.

Misra, Amalendu. *Afghanistan: The Labyrinth of Violence.* Cambridge: Polity, 2004.

Muhajir, Abdul Qadeer. *The Warlord Abdul Rasheed Dostum: A Blood-Stained Chapter in the History of Afghanistan.* 1st ed. Lahore, Pakistan: Azad Consultancy, 1997.

Nair, S. V. *Afghanistan: Perspectives for Reconciliation & Peace.* New Delhi, India: Panchsheel Publishers, 1988.

Odom, William E. *The Strategic Significance of Afghanistan's Struggle for Freedom.* Coral Gables, Fla.: Institute for Soviet and East European Studies, Graduate School of International Studies, University of Miami, 1988.

Shai, Shaul. *The Endless Jihad: The Mujahidin, the Taliban and Bin Laden.* Herzliya, Israel: International Policy Institute for Counter-Terrorism, Interdisciplinary Center Herzliya, 2002.

Singh, Jasjet. *Superpower Detente and Future of Afghanistan.* New Delhi, India: Patriot Publications, 1990.

Smith, Mary. *Before the Taliban: Living with War, Hoping for Peace.* Aberdour, U.K.: IYNX Publishing, 2001.

Whitehead, John C. *Afghanistan's Struggle for Freedom.* Washington, DC: Department of State, Bureau of Public Affairs, Office of Public Communication, Editorial Division, 1985.

The Taliban Era (1996–2001)

Brentjes, Burchard, and Helga Brentjes. *Taliban: A Shadow over Afghanistan.* Varanasi, India: Rishi Publications, 2000.

Crist, John T. *The Future of Afghanistan: The Taliban, Regional Security and U.S. Foreign Policy.* Washington, DC: United States Institute of Peace, 1997.

Gohari, M. J. *The Taliban Ascent to Power.* Karachi, Pakistan: Oxford University Press, 2001.

Griffin, Michael. *Reaping the Whirlwind: The Taliban Movement in Afghanistan.* London: Pluto Press, 2001.

Marsden, Peter. *The Taliban: War and Religion in Afghanistan.* New expanded ed. London: Zed Books, 2002.

Matinuddin, Kamal. *The Taliban Phenomenon: Afghanistan 1994–1997.* Karachi, Pakistan: Oxford University Press, 1999.

Nojumi, Neamatollah. *The Rise of the Taliban in Afghanistan: Mass Mobilization, Civil War, and the Future of the Region.* 1st ed. New York: Palgrave, 2002.

Rashid, Ahmed. *Taliban: The Story of the Afghan Warlords Including a New Foreword Following the Terrorist Attacks of 11 September 2001.* London: Pan, 2001.

Singh, Vijay K. *Security Implications of the Rise of Fundamentalism in Afghanistan and Its Regional and Global Impact.* Carlisle Barracks, Pa.: U.S. Army War College, 2001.

Yousef, Ayman Talal. *Taliban: The bane of Afghanistan.* Delhi, India: Kalinga Publications, 2002.

The Legacy of the Civil War

Armstrong, Sally. *Veiled Threat: The Hidden Power of the Women of Afghanistan.* New York: Four Walls Eight Windows, 2002.

Benard, Cheryl. *Veiled Courage: Inside the Afghan Women's Resistance.* 1st ed. New York: Broadway Books, 2002.

Brodsky, Anne E. *With All Our Strength: The Revolutionary Association of the Women of Afghanistan.* New York: Routledge, 2003.

Christensen, Hanne. *Afghan Refugees in Pakistan: From Emergency Towards Self-Reliance: A Report on the Food Relief Situation and Related Socio-Economic Aspects.* Geneva: United Nations Research Institution for Social Development, 1984.

Citizens Commission on Afghan Refugees. *The Challenge of the Coming Afghan Refugee Repatriation: Fulfilling Our Commitments in the Final Chapter of the Afghanistan War, a Report on a Fact-Finding Visit of 1988.* New York: Citizens Commission of Afghan Refugees, 1988.

Coursen-Neff, Zama, and John Sifton. *We Want to Live as Humans: Repression of Women and Girls in Western Afghanistan.* New York: Human Rights Watch, 2002.

Doubleday, Veronica. *Three Women of Herat.* London: Cape, 1988.

Dupree, Louis. *The Burqa Comes Off*. New York: American Universities Field Staff, 1959.

Dupree, Nancy Hatch. *Seclusion or Service: Will Women Have a Role in the Future of Afghanistan?* New York: Afghanistan Council, Asia Society, 1989.

Emadi, Hafizullah. *Repression, Resistance, and Women in Afghanistan.* Westport, Conn.: Praeger, 2002.

Goodson, Larry P. 1990. *Refugee-Based Insurgency: The Afghan Case.* Ph.D. diss., University of North Carolina at Chapel Hill.

Iacopino, Vincent. *The Taliban's War on Women: A Health and Human Rights Crisis in Afghanistan.* Boston: Physicians for Human Rights, 1998.

Jones, Allen K. *Afghan Refugees Five Years Later.* Washington, DC: U.S. Committee for Refugees, 1985.

Khattak, Saba Gul. *In/Security Afghan Refugees and Politics in Pakistan.* Islamabad Pakistan: Sustainable Development Policy Institute, 2003.

————. *Violence and Home: Afghan Women's Experience of Displacement.* Islamabad, Pakistan: Sustainable Development Policy Institute, 2002.

Mayotte, Judy A. *Disposable People? The Plight of Refugees.* Maryknoll, N.Y.: Orbis Books, 1992.

Omidian, Patricia A. 1992. *Aging and Intergenerational Conflict: Afghan Refugees Families in Transition.* Ph.D. diss., University of California.

Rose, Carol. *Making the Move: Repatriation of Afghan Refugees.* Peshawar, Pakistan: Institute of Current World Affairs, 1991.

Saikal, Fazel Haq, and William Maley. *Afghan Refugee Relief in Pakistan: Political Context and Practical Problems.* Canberra, Australia: University College, University of New South Wales, Australian Defense Force Academy, Department of Politics, 1986.

Shahrish-Shamley, Zieba. 1991. *The Self and Other in Afghan Cosmology: Concepts of Health and Illness Among the Afghan Refugees.* Ph.D. diss., University of Wisconsin.

Shalinsky, Audrey. *Long Years of Exile: Central Asian Refugees in Afghanistan and Pakistan.* Landham, Md.: University Press of America, 1993.

Turton, David. *Taking Refugees for a Ride? The Politics of Refugee Return to Afghanistan.* Kabul Afghanistan Research and Evaluation Unit, 2002.

Weinbaum, Marvin G. *Pakistan and Afghanistan: Resistance and Reconstruction.* Boulder, Colo.: Westview, 1994.

Overcoming the Legacy

Barakat, Sultan, ed. *Reconstructing War-Torn Societies: Afghanistan.* Houndmills, U.K.: New York: Palgrave Macmillan, 2004.

Center of Military History. *Operation Enduring Freedom: October 2001–March 2002*. Washington, DC: U.S. Army Center of Military History, 2004.

Cronin, Richard P. *Afghanistan: Challenges and Options for Reconstructing a Stable and Moderate State*. Washington, DC: Congressional Research Service, Library of Congress, 2002.

Donini, Antonio, Norah Niland, and Karin Wermester, eds. *Nation-Building Unraveled? Aid, Peace and Justice in Afghanistan*. Bloomfield, Conn.: Kumarian Press, 2004.

Friedman, Norman. *Terrorism, Afghanistan, and America's New Way of War*. Annapolis, Md.: Naval Institute Press, 2003.

Human Rights Watch. *Enduring Freedom: Abuses by U.S. Forces in Afghanistan*. New York: Human Rights Watch, 2004.

Latifa, with Shékéba Hachemi. *My Forbidden Face: Growing Up Under the Taliban, a Young Woman's Story*. Translated by Linda Coverdale. 1st ed. New York: Hyperion, 2001.

Logan, Harriet. *Unveiled: Voices of the Women of Afghanistan*. 1st ed. New York: ReganBooks, 2002.

Mackey, Chris, and Greg Miller. *The Interrogators: Inside the Secret War Against al Qaeda*. 1st ed. New York: Little, Brown, 2004.

Mehta, Sunita, Esther Hyneman, Batya Swift Yasgur, and Andrea Labis, eds. *Women for Afghan Women: Shattering Myths and Claiming the Future*. Houndmills, U.K.; New York: Palgrave, 2002.

Mukarji, Apratim. *Afghanistan, from Terror to Freedom*. New Delhi, India: Sterling Publishers, 2003.

Pain, Adam. *Understanding Village Institutions: Case Studies on Water Management from Faryab and Saripul*. Kabul: Afghanistan Research and Evaluation Unit, 2004.

Peimani, Hooman. *Falling Terrorism and Rising Conflicts: The Afghan "Contribution" to Polarization and Confrontation in West and South Asia*. Westport, Conn.: Praeger, 2003.

Pinney, Andrew. *National Risk and Vulnerability Assessment 2003: A Stakeholder-Generated Methodology*. Kabul: Afghanistan Research and Evaluation Unit, 2004.

Reddy, L. R. *Inside Afghanistan: End of the Taliban Era?* New Delhi, India: APH, 2002.

Saigol, Rubina. *At Home or in the Grave: Afghan Women and the Reproduction of Patriarchy*. Islamabad, Pakistan: Sustainable Development Policy Institute, 2002.

Schutte, Stefan. *Urban Vulnerability in Afghanistan: Case Studies from Three Cities*. Kabul: Afghanistan Research and Evaluation Unit, 2004.

Skaine, Rosemarie. *The Women of Afghanistan under the Taliban.* Jefferson, N.C.: McFarland, 2002.

"Sulima" and "Hata," with Batya Swift Yasgur. *Behind the Burqa: Our Life in Afghanistan and How We Escaped to Freedom.* Hoboken, N.J.: John Wiley and Sons, 2002.

Women Living Under Muslim Laws. *Women's Situation in Afghanistan.* Grabels, France: Women Living Under Muslim Laws, 1998.

INDEX

Note: Page numbers in *italic* indicate illustrations. The letters *c, m,* and *t* indicate chronology, maps, and tables, respectively.